A PLUME BOOK

MISS FORTUNE

Sean Rainer

LAUREN WEEDMAN is a comedic actress, author, and playwright. Her first show, *Homecoming*, began as a fifteen-minute performance art piece at Seattle's On the Boards and went on to go off-Broadway in New York City. *Bust*, about her work in the LA county jail, was awarded a MacDowell fellowship for playwriting by the Alpert Awards, as well as several "best of the arts" across the nation. She has written and performed ten solo plays: *Homecoming, Amsterdam, If Ornaments Had Lips, Huu, They Got His Mouth Right, Rash, Wreckage, Bust, No . . . You Shut Up*, and *The People's Republic of Portland*. Her television credits include *The Daily Show, True Blood, United States of Tara, Reno 911!, Curb Your Enthusiasm, New Girl*, and *Arrested Development*. She played Horny Patty on HBO's *Hung*, and most recently she played Doris in HBO's series *Looking*. Weedman's first book, *A Woman Trapped in a Woman's Body: Tales from a Life of Cringe*, a collection of comedic essays, was named by *Kirkus Reviews* as a top ten indie book for 2007. Weedman is the host of the popular Moth storytelling series in Santa Monica, California.

Miss Fortune

Fresh Perspectives on
Having It All from Someone
Who Is Not Okay

Lauren Weedman

A PLUME BOOK

PLUME
An imprint of Penguin Random House LLC
375 Hudson Street
New York, New York 10014

P REGISTERED TRADEMARK—MARCA REGISTRADA

Library of Congress Cataloging-in-Publication Data

Names: Weedman, Lauren.
Title: Miss Fortune : fresh perspectives on having it all from someone who is
    not okay / Lauren Weedman.
Description: New York : Plume, 2016.
Identifiers: LCCN 2015040359 | ISBN 9780142180235 (paperback) |
    ISBN 9781101620564 (ebook)
Subjects: LCSH: Weedman, Lauren. | Actors—United States—Biography. |
    Comedians—United States—Biography. | Conduct of life—Humor. | BISAC:
    HUMOR / Form / Essays. | HUMOR / Topic / Adult. | PERFORMING ARTS /
    Television / General.
Classification: LCC PN2287.W45557 A3 2016 | DDC 818/.602—dc23
LC record available at http://lccn.loc.gov/2015040359

Printed in the United States of America
10 9 8 7 6 5 4 3 2 1

CONTENTS

This book is dedicated to Leo,
who helped me stop spitting into the wind
(but only metaphorically, since I know how much he enjoys spitting)

AUTHOR'S NOTE

Hello. Thank you for reading these few sentences of my book. Or maybe you're in a weird period of your life where you've found yourself reading entire books. Or maybe you want to write a book and you needed a "Geez, she did it, I certainly could" jolt of inspiration. Whatever brought you here, I'm incredibly glad for it. One thing you should know is that this book is based on my life. It's true, but I've also exaggerated a bit for the sake of the jokes, in order not to cause any human harm, and to avoid being sued. Just like Tolstoy.

That is my principal objection to life, I think: It's too easy, when alive, to make perfectly horrible mistakes.

Kurt Vonnegut

Miss Fortune

Love of My Life

My boyfriend, David, is organizing his sock drawer when I say to him, "You know, it just hit me: If we end up staying together, you will go down in history as the love of my life." I lean back and position myself on the bed—fan out my skirt and fluff my hair—so that when he turns around and says it back to me, I'll look worthy. But he doesn't follow the script. Instead, he says, "*Aww*," like he just saw a little baby with hearing aids.

We've been together for four years. It shouldn't feel like I just took a gigantic risk and told him that I had a crush on him. We are at the point in the relationship where we are supposed to say either "You are the love of my life too!" or "You are *not* the love of my life but you *have* helped me figure out that I don't like bossy women."

Lately, David's been bizarrely excited about how his senses are starting to fail. He likes to demonstrate this like it's a magic trick. "Do you see this lemon? Okay . . . I'm bringing it to my nose . . . and"—sniff, sniff—"*nothing! I smell nothing!*"

I wonder if he's losing his hearing as well as his sense of smell and maybe didn't hear me properly. "That kind of blows my mind to think that you are the love of my life," I try, a little louder.

I'm fairly certain he hears me because he stops balling up his socks, and it looks like he's just staring at the wall. All I wanted was for him to simply cup my face in his hands and sob, "You are the love of *my* life." I thought it would be a nice midday perk. I almost feel a little cruel. Like I've thrown the "you're the love of my life" ball to the kid with no arms and watched it bounce off his head.

True, I was probably fishing for a little reassurance since that evening we were going to dinner with Jessica, an old friend of David's whom I find completely petrifying. Not only because she's a yoga/healer person for whom David always makes time for long walks when we visit her hometown of Seattle, but because she used to do massage on Hannah, David's wife, before Hannah died of cancer eight years ago.

Thanks to David's habit of confusing the speaker for the volume button on his cell phone and having entire conversations holding his phone to his ear and oblivious to the fact that everyone can hear every word, I was able to get a sense of David and Jessica's relationship without having ever met her. I, along with everyone in line at the Subway sandwich shop, heard her telling David, "I miss her hair, don't you?" For half a second I thought, That's sweet, she's never even seen my hair. Then I realized what they were talking about, and I knew why I'd never be invited on one of their walks.

Jessica is in town for an acupuncture conference, and we are going out for Indian food. I'm not so hungry. It doesn't feel like something I should be going to, but David insists.

We all meet in the parking lot of the restaurant and slowly make our way toward one another, David's and Jessica's arms stretched out in front of them ready to embrace. I encourage David to "run to her!" He laughs, somewhat nervously, which is good, because when Jessica walks up she sees the two of us laughing together. You see, Jessica, I make him laugh. I'm good for him. Jessica is attractive. She's not what a girlfriend wants to see when she's feeling a little jealous. If she was a real nurturer type, like David says, she would have taken care of my fragile feelings and been a stout, ruddy tree dweller wearing fanny packs full of essential oils, and with thick black hair covering her arms and legs. In reality, Jessica is a tiny blond girl wearing tan parachute pants and a sleeveless David Bowie T-shirt. She's got that healthy shine that could only come from two-hour headstands and a strict yet "thoughtful" diet of deep breathing and sprouted nut butter. All of Hannah and David's friends are so attractive. Why is that? Do attractive people hang out with other attractive people so they don't have to feel bad about never paying for drinks or newspapers?

I'm tempted to reach out and touch her skin to see if it's as soft as it looks, but my fingers are sticky from the gum I took out of my mouth in the car and am still holding until I can find a trash can.

David introduces me to Jessica. She stares at me with big blue eyes, startled. She looks freaked out. I'm not sure why. Is it because she was close to Hannah and now she's being forced to move on? Forced to let go of Hannah even more? Another step in the grief process would be seeing the person's partner move on. That's got to be hard.

Her stunned gaze is making me uncomfortable. I break the silence: "I need a trash can." My voice sounds like Godzilla's footsteps.

Jessica reaches out her hand and offers to take my gum. I give it to her. I thought it would be funny. It wasn't. It was like a child handing her gum to an adult.

The naan hasn't even hit the table and Jessica is reaching over and giving David little massage-y squeezes. "Oh, hey," she says. "Thank you for visiting me in my dream the other night! It was a really fun place to see you. The only tough part was waking up!"

Did she miss the part where David introduced me as his girlfriend? Am I so far from the type of woman that she imagined David being with that she's making a move on him right in front of me? I'm sure David must be as irritated by her New Age hooker talk as—

"Wow! That's so cool." He jumps right in. "I wonder if your dream happened while I was meditating, because I can go to some pretty deep places. Wouldn't that be wild?"

David is the most stressed-out meditator I've ever seen. The very first time I saw him "meditating" I thought he had a migraine and was rocking back and forth to help the nausea pass. If he's in the middle of his daily twenty minutes of "getting right with the universe" and hears me in the kitchen, he'll call out, "Are you making popcorn?" But he keeps his eyes closed and yells in a whisper voice, so he still counts it as meditation. He always seems tenser after meditating. Like meditation is just uninterrupted time to go over whom he's angry with. His eyes pop open when he's done and he'll be right back in the middle of a fight he started in his head—"Yes, I did tell you that I was selling that bookcase on eBay—I know I did!"

"Go back in," I always tell him. "I don't think it took."

But at the mere mention of the word "meditation," Jessica scoots her chair closer to David and asks him, "How are you . . . David? I mean, how *are* you?"

David is handsome and charming; that's how he is. I'm glad to see he's enjoying himself. He gives me a quick glance before he launches into his graphic response.

Remember I'm at the table, David. Remember I'm at the table.

"Well, I had a little blood in the stool."

Oh no, he didn't. Oh my god.

Blood in the stool is like a mating call for yoga people, and Jessica's chakras just swelled up and released an egg. "Oh, David! David! The rectum is a warehouse for unresolved emotions . . . like grief."

I have to break this up.

"You know, he's fine. He got scraped by an angry peanut or something—he's really fine." Which was true.

His doctor had confirmed that the source of the injury was the bucket of peanut brittle my parents sent him for his birthday that he finished off in two days.

But for some reason David has forgotten this.

Jessica puts a protective arm around David as she explains to me how "David had a scare. It's really scary." I didn't throw my three-year-old into the deep end to teach him how to swim. I was simply ribbing David a bit for bringing up anal bleeding in a fine dining establishment. That's all.

Leaving the restaurant, Jessica tells David how much she'd love to be able to do some "work" on him. "It would be pretty intense, but if you trust me . . ."

Back at home, I vow not to say anything negative about the night. The two of them have a connection that cannot be denied. Perhaps it's slipped into a sexual realm. These things happen. Sure, it would be nice if David admitted that Jessica is in love with him, but it's not necessary. Jessica looked at me like she loved me a few times. And her menu. It's what healer folks are trained to do. I'm going to say nothing. Whatever I say is going to make me sound jealous. That's not the person I want to be. It's so unattractive. One little tap of the jealousy wand and *poof*—you're a tiny mean troll with brown teeth. The best thing for me to do is to pretend I'm not jealous.

David is brushing his teeth.

"Jessica is the most incredible person I've ever met," I say. I'm already going too far. "She's amazing. I love her." I'm laughing as I talk, like a manic teenage girl. "David, I'm not kidding. I think I'm a little in love with her!" Next thing I know, I'm begging David to tell me how soft her skin is and celebrating that I've finally found the love of my life, and the aggression is back in my voice.

This always happens. If I'm not honest about what I'm feeling, the truth finds its own little path to get out. My mother lied about loving her kids more than her cats and now she's a tiny eighty-year-old woman with the face of a giant Persian cat.

Better to be myself and overtly make fun of her.

Half an hour of taint massage jokes and imitations of her chewing or as she called it "exposing her food to her saliva," later, David informs me that Jessica is a mock-free zone.

Got it. Her and 9/11.

Not being able to make jokes frees my head up, which is unfortunate because I get hit by a huge realization that I don't want to have: It's not Jessica I'm jealous of. It's far more vulgar. It's Hannah. David can't tell me I'm the love of his life because I'm not the love of his life. Of course I'm not. Hannah, his wife for thirteen years and mother of his first child, is the love of his life. In fact, even if they ever discussed David "moving on" after she died, I would hope he told her, "I will try to be happy for my sake and for our son Jack's sake. But you will always be the love of my life. No matter what."

Two weeks later, David and I are on the bluff overlooking the ocean by our Santa Monica apartment. I'm leaving in the morning to do a play in Pittsburgh for six weeks, and I'm in a horrible mood. This morning, I'd decided that before I left I wanted to give Jack, David's son, his first driving lesson. Committing to teaching Jack to drive meant that if something happened, like, oh, David and I broke up before I got back, he and I would still have our thing. Plus, David didn't want me to teach Jack to drive. He felt that he was a young fifteen and not ready. I thought doing it anyway would show Jack that I was a cool girlfriend who rebelled against authority. No matter what happened with David, I wanted Jack and me to have a relationship. Of course I couldn't replace his mother, but maybe I'd end up being the one adult in his life who tried the hardest to be there for him in a non-mother-y yet mother-wannabe way.

You can't be a part of a kid's childhood for any extended period of time and not feel some sort of investment. Well, you could, but it would take a deep commitment to alcoholism and other modes of forgetting. Jack and I have developed a "just a couple of bros hanging in an apartment drinking fizzy water and making fun of the other guy who lives here" dynamic.

My attempts to learn about his life are answered with "your face." Examples: "Do you think you'll try out for baseball?" "Your face will try out for baseball." "Does Jaxon have a girlfriend now?" "Your face has a girlfriend now." It's your standard teenage response, which I happen to find hilarious. "Jack, did you drop this sock?" "Your face dropped that sock." My face doesn't have hands; get it? I wish Jack was able to relax more around me, but I get it. The first year of college I was so freaked by having a roommate that I didn't fully breathe or poop for the entire first month.

David thinks that Jack and I are alike, and we are, in that we both love to laugh at David. It's nice to have that connection, even if it's more of a laughing *at* than a laughing *with*. David feels things far more dramatically than most mortals. If I'm exhausted, David is "*Literally* losing his mind from lack of sleep. *Literally.*" The other night, David was doubled over, clutching his stomach, yelling, "Oh my god! Oh my god!" holding on to the stove for support as he made his way to a box of cereal. Jack and I laughed for days about that. We still take turns trying to fake the other one out. At any point in the day, one of us will cry out in pain, fall on the floor, and as soon as we've caught the other one's attention, pop back up and say, "Whew! Hungry."

The lesson had taken place on a very wide residential street in our neighborhood. For thirty minutes, I'd covered the basics: driving in a straight line and slamming on the brakes when I yelled, "NOW! NOW! MOTHERFUCKER! NOW!"

Maybe it was my stress over leaving, or the fear of Jack hitting the gas pedal instead of the brake and slamming into a palm tree, but I wanted to tell Jack how deeply I cared about him. How after four years together, it wasn't just his dad I had a connection with; it was him. I wanted to tell him the story about working with his mother's best friend, Nina, on a comedy show in Seattle. About how Nina would give all the writers updates on how Hannah was doing after she got sick. About the day she came into the middle of a pitch session, her eyes puffy and red, and told us how Hannah had accepted the fact that she was going to die, but what she couldn't accept was the fact that she was going to leave Jack and David.

It had been established early on that any talk of Hannah in front of Jack that was not initiated by him was forbidden. I told him anyway. When I got to the end—"and, Jack, at that moment, I can remember so vividly, even though I'd never met you guys, thinking 'Give them to me, Hannah. I'll take care of them'"—Jack didn't move. He sat staring out the window. A teenage warrior, blank of emotion.

"Maybe that wasn't a great story for you to hear," I finally said.

He got out of the car and waited for me to turn it around so he could drive it back down the street. The quiet in the car for the rest of the lesson was very loud. I was so desperate to know what he was thinking that I considered offering him fifty dollars if he told me how hearing the story made him feel, but he was with me the last time I took money out of the ATM. He knew I'd have to "wait for a few checks to clear" before I could make good on my bribe.

On the bluff, I'm convinced that I've ruined my relationship with Jack and probably with David. I realize I will never be a "wife" or a "mother" to them because those titles have already been taken.

Here's what's going to happen: I'm going to go do a show in a new town—be a big hit, feel like a big star, and ride that confidence into the courage to be on my own again. I'll use the money I earn to move out. It's all too hard. Who knew that being part of a family would matter to me so much?

During Joe Biden's inauguration speech he spoke about how after he lost his first wife in a car accident he'd gone through hell but was able to love again, and when he brought home his next wife he said in his direct "everyone calls me Joe" style, "Boys, you see this woman? I love her. She's my wife now and your stepmother. That's how this is going down. We're a family now. Boom." Boom. And they were. Because he said it. Boom. This was not something I could ever imagine David doing. The only thing he had in common with Joe Biden was his hairstyle. Of course, maybe I didn't warrant that kind of statement. Maybe Mrs. B. was such a great lady it brought it out in him.

David doesn't seem to be making any effort to make our last day romantic. He's lying on his back, shoving salami in his mouth.

"Jesus, the ocean bugs me. It's so endless," I say.

David's eyes are closed and he says nothing . . . to me anyway.

In his head I'm fairly sure he's saying, "Don't worry, Hannah. She's almost gone."

My first night in Pittsburgh, I listen to a girl sobbing in her car. The only words I can make out are "*noooo*" and "*whyyyyyyy?*" It's been going on for so long I've started to sing along with her like you do with a car alarm that's been going off for a long time. "*Nooooooo . . . whyyyyyyy?*" There is also the occasional sound of throwing up and beer bottles being thrown. By the time it starts to get light out, I'm in bed thinking, forget this "love of my life" shit. I just want a warm body next to me.

Staying in bed and eating the smooshed PowerBars I brought with me sounds good, but I think about how David would have us up and out the door looking for a little Pittsburgh joint to have some breakfast. In his honor, I set out, forgetting the most important rule of exploring a new neighborhood—stay away from the streets that are littered with beer cans, crusty throw up, condoms, and dead baby birds.

I see two dead baby birds, which seems like one too many. It's the "morning after" on Carson Street, the city's biggest party stop. The only "joint" that is open is Schultz's market. When I walk in, I suddenly miss the dead birds and dried throw up. The market is what my friend Narver would call "an ice cream and porno store." I don't see any porno—but I feel it. Later, the people at the theater tell me, "Oh, don't buy anything from Schultz's. They make their own meat."

After five weeks, I'm finding being in this city tougher than I'd imagined. David and I talk on the phone every day but don't say much. Performing eight times a week for audiences that are shuttled in from their convalescent homes hasn't quite been the diva-making machine that I'd hoped. During my curtain calls, I start mouthing "I'm sorry" as I bow to an audience of confused-looking old people. I've gone from deeply depressed to morbidly depressed.

After shows I start making videos of myself where I look in the camera and say, "I'm so lonely. I've never been so lonely in my life." They're just three-second videos of me staring into the camera—"I'm so lonely"—looking around the room for someone to talk to, and shutting it off. Gradually the videos get longer as I add a second on each night: "I'm so lonely . . . I want a dog." In my thirst for knowledge, also known as filling up the endless eternity of my days, I was on *Huffington Post* reading about a woman who'd found a slug in the bottom of her juice carton when I noticed an article about Joe Biden. The article talked about Joe Biden's second marriage and how nervous he'd been to introduce Jill to his kids. He hadn't pushed Jill at his sons, with some "This is my new wife, call her Momma!" demand. In fact, it was the opposite; he'd waited months before introducing her to his sons and worried constantly about bringing her into their lives too soon. What? How was it that I remembered what he'd said as being so completely different? I must have stopped listening right after he said they'd gotten married and shut the curtains on reality and spun off into my own "Everybody gets married and has a family except for me" story line. It makes no sense, though, because I don't want to get married. Only weak girls who want to feel "loved" and "safe" need that ceremony of lies. Not me. I don't need that. I'm NEEDless. It's one of my selling points right before beatboxing and speaking Dutch.

The article also mentioned how Jill had slowly carved out a relationship with his sons, cooking them meals, driving them to their sports games. She earned her position as a family member. The only thing I'd done was teach. I'd taught Jack how to drive to one end of an empty street.

It's closing night. The show is sold-out—most of the tickets were bought by one woman bringing a large group. Hopefully, she's one of the wealthy Pittsburgh patrons of the arts I've been hearing so much about. Perhaps she's looking to produce a show in New York to impress all her friends. You never know. Plus, the theater is having a closing-night shindig for me, so people will at least pretend to love me for the sake of a good farewell party.

The patron of the arts turns out to be a twenty-four-year-old who brings twelve of her closest drinking buddies for a bachelorette party. Apparently, she thought the show, *Bust*, would be a madcap comedy about boobs. It's actually about my experience volunteering with women at the Los Angeles county jail. The bachelorette crew has clearly been out drinking on Carson Street since eleven A.M.

They sit in the middle of the theater and spin their lit-up whips and yell "woo-hoo" whenever they think the show has gotten remotely sexual. A character in the play who's been arrested for prostitution reveals that she'd been molested, and there are "woo-hoos" and twirling whips lighting up the audience. When the prostitute character gets released from jail, I hear one of them drunkenly whisper, "This isn't like ha-ha funny. I have to pee." They all click their way out on high heels and take a group of men from the front row with them. One of those girls is about to be married. She's the love of somebody's life.

Chances are, by the time you meet anyone at any time, they have already had a love of their life. You will never be their first love. Nor do you have to be.

That's the problem with the "love of my life" thing. I'd never thought I was worthy of it. I do not expect to be someone's anything. I'm the funniest person in some of my friends' lives; there are definitely people I know who can claim me as the only person they know who took a shit in her own hand. So I'm not without note. Not without some stature. But love of a life? No.

"Loves of lives" are a type. They're quiet. Mysterious and unattainable. I'm done with this love thing. I'm into like. "You're the thirtieth like of my life." Who needs more? If you're the love of a life, all you can do is go down, be demoted. Being the thirtieth like of a life means you can go up the list. "After you picked me up from the airport you became the twenty-second like of my life."

In the dressing room after the show, the house manager apologizes for letting in a group of drunk women. "You know, when I saw that one girl sucking on that penis straw, I thought, uh-oh."

My phone rings. It's David.

"Something horrible has happened. Oh my god, Lauren. I'm not even sure how I'm supposed to tell you this."

He sounds completely hysterical.

My first guess is that he left the clothes in the dryer. Or that he lost his water bottle.

"Jack crashed your car," he says. "He stole it and he totaled it. Oh my god, I can't handle this. I honestly can't handle this . . ."

The words "crash" and "Jack" stun me. The image of him even wincing in pain makes me feel sick. I cannot stand to think of him in pain. This isn't David doubled over, clutching his sides, hungry for breakfast—this is graphic, real pain. I'm longing for the simple times of misunderstood molestation and penis straws when David finally lets me know that Jack wasn't injured.

Thank you, Jesus and Mary and Peter, Paul and the Mamas and the Papas, he's okay.

Here's the story. David was out of town for a few days working in Seattle. Jack's grandma came to stay with him. Her flight left at four P.M. to go back home and David's flight was arriving at five P.M. Jack was alone for two hours. During those two hours, he invited his friends over, took my keys, and pulled out into traffic.

Cops immediately identified teenagers behind the wheel and turned on their lights and came up behind them. Jack saw the cops and took off. As if he was going to lose them. As if he knew how to drive. The first corner he took, he lost control of the car. The car smashed into the gate of a Jewish preschool. Nobody was hurt, thank god, but now it was bordering on a hate crime. His friends were screaming for Jack to stay in the car, but Jack jumped out and started running.

The cops formed a perimeter around the area and when Jack tried to pass through it a cop asked his name and where he lived, and Jack said his name was "Lucky Lightening" and he lived on Castle Street. With that, Lucky was arrested, and when no guardian could be contacted, they put him in juvie.

"I can't take it. I'm going to faint. I'm going to pass out. I can't handle this." David was losing it waiting for his flight to LA.

"Don't cry—get up and go take care of it," I commanded him. Go get him out. You're not collapsing. You're getting it taken care of. You can handle it.

Of course this happened! Nobody taught Jack the life lesson of how when the cops show up, the party is over. My car is dead. Who cares? Everyone could have been dead. Jewish preschool children, Jack's best friend . . . Jack.

Why did I have to be the one who was teaching him to drive? Why didn't I just buy him some condoms or something?

"We can figure this out." I hang up, walk out of the theater, and collapse on a stoop next to a drunk girl who looks like she's going to be sick. The main thing is that Jack is okay. No point going over all the variations of tragedies that could have happened. This is what happened.

The next day, before my flight home, I'm in a coffee shop when a call comes in.

A detective calls me to ask if I want to press charges. In a way, this is the moment I've been waiting for. A chance to show David and Jack what I'm willing to do for them. If only there was a way to videotape myself and talk on the phone at the same time. "No, no. Of course not. He's learned his lesson. I'm actually glad this happened, because now he will get some extra guidance and care. The only thing I ask is that he pay me back for the car, or make some gesture to pay me back. Not that I care about the money. It's not about that. It's about what he's learning from this. How this experience will help him mature."

"You're not doing him any favors by not pressing charges. If you press charges, he'll have to do the things you're talking about. I can suggest the other things in court, but it won't necessarily happen. Not if you don't press charges. Are you his stepmother?"

"No, no. I'm the girlfriend."

"Oh, okay." He says it like now it all makes sense. As if I'm only not pressing charges because it's hard enough to get a boyfriend's teenage kid to like you without pressing charges.

"I have to pay for my coffee. Thank you for the call." I hang up.

Back in Los Angeles, we're not allowed to visit Jack until he's brought to court, which is in three days. In order to not be charged for the storage for the scrap heap of a car, we have to get the car out of the police department lot and pay to have it towed to a junkyard. It's late at night and nobody is around. The officer on duty smiles when we give her the case number. "Oh yeah, Jack. I was a part of the perimeter." She then tells us about Jack leaping from the car—dodging traffic and giving a false name.

"It's hard to run in all this gear," she says, tapping her bulletproof vest.

I say, "I bet." So does David, but the policewoman can't hear him because he's squatting on the floor with his head in his hands waiting for his dizzy spell to pass. David feels responsible for Jack being in there because he was out of town when it happened. That's why he was put there. If David had been home. Or if Jack had a second parent . . .

The detective I spoke to on the phone had pretty much pinned the blame on David for not being home in the evenings to supervise Jack and for not being stricter with him. Normally, I'm happy to throw David under the bus and even add a "Guess what else he's done?" or two for good measure, but the image of Jack in juvie takes the fun out of it.

The next morning we get a recommendation for a lawyer from Jack's girlfriend's father and are sitting outside his office waiting to meet with him so we can get Jack out of juvie ASAP.

The lawyer opens the door to his office and motions for us to come in. We both stand, and he asks David if it's okay to speak with me alone for a moment.

"As Jason's stepmother, is there anything about this incident that you'd like to let me know about before I speak with you and David together?" The lawyer is thumbing through papers in his file and seems to be half listening and half thinking about lunch.

"Well, I'm not his stepmother, and his name is Jack, and no, I don't think so. I just know that this whole thing is going to be tough on David. I mean, he's been scared to set boundaries with Jack because of the guilt from Jack losing his mother. I've been begging David to bring Jack to therapy, but he just won't do it, and now, well, here we are."

I nod toward the door, knowing that David is seated on the other side having a mini nervous breakdown.

The lawyer looks up from the file and asks me, "So you're a performer?"

His question strikes me as a bit out of left field. Perhaps I'll follow suit and ask him if he's ever seen a grown man cry.

I'm about to tell the lawyer that, yes, I am a performer, but today is maybe not the best day to discuss that, but if he wants more info he can look me up on IMDb after we leave. Before I can, though, he takes out a piece of legal paper from the file and starts reading it aloud.

"His dad's girlfriend had made a joke in a newspaper article about wanting to move a photo of his mother, who is dead, during sex, and when his dad confronted the girlfriend, Lauren, about making jokes like that in interviews, she brushed him off." The lawyer stops reading and looks directly at me with his eyebrows raised. I want to speak but my throat is constricting. What is happening?

He continues, "According to Jack's girlfriend, whom we spoke to, to get some background, you were also interviewed by a newspaper for a theater show in New Jersey, and he read it online and saw that you made the same joke about Jack's deceased mother and when Jack told you how upset he was about it, you ignored him. Does that sound right?"

New Jersey. The lady from the Trenton paper had chided me for not providing better "newspaper-friendly quotes" about the play. To win her over, I'd started telling her my life story. Including the one about how when I was first dating David, I had to ask him to move the photos of Hannah that were right by his bed while we were having sex. She'd printed everything I'd said. Jack read the article and came into my room one night when David was gone and told me that he didn't want me writing or talking about his mother.

Oh god, now I'm remembering how I said to him, "I'm an artist, Jack. I write from my life. I talk about my life." Oh god. How awful. He asked me why I did that. Why couldn't I make things up? Wasn't that what a good writer was? Someone who could create something? I'd defended myself instead of listening to what he had to say or caring about how hurt he'd been.

Now Jack is in juvie being ordered by gang members to hand over his pudding or else because of me.

I open my mouth to say "Excuse me" to the lawyer but no sound comes out. I mouth the words and run from his office. I run past David and out into the street and start sobbing.

David follows me out. He sits in the car with his arms around me.

"I really thought that this was all going to be pinned on you," I cry into his shoulder.

"I know . . . ," David says. "Me, too. And, listen, it's not you. He didn't steal your car to get back at you. I promise you that." David's the calmest he's been since this whole thing began. I should have started sobbing years ago.

Jack's day in court is endless. Waiting for the trial to begin is almost as traumatic as the trial itself, because we're stuck doing nothing but sitting and worrying that the judge will send him to a work camp.

At the beginning of the trial, the judge asks for the family of Jack Thane to please stand. David stands up and I stand up right next to him. It's the first time that anyone has officially called us a family.

Eventually, Jack is released and we all walk out together into the blinding Los Angeles sun. Jack hugs his father and then, unable to look at me directly, tells the concrete sidewalk, "I'm sorry." I can't look at him either, so I tell the sidewalk to tell him, "It's okay, Jack. It's really okay. Now, let's eat."

We find a Jamaican restaurant a block away from the jail. Jack tears up at lunch from the stress of what's just happened.

David and I wait until Jack's hands and eyeballs stop shaking and ask him what we've been dying to ask him: Why did he do it?

"Okay, first of all, Lauren always leaves her keys right out on the table, so I just grabbed them—that's why I took her car." David kicks me under the table. "And I know I'm gonna get in trouble for saying this, but in the movies and stuff, nobody just pulls over. Everybody runs. Everybody."

If only I had some pudding or a Jolly Rancher I could give to Jack. Some gesture of jail respect that spoke to him. Jack could so easily pin this on me and nobody would have blamed him for doing so, not even me, and he didn't.

"I'm so incredibly glad you're okay, but no, Jack. You don't run. When the cops show up, the gig is up. You aren't Lucky Lightning. You are Jack. Fifteen years old. You are not in a movie. You are like the rest of us assholes who have to follow the rules."

Normally if I say or do anything remotely stern or parent-like with Jack, I run away right after I do it so I won't have to see the look of "Who do you think you are?" on his face. But considering the circumstances, running away now wouldn't be the best choice.

Jack nods. He looks tired but I can tell that he's so incredibly grateful to be sitting with us at a Jamaican restaurant across the street from juvie that he'd agree to anything.

Three months later, David and I are engaged. Every few weeks I still find a reason to scream "DISENGAGED!" But David and Jack both know I'm not going anywhere.

On a trip to visit Hannah's parents, Jack's grandparents, in Berkeley, California, David asks me to marry him. Looking out over the East Bay Hills at a spot called Inspiration Point, he tells me how he's tired of living in fear. Tired of waiting to get things together before he goes after what he cares about. He tells me how difficult it was to find parking downtown when he went to pick up my engagement ring and how Abraham Lincoln's marriage to Mary was a rocky one mostly because he struggled with depression, which David was fairly sure he didn't struggle with, but man, did Lincoln go through a lot in his life.

His proposal covers a lot of different topics and goes on for so long I almost forget what his point is. But thank you, Jesus and Mary and Peter, Paul and the Mamas and the Papas he never once feels the need to tell me that I'm the love of his life. It's not necessary. I don't want to be the love of his life. I just want to be loved by him, preferably during my lifetime. If he had tried to stick that in, it would have felt scripted and forced, and I would have run like Lucky Lightening whether the police were chasing me or not.

Carlos the Dog Learns to Juggle

At one point in my adult life, I owned a dog. He was a border collie mix named Carlos, who survived on a diet of couches and cat poop he dug out of the kitty litter.

Dog ownership wasn't something I understood. In my simple mind, owning a dog meant petting it, feeding it, and once in a while tying a sock around its head, hiding, and making it find you. That's what it had been like growing up with our schnauzer, Katie, so that's all I knew. Strangers would see me trying to walk him and yell, "Don't let him pull like that!" Carlos taught me a lot about what it meant to care for a living being. He also taught me that you can't choose a dog based on how soft their ears are—the breed is important.

Carlos taught me many life lessons, which is why when a certain storytelling show that airs on NPR asked me if I had a true story about pet ownership, I said, "Yes!" I'd always wanted to be on a radio show like *This American Life*. I'd actually come close a few years earlier but was bumped at the last minute when David Sedaris turned in a poem about Christmas told from the viewpoint of a squirrel.

It worried me that after I recorded the story for the show I'd be cut because my voice wasn't nerdy-sounding enough or, worse, that I sounded like a stand-up comic. My "fully covered by mediocre insurance" therapist, Judy, who I went to years ago, opened the door before each session and burst out laughing as soon as she saw me. "Oh, get in here, Lauren! Now what happened?" She referred to stories from my childhood as "bits."

NPR is trustworthy. Good enough for Cokie Roberts, good enough for me.

The Carlos the Dog story had some "jokey" bits, but it was mostly just the journey of one misguided, self-absorbed womanchild in her twenties who adopts a dog. The theme of the episode was "domestication." The host of the show told me that my story would be sandwiched between a woman talking about the greatest cat that ever lived and a story by a man whose pet chicken had been his childhood companion and role model.

The day after the show aired, I went to the NPR website to listen to it. "I'm so curious how they ended up editing it," I said to myself.

This was a lie. I had no intention of listening to it. All I wanted to know was if the show had a message board and if people were talking about my story. I've read enough message boards in my life to know that there's always going to be a crazy man who lives in his basement reading the Bible to dolls he's dressed up in his mother's clothes who is going to write comments demanding that I burn in hell for not loving Jesus. My stepson, Jack, says that people talk shit about Martin Luther King Jr. on YouTube message boards. He shared this with me after he caught me collapsed on my keyboard mumbling, "Can't I have saggy titties *and* be a good actress?"

The comments loaded. I prepared myself.

I certainly wasn't a hero in the story, but who needs more

heroes? Apparently NPR does. I was not prepared. After the story aired, I received death threats from dog owners all over the world.

I'd assumed at least some of the comments would be at least sort of positive, maybe, if not glowing.

The less death-threaty ones went like this:

> "What a self-centered obnoxious person. Not fun to
> listen to. She didn't learn a thing from it."
> "Her story was predictable and tired."
> "It was hard to listen to. Selfish nightmares like her
> shouldn't be allowed to own a dog."

The rest of the comments were in praise of the chicken story.

> "Loved the chicken story! What was the music used at
> the end?"

What? I didn't try to drown Carlos in the river or sell him to a football player! I told myself it was because I'm a woman. People don't like stories about women who aren't sweet and nurturing. If a lady isn't a cat lady, then she's a bitch. Maybe what I needed was someone to offer to tenderly guide me through my next dog ownership. Someone to grab my hand and show me how to pet a dog properly, to guide me like Patrick Swayze teaching Jennifer Grey how to dance, "Shhhh . . . relax. It goes like this: [Pat, pat, rub. Pat, pat, rub.] See? Now you try it." I immediately decided that the best way to deal with the onslaught of hate was to pretend it never happened. If anyone I knew actually had heard the story when it aired, I'd tell them it was Paula Poundstone and deny any involvement.

Two years later, I ran into Gary, the chicken-story teller. The first thing I did was ask him if he'd had any backlash after our stories aired. I hadn't gone back to read the rest of the message boards after I'd read the comments about myself, but it was NPR—he must have offended somebody. Surely there was a community college philosophy professor out there, busy knitting sweater vests for his chicken companion, who didn't even hear the story but was set off by hearing the word "chicken," assuming it was yet another story of chicken contempt.

Gary was too busy traveling the country getting paid to tell stories for the Moth storytelling series, and writing a movie for Disney about a chicken family, to indulge in self-flagellation.

"I didn't even know that NPR had message boards."

He'd been back on the show several times, a fan favorite. There was a wealthy lady in the Palisades who after hearing his chicken story starting paying for him to tell stories at her cocktail parties.

Nobody was asking me to do anything like that.

All I got were people asking me how I got on the show.

Maybe I needed to be the hero after all. Maybe I was the hero but I was so opposed to coming off as the hero that I'd exaggerated myself into an abusive idiot for a laugh.

I went back and listened to the story itself for the first time.

Next time I consider revealing my character flaws or mistakes I've made, I'll know how to do it in a way that makes me sound charming, like when an especially cute toddler says, "I pooped."

Cue tape . . .

So during my first marriage I was touring with a solo show . . .

Boom! Right off the bat I see mistakes. A better beginning would have been "So, there I was in the Congo, building a library out of mud bricks . . ." Or "So, there I was teaching blind teenagers how to fly on the trapeze . . ." Solo theater *and* a "first marriage"?

I'm surprised I've been able to travel freely within the United States. There's also a cockiness in my voice that is off-putting. A little more sad, nervous laughter wouldn't hurt, or maybe more of a "help me, I'm so hungry" nasal tone.

> *I was with some of the crew in the touring van driving around Aberdeen when we saw a bunch of dogs in a parking lot by a sign that said* PAWS PET ADOPTION. *Every single dog was completely insane. It was a madhouse of out-of-control dogs barking, lurching at passing people, squirrels, leaves. They all looked completely unadoptable.*

Boom *again*. Why didn't I say how the dogs were acting out because they were scared? They'd been abandoned or possibly abused. I sound like the woman on the playground who complained about homeless people: "I hate bums! They drink too much, they're lazy, and they're always fighting!"

This was for NPR. To fail to acknowledge *why* the dogs were acting insane makes me sound like a Republican. Also, the show I was on tour for was actually a show about being adopted! I should have mentioned that! *I* was adopted! That very day in Aberdeen, Washington, I'd had a line of kids waiting for me after the show to tell me their stories of their nontraditional families— "My sister is my aunt but she doesn't want my mother to know because she never knew her dad but she lives with his ex-wife now who calls her Bunny even though her real name is Nora."

Instead of saying those dogs looked unadoptable, I could have mentioned how my heart went out to adopted things, like children. And highways . . . and dogs.

Most important, I forgot to mention how country-song lonely I had been at that time in my life. How I was married to a bartender who came home at four o'clock every morning. It had been so fun to date a bartender I hadn't really thought about how down to my last lonely teardrop it would be to be married to one.

> *Anyway, in the middle of all the chaos sat a little sweet black-and-white dog. He looked confused by it all, like, "Why am I here? These other dogs are insane. There's been a horrible mistake." He was a half border collie, half springer spaniel. Very cute.*
>
> *I go up to the lady in charge of the adoptions and say, "I'd like this dog."*

Thank god I kept this part short. At the time, I'd seen the woman as off-puttingly severe, with eighties hair and eyebrows drawn on with a Sharpie. Now I know these women are angels who are doomed to live in tiny studio apartments filled with the animals they save. They will never get laid or have a meal without a cat hair in it.

> *She tells me that I don't want that dog.*
> *"Oh, but I do."*
> *"You can't handle this dog," she tells me. "Border collies take a lot of work."*
> *"Excuse me . . . I can handle a dog."*

Actually this part is okay. It was a big deal to adopt a dog. It felt good to get one off the streets of Aberdeen and into my theater touring van. There was a chance it was the kind of rural small town where they fed any dog that wasn't a pit bull to a pit bull.

> *And I adopted him. He walked to the touring van very calmly. It was his last calm moment the entire time I owned him. As soon as we got to the van, he was out of*

control. Out. Of. Control. He jumps into the van. Jump-
ing everywhere. Barking, scratching. People are scream-
ing like they're being attacked. Nobody could control
him. We couldn't get him to sit down. The driver felt
unsafe. Nobody knew what to do. I was in tears within
five minutes. Why did I adopt him? I can't take him back.
Oh my god, what have I done?

This was all true, but at the time, I had made up my mind to apply myself to the task of owning a dog. I was going to have to really learn how to take care of a dog. Take him to obedience school. Read that book by monks about raising dogs. Here may have been the time to talk about my beloved grandfather, the vet. He had scars on his head from being run over by a bull during a house call. He called me by the wrong name my entire life. My parents tried to convince me that Jason was his nickname for me, but I worshipped him. He was a vet, for god's sake.

The entire time I owned Carlos he was a stress to
me. He needed constant attention. He ate a bag of makeup.
He ate a couch, not an entire couch, not a full couch,
half a couch . . .

Okay, here the producer saved me and didn't include the details about how Carlos loved to eat kitty poop. I'm sure I mentioned it when I was recording the story. "Kitty roca" was one of my favorite lines about the whole Carlos story. He'd come out of the bathroom with kitty litter all over his lips. Carlos also ate a lot of other dogs' poop.

Thank god I didn't get into how much Carlos was alone during the day, though actually that would have been okay as long as I mentioned how awful it made me feel, which it did.

Anytime he was actually sleeping, it was like having a newborn baby around. We'd whisper, "He's sleeping, let's get some stuff done." My sister came to visit at one point. She tried to convince me that he was a good dog, that he just needed more structure. He peed on her in the middle of the night. My husband liked him. My husband took him to the dog park a lot.

At the dog park, I'd see Carlos chewing on something and reach inside his mouth to discover a mound of wet dog shit. I'd scream, "Oh my god!" and hurl it away from me. The other dog owners informed me that when Carlos had dog feces in his mouth he was simply masking his scent. It wasn't that I didn't understand that dogs were animals; I was just at an age when I found things entertaining rather than enlightening. The other dog park people had rational "That's very common in the animal kingdom" responses, and I would say, "He had another dog's shit in his mouth!" and burst out laughing.

Listening again, I feel like I showed great restraint here in my storytelling. If I'd included more of what really happened, I would have had to live like Salman Rushdie.

Every aspect of owning a dog stressed me out. The dogs would be in a long conga line of humping each other and I would get the giggles. The other owners would say, "They're showing their dominance . . . that's all that is." I was like, "I get it, but it's hilarious."

We decided to move to New York. I was secretly excited that we couldn't take Carlos but I tried to hide it by saying stuff like, "This is a tough decision, but I don't think he should go." I had a friend who lived in a tiny studio apartment in New York with her golden retriever. She told me that dogs don't care where they are as long as they are with you. Her dog spent her days on an Ikea futon waiting to walk down a sidewalk. She was just saying that to justify her choice.

I gave him away to a woman who had never owned a dog before. Perfect. She didn't know about the whole border collie thing. I was excited about not having to deal with all the dog drama anymore.

Excited?

Bam! Bam! Bam! What in the hell was I doing!? How dumb could I get?

It was horrible. I was trying to really play up how immature I was as a pet owner. I thought that if I had shared how painful it really was, deciding to move and figuring out what to do with him, it would have weakened the story.

It was about telling a good story. Who needed to be a hero? How boring. Not boring when you're living it but boring to hear about it. Though humanity does need heroes, it also needs demons to compare themselves to and realize what a hero they are. I've fought so hard against painting myself a hero I'm starting to wonder if I'm getting stuck in this idea of being an asshole that's not the real story. Reality may be getting a little lopsided simply for the sake of making sure everybody knows that I win—I hated me first.

I thought the best way to approach anything in my life that was the subject of failure—marriage, jobs, dog ownership—was to put all the responsibility on myself. That way I'd avoid lawsuits and bitch slaps at public appearances and family gatherings. Aren't we supposed to bitch slap ourselves in order to grow? Not play the blame game?

Perhaps the guilt I still feel about Carlos made me tell the story from the "greatest mistake from the biggest piece of shit on earth" viewpoint. I didn't want to give myself an out. I wanted to be harsh and awful to myself so nobody else would do it. I'd simply rather not be trying to save myself for the sake of a good story. Why not be the antihero? Why not be the voice of the mistakes we have all made? There's a lot of time to be gained by getting other people to kick your ass for you so you don't have to, and I'm really busy. Some people are scared to admit they've done something wrong, and I'm scared to admit I've done something right.

> *The woman, Liz, who was going to adopt him was on her way to pick him up. My husband at the time, Mathew, says he's going to the hardware store.*

Just say "husband," Lauren. Jesus, I'm over you. Where are the message boards so I can vent?

> *And I'm, like, "You can't go now." I'm stressed getting him ready to get picked up. I've got to get his toys, his food, and his pillow that he would sometimes lie on.*
>
> *Mathew says, "Don't worry, I'll be right back," and leaves. He's gone forever. Liz shows up and I'm mad. Mathew did this on purpose. Maybe he was too emotional about it. So, Liz comes in and we gather up the stuff. I'm on point. I've got the pillow. Likes the chewy stuff. Here we go.*
>
> *We go out to the car and start to load up the back of the Subaru.*

The minute I put the pillow in the car, Carlos, the cat-poop-eating crazy dog, who was able to communicate only his most basic animal needs, turns into this incredibly wise, communicative animal. He had been faking dumb like Suzanne Somers playing Chrissy on Three's Company. *She acted dumb because it's the part she had to play to make money and survive, but in reality she was capable of creating hormone therapy and machines that tone the hard-to-hit inner-thigh area.*

Carlos sits down on the ground next to the car and I swear to god, he gives me a "That's odd. Why did you just put my pillow in her car?" look. He understands what's going on.

I start to cry, so hard. I'm sobbing. It's embarrassing. Just sobbing. I can't breathe or talk.

Liz says, "Just go inside. Go inside. I'll come back later and get his toys."

As they're driving away, I see him looking at me through the window.

Carlos was, according to Liz, a perfect dog. Once she changed his diet, he calmed right down and became so sweet and docile he could have been a pug.

He had a good life.

That had been the end, but the producer of the show suggested that maybe I could talk about any regrets I had. Or what I'd learned from the experience. I thought, no, that's not a good story. Let the radio listeners beat their steering wheel and scream at what a horrible person I was. Because I was. I don't need to be liked. Who cares? In fact, if I go on to explain all that I've learned, it will feel like an after-school special or a typical Hollywood movie . . . "I guess what I've learned is that whales need to live in the ocean and that you don't need to spend a lot of money on a wedding if you're in love . . ."

No, let them feel what they want.

I'm still traumatized from the moment when Carlos got into the car, basically stood up on two legs, took my hands in his paws, and said in the queen's English, "You poor Germanic-looking woman. Don't you see? Dogs don't care where they are. As long as we are with you, we are content. I trusted you. You abandoned me. Your excuse—'but I'm adopted, I'm all messed up'—doesn't move me. It should have opened your heart to my plight. Good day."

I'd been his owner. I had taken care of him. Went to obedience class. I slept with him, fed him, walked him, and loved him. I'd put so much effort into playing the "I'm an asshole with a dog who's causing mayhem!" comedy that I hadn't let myself feel what was really going on. I was in love with that dog.

Don't NPR listeners have the liberal sensitivity to understand that if I describe my love, or get too showy with it, if I bring it out into the open, someone will grab it and run away with it? My love will be exposed, hovering in the air in front of me until it's karate kicked away. If I love openly and fiercely, I'll be left looking like an asshole. It's far better for me to tune out the chatter of my heart because what is real is that I don't really trust people, or maybe it's that I love them so much I'm sure that love will destroy me.

Complaining is easy. Admitting to doing awful things is easy. I like it! I'm the one who didn't flush the toilet, who stole from people I babysat for, who did coke in the elevator of the Standard! Loving something is awful. Like that scene in *Harold and Maude* where Harold gives Maude a fancy ring, and she takes it and hugs it to her chest lovingly, then leans back and tosses it into the lake. He looks at her with horror—what did she just do? "That way I'll always know where it is," she says with a deep, relaxed sigh. That's how I feel when something I care about, something beautiful, is in front of me that opens my heart. I worry about losing it the entire time I have it. I'd rather throw it away and know that exactly where it landed is where it remains. It won't go on any journeys with me; it won't change. It won't get damaged or sold or lost and it won't age.

Those message-board folks should be glad I didn't throw Carlos in a lake. The joke would have been on them, though: Carlos loved swimming in Lake Washington. He'd leap in and swim and swim and swim. Sometimes, it looked like he was never going to come back. "Will he swim too far and drown?" I asked Mathew in a total panic, watching him swim after a goose that was heading toward the opposite end of the lake by Bill Gates's mansion. "Well, I don't think so," Mathew had said. "Go after him, Mathew! Go get him!" I'd panicked and made Mathew swim out to get him, which he did. As soon as Carlos saw him, he swam toward him and followed him back to shore. From then on, I didn't take him to the lake because I was too worried he'd swim away and never come back.

Dear god, listening to this story is going to change my entire life. I'm going to let myself love something and admit to it. I've already started with my son, Leo. Next I could move on to a dog, and then a man and after that an outdoor deck. If I can do this—it will change my life. It won't change the story or the message boards from that show, because that shit is on the Internet and written in Internet stone.

I'm not just saying that now to prove to the four people on the message boards that I'm not bad. Well, maybe I am. There's sometimes something to be learned from those four people. But don't get all happy about it, Vermontbeerboy09.

For all the animal lovers reading this, I'd like to add that as I write this there's a black-and-white bunny named Liza under my couch, a kitty named Arthur nursing on my earlobe, a dog named Georgia at my feet eating its own throw up, and a potbellied pig named Inez soaking in my bathtub.*

* All of these are names of animals that I have had who ran away or whom I sold to college kids in the past year. *I'm kidding.* They've all been eaten by coyotes.

Piles of Idiots

David and I are in the car on our way home from a pool party, trapped in a classic 405 traffic jam. It's the hellish kind that makes people either jump out of their cars and start sucker punching anyone with their window down or turn on the radio and listen to *The Dr. Laura Program*. Dr. Laura is a conservative talk show host who loves to yell at young girls. She's the Bobby Knight of self-help, a feminist nightmare, and I listen to her every chance I get.

Today she's taking a call from a young girl from Arkansas looking for advice about inviting her uncle to her wedding.

"Well, my mom doesn't want him to come to the wedding because he used some inheritance to buy cocaine, but it's *my* wedding and—"

Dr. Laura cuts the caller off. "How old are you?"

"I'm twenty-three but I'm—"

"I'm not having this discussion with you."

"I know you say not to get married in your twenties but—"

Dr. Laura cuts her off in voice so calm it gives me a chill. "Ask me the names of the boys I dated in my twenties."

"I know, but—"

"Ask. Me. The. Names."

There's an inhale that sounds like the girl is about to burst out sobbing. "Uhm. What were the—"

"*I don't remember because they didn't matter because I was in my twenties!*"

Normally, when Dr. Laura lays into a caller I start banging my tin cup on the bars: "*Get her, Dr. Laura! Cut her!*" But I couldn't have disagreed more. I'm grateful that I didn't marry any of the boys my path crossed with way back in the 1990s, but I certainly would never say they didn't matter.

David has always maintained that anything that happened to me between the ages of twenty and twenty-nine is either too sexual or too depressing or both. Given a choice, he'd rather not hear about any of it.

I just went to a pool party in a practical, long-sleeved, fully skirted swimsuit made popular by lesbians in 1910, yet David still has this idea of me as a crazy party girl with my shirt flipped up *Girls Gone Wild*–style. Yes, he's found things like "anorexic workout" in my browser history, but I'm still at my core an empowerment feminist. In my twenties, I had hairy armpits and believed that stilettos were invented by men to ensure that women would be rendered wounded animals that wouldn't be able to run away too quickly. I've always found David's image of me as this vapid blond sexpot a little flattering, though, so how good a feminist could I really be?

There *is* one story that I could see him using to build a case that I was a crazy wild child. If he could get past the part of the story that begins "This one time I had sex with two guys in Amsterdam," he'd see that my three-way story isn't an after-hours story. It's a coming-of-age story. A story about self-discovery and two friends, Emad and Mikhas. A story about learning to listen and Muslim values.

Before I start, let me tell you that having a threesome is not what you think it's going to be.

It's not sexy.

For me, having a threesome was like living in New York. When I lived in New York, I was always having to tell myself, "I mean, look at you. You're in NYC!" A cab could drive by and splash gutter water into my mouth and I'd say, "Sure it's disgusting, but look at me! I'm in New York City."

My threesome was not planned. At least *I* didn't plan on it.

Once upon a time, I was a twenty-one-year-old American living in Amsterdam with the low self-esteem and poor personal boundaries that only a cult leader could love. My Dutch boyfriend and I broke up, I wanted to go back home but didn't have enough money for a plane ticket, so I stayed. After a few years of doing experimental theater and learning important acting techniques, like how to breathe in through my vagina and out through my asshole while reciting William Blake, I had a regular job at a five-star hotel called the Pulitzer, a converted seventeenth-century canal house.

Initially, I was hired on to work room service, but since I'd learned how to say things like "I'm sorry, junkie, but you can't hide in the linen closet" in Dutch I'd been promoted to the café. The café wasn't as fancy as the hotel's formal dining room, the Sun Flower, where Swiss royals drank thousand-dollar bottles of wine and ate elk. But it wasn't considered as rough as what happened in the hotel's Breakfast Buffet. The Breakfast Buffet was a tiny eatery crammed into the hotel's attic space.

The café people and the Breakfast Buffet people rarely interacted. The Breakfast Buffet had its own little sad space, and its Anne Frank tiny attic working conditions meant they had to hunch over for most of their shifts so they wouldn't bang their heads on the low-hanging ceiling. Meanwhile, the café staff would complain if they had to actually wait on a table. "I have to have a cigarette before I work. I'm not an animal." The Buffet Boys, who were all, with the exception of Mikhas the Greek manager, Middle Eastern, started their shift at four A.M. and ended five hours later, whistling, winking, and throwing plates up into the air and catching them behind their backs. "Ha-ha!" My theory was that they loved their jobs. My coworker Yolanda's theory was that they partied until the clubs shut down and came to work to get free coffee and sober up before they went home to their families.

She was probably right, since there were many days when they started their shift sweaty, bleary-eyed, and reeking of hashish.

They could hardly keep a grip on the coffeepots, yet they still found the energy to hit on every single hotel guest who showed up for breakfast. The womanizing ways of the Breakfast Buffet Boys were infamous.

"Good morning, beautiful woman. Normally I'm not aroused so early in the day, but hello there. Coffee?"

The daily job of setting up for lunch in the café always included checking to see what the Breakfast Buffet Boys had stolen. Instead of walking all the way down to the supply closet in the hotel's basement, they usually made the shorter trip to the café and grabbed what they needed from us.

My hand was always the first one up when Steffan the café manager asked, "Who wants to go up to the Breakfast Buffet and retrieve the coffee cups, sugar packs, and whatever else you notice doesn't belong to them?"

Nobody else liked having to traipse up three flights of stairs, but even if there had been an elevator I would have volunteered, because only buying a jumbo box of tampons made me feel as solidly female as being sexually harassed by the Buffet Boys.

Being sexually harassed was something romantic that happened to pretty girls on summer days in Brooklyn whose Love's Baby Soft perfume made the construction workers fall off scaffolding to their deaths. In Indiana, boys would let girls know they thought they were pretty by driving by them and throwing a beer can at their heads, and that had never happened to me. The closest I'd come to being sexually harassed was at the Indy 500 racetrack when a man with the command SHOW ME YOUR TITS written across his T-shirt walked past me. It was so crowded I wasn't even sure he was talking to me.

The minute I set foot in the Buffet attic, Mert, the fifty-five-year-old Turkish busser, yelled my name. How he was able to see me at all through his butter-smeared glasses is a mystery.

"In my country you would be a movie star!" he shouts.

Italian guests would look around trying to figure out whom on earth he could be referring to. Mert asked guests to take pictures of me and wrote down his family's address on the place mats so they could send the photo directly to his family back in Turkey. "Just write a note—'This beauty works with Mert. You see, he is okay.'"

Emad, the headwaiter of the Breakfast Buffet (or head bin refiller, since most of the work in the Buffet involved keeping the *pannekoeken* piled high), looks like an Egyptian Burt Reynolds. Big, wide-open face. Black mustache. Emad had a never-ending look of alertness, which made him a good breakfast waiter. He'd seen me only during the daytime—and he still liked me.

We came from different worlds. According to Yolanda, a stern waitress with no eyebrows and an accent that I'd thought for months was a speech impediment (turns out she was just Belgian), it was forbidden for us to be together. She didn't actually say the words "It is forbidden." It was more like, "Dey thmell dike hash-ish! Blah!"

Emad made an effort to come down into the café at least once a day to tell me, "I like you, Lauren, I really like you." It made Yolanda furious. She furrowed her eyebrow ridge and told him to "go ayay! Doo can't be dow here!" None of the pale, floppy Dutch depressives I worked with liked the dark Middle Eastern (and one Greek) boys of the Breakfast Buffet. That bothered me. "You guys are racist," I'd say, and then quickly add, "Just kidding!" for job security.

Emad was funny. He made jokes about being Muslim the same way I made jokes about being American. I ran around screaming, "Everything is just too *different* in Europe!" in a Texas accent and acted like I was going to eat a bowl of ketchup, while he threw napkins at the female kitchen staff and asked them to "Cover your face—stop tempting me!"

The day he tied a tablecloth around my face I fell a little bit in love with him. Maybe it was the contrast between his humor and the café staff's lack of it. The café staff aggressively fought against the idea of laughing. "Ja, you told a joke, so what? Big deal. Am I supposed to lose my mind now? Oh, ha-ha-ha. No, I'm not doing that. Sorry."

Emad cornered me after his shift one day. "I like you, Lauren, I really like you," he said, and asked me on a date.

Sure, it was his catchphrase. I'd overheard him saying it to an eighty-nine-year-old, limp-necked German woman, but nobody had told me they liked me, really liked me, in a long time. They'd told me I had the figure of a mole or that I needed to stop laughing so loudly. Mert had referred to me as a movie star, but movie stars are admired from afar. Being asked out on a date pulled me back into the world of hopeful romance and delusional dreams. He could be the one. What if he fell in love with me? (I never thought, "What if I fell in love with him?" because I was very polite and wanted him to go first.) Having a Dutch boyfriend was an item of exotic interest for three months in Indiana. An Egyptian boyfriend would be exotic forever. Hans taught me how to keep with the flow of bike traffic in Amsterdam and buy hard cheeses. Emad would teach me to ride a camel and buy spices from men in robes with monkeys on their shoulders. I'd come home for the holidays with dusty suitcases full of magic lanterns and beads and dried mice. "They eat them like peanuts over there," I'd explain. Thanks to Disney's version of *Aladdin*, I knew exactly what my future held.

Best of all, I'd finally have a compelling reason to go to work besides free cookies: to see my boyfriend.

Heading out the door for our date, I was excited because Emad had never seen me in anything except my hotel uniform and I was looking goooood. It was a rare moment where my chin wasn't broken out, my hair was taking the curl, and my skirt and shirt were the same shade of black. The gods must be pleased with the coming together of Emad and me.

My phone rang. It was Emad calling to ask if I could bring a friend for his best friend, Mikhas. "Listen, Lauren, it's Saturday night and Mikhas really needs to go out. I have to bring him." Mikhas is Emad's boss.

It was flattering that someone from upper management wanted to tag along, but a double date was not really what I'd been hoping for, and it was a little last-minute.

None of my expat, artsy girlfriends were the "Hey, put on your stockings, his friend wants a gal too, Madge!" sort. They were far too busy creating dance pieces about the AIDS epidemic as dreamt by Rumi. For a second, I thought about calling my single friend Rachel, an English painter who had just finished painting a series of "lonely flowers," but she'd just broken off a relationship because she didn't like the guy's hands. "He's got funny knuckles," she'd said. I couldn't remember what Mikhas's hands looked like, so I didn't call, a decision I would deeply regret later that night when Mikhas was behind me in that sexual position made popular by sheep herders and the morbidly obese, and Emad was under me whispering, "I like you, I really like you. I mean, besides all of this."

Emad is giggly on the phone as he says good-bye. He's nervous about our date, I thought. Or very high.

We met at Rum Runners. Nothing says romance in Amsterdam like Jimmy Buffett blasting in a Caribbean tourist bar. Also nothing says romance like bringing your manager from work with you. On the barstool next to Emad was Mikhas.

Emad continued to refer to the night as "our date" while the three of us sat and did round after round of Laser Beam shots—a neon-green concoction that gives you that "laser beam melting your organs" feeling that the kids love.

Before the Laser Beams liquefied my insides, Emad told me he used to be an agricultural engineer back in Egypt. He lived in Libya for a while, married and divorced a white African woman, and moved to Holland.

I like him.

Mikhas and Emad kept excusing themselves to use the bathroom every few minutes. Any time one was gone the other would scoot his barstool over and whisper, "I like you, Lauren. I really like you. Oh! Here he comes!" It was hard enough for me to think of dealing with one guy falling in love with me, but two! Best friends and on the same night! I'd read about this sort of thing in *Seventeen* magazine, but I never thought it would happen to me!

"Tutti frutti, man!" Mikhas yelled as he ran out of the bar bathroom with a handful of flavored condoms. Mikhas and Emad high-fived each other.

Oh, wait a minute. Do these guys think . . . ?

By the time we got to my flat I was feeling woozy. All I'd eaten that day was a stack of sugar cookies called *Jodenkoek*, which in Dutch means "Jew cookies." I hate to blame the Jews for everything, but those cookies didn't quite have the absorption power that six Malibu rum shots needed.

I didn't care about who liked me more. To overcompensate for my head spins I invited them both up—assuming they'd decline.

"Please join me for a nightcap. I'll be right back. Just want to powder my nose!"I ran inside. After I'd thrown up so hard my eyeballs got shoved out of their sockets, I opened the bathroom door and was shocked to find Emad standing there. Waiting. I'd been in there for three hours. Or maybe it was ten minutes.

"Hello, Lauren!" Emad was waiting right outside the bathroom door, and he looked so sober and wide eyed. He told me that if I wanted them to go home right now they would, no problem. Or—big wide-open-face smile—"We could stay and make you very happy."

He assured me, "We've done it before, and it's a guaranteed success. Mikhas is good guy. I trust him more than my brother."

I'd hate to meet his brother.

Before answering Emad, I needed to ask myself the two questions that have launched every hero's journey: "Didn't they hear me throwing up?" and "Will my mother ever be able to find out about this?"

The answer to both of those questions was "*No.*" I hoped.

That's what you do in your twenties, I told myself. You explore.

If I did this, did it mean I was going to have horrible boundary issues and do whatever men asked me to do? No. It didn't.

I don't remember saying yes, but I do remember saying "Okay." Let the wild rumpus begin.

What happened then was that we all made sweet, beautiful love. Smiling at one another and checking in to see if everyone was feeling connected. There were a lot of "Are you okay?"s and "Does that feel good?"s.

Oh no, wait, I already spoiled the ending, so you know that it was the most unsexy thing that was supposed to be sexy that I've ever done. It was an exhausting forty minutes that felt like seven hours of "Okay, so who needs a leg? Could you get by with just a foot? Emad, let him have my arm and then you take this leg . . ."

Every few minutes there was an "Okay, now, everybody *flip*!" It was like a drunken game of naked Twister. Fumbling and losing balance. The worst part of it for me was that I felt out of control of what parts of my body were being exposed. Normally, during intimate encounters I like to make little mountains out of my comforter to hide certain areas of my body. Or demurely cover my entire body with pillows, leaving just an ankle sticking out, which could make actual sex impossible, but at least I was in control. Sex with two people is like doing theater in the round; no matter which way you turn, someone is looking at your ass and there's nothing you can do about it.

The night ended when Mikhas checked his watch and announced that he had to get home because his wife got nervous being alone with her newborn baby at night.

He had a newborn?! What kind of person left his wife at home with a newborn while he . . . ech. Ech-ech. Awful people making disgusting choices, and there I was in the thick of it. They shouldn't call them three-ways. They should call them "piles of idiots."

What the hell was wrong with me? Everyone out! Out so I could wash the smell off of me, so I could journal and re-hang my flying pigs sculptures that they took down in case someone hit their head. How dare they take down my flying pigs! They were the symbols of my "magic is possible" life in Amsterdam.

I was convinced that this was the darkest night of my life . . . until they were gone.

The minute the door shut behind them I got up and sauntered over to the mirror. "Look at you—you're *insane*! What's next, Anaïs Nin? What is *next*?!"

My breezy "anything goes, I'm in my twenties in Amsterdam" façade worked until I was at breakfast the next morning telling my English painter friend, Rachel, about my night and she burst into tears. "Why did you let them do that to you?" she sobbed.

I told the story to another friend that day, an African American experimental dancer, and even though I presented it with all the "dark night of the soul" affectations I could muster, she thought it was the best thing she'd ever heard. She high-fived me throughout the story. "Next time something like that comes up, call me!" she said.

What did happen? I have two minds about it. Everything's in twos. Two minds. Two penises. Hopefully the tutti frutti didn't break, because if it did I'd be having twins.

No good relationship starts with a three-way, but Emad "likes me, really likes me" and I "like him, kind of like him," so we started dating. It wasn't what I would have called a romantic, lovely relationship. It was mostly just fun. And exotic. Emad had been a wedding singer back in Alexandria, Egypt. After sex, we'd lie on his bed under the mosquito net while he sang songs about brides feeling like the queen of the Nile who finally found their kings. "It's our story," I'd say to him, and he'd laugh and jump up to wash his hands, face, neck, and feet for the ninth time that night. The man was so clean he sweated soap bubbles, and I popped them with my kisses.

At work, Mikhas tried to return coffee mugs that he knew didn't belong in the café a few times to let me know that he was always up for bringing back the magic, but after I asked him if that meant his baby was sleeping through the night now, he left me alone.

After a month of dating, Emad and I both had trips planned to go home to visit our families. The first chance we got once we were both back in Amsterdam, we went out to dinner. I'd worked in my mother's year-round Christmas store helping her glue together cotton balls to make fake snow for her window displays and drank large tumblers of Diet Coke that made me feel sick. It was hell.

I asked Emad how his trip was.

"I got married!"

"What?"

"I got married!"

He burst out laughing, and because I was so disoriented, I joined in.

"That's crazy!"

He laughed harder. "Yes! Crazy! And, Lauren, I can't wait for you to see her. You won't believe it. You're going to love her. You think I'm Muslim? She's got the veils and everything!"

Emad's parents had surprised him with a wife as soon as he got off the plane. He'd never met her before, so it was "very exciting!" His wife had never left her country before and she was a little nervous about joining him next week.

"But it doesn't matter. We can still see each other."

What would have made him think that I'd be the kind of girl who would continue to see someone who was married? Oh, wait.

I sighed. "No, Emad. I'm not going to see you anymore. This is where I draw the line."

He gave me an "Oh, *this* is where you draw it?" smirk. Fair enough.

It had felt good to turn him down. It wasn't a hard call, but it still felt good, like proof that I'd finally taken control of my life. I didn't have to date the man I had a threesome with who now had an arranged bride. I was really growing up.

Maybe that's what the three-way had been, too! A way of saying, "Guess what, Mom? I don't have to Windex all the bathroom windows just because it's on my chore list."

The moment I ripped up my return ticket to America and decided to stay in Amsterdam, I took control. Of my life.

Back in the car with David I finish the story by telling how what I'd really wanted back then was some hand-holding, a nice dinner, and back-tickling with one boring unmarried person. I'm not Anaïs Nin.

"I'm with Rachel," he says. "Why would you let someone do that to you?"

Honestly, I feel the same way. A little sad and embarrassed for the girl who couldn't say no but also jealous of the freedom to catch whatever crazy ship sailed past me. That pretty much sums up my twenties.

David gets his revenge and manages to tell three stories from his twenties that highlight his taste for danger and his attraction to exotic women before we've even reached our exit on the highway.

By the time we pull into our driveway, we agree that any story that starts with "Once, when I was in my twenties . . ." is a story, as meaningful and life-changing as it may be, we were going to have to pay a professional to listen to.

BFF

According to the little red clock above the stove, I've been lying on the floor of Magda's kitchen for thirty-five minutes. I fell off her kitchen counter trying to sponge-clean her ceiling. I'd tried to move, but the ache of my spine and the intense swelling of the brain-like pain in my head wouldn't let me. Magda's note had a list of specific areas of her flat she wanted cleaned. People normally leave their instructions for me in English, but Magda wrote her note entirely in Dutch, and I didn't bring my dictionary. It's never been a problem before since I've been able to figure out the words for "dried pee" using context clues. Five minutes after I fell I remembered the Dutch word for "front steps" and screamed to nobody, "Steps! 'Stoop' means front steps! Clean the front steps!"

It would be a lot easier to be dying slowly from a concussion if Nina Simone wasn't on the radio singing "Porgy and Bess." In the best of circumstances my heart can't handle listening to her sing. Her voice is so pained and haunted. It makes me feel so alone.

"Porgy . . . if you can keep me, I wanna stay here forever . . ."

If I'd known I was going to fall and suffer what could be a broken back or a mild concussion, I would have put on Billy Joel's spiritual and uplifting "River of Dreams" or U2 or Paul Simon. Really, any song with a white man singing with a gospel choir would work.

Life had been so good a few hours ago, dancing my heart out to Prince in my little apartment, laughing hysterically at how many grapes I could fit in my mouth (twelve). I'd smoked half a joint by myself, so it was drug-induced, but joy is joy no matter how much you pay for it, and I'd found the joint on the ground next to my bike this morning, so my joy was the best kind of joy—the free kind. Now I was paying for it.

Pot is usually my perfect Buddhist boyfriend, taking me gently by the hand and showing me how to turn a dirty menial job into a spiritual practice by cleaning the too-often-ignored objects in a home, like pen caps. Today, he turned on me. I don't want to blame pot. I blame that photo of Magda and her boyfriend, Dick, standing in front of a waterfall with their arms around each other. They're completely naked. Of course. You cannot keep clothes on Dutch people. The glass covering the picture is thick with grease because Magda hung it right above her stove and filthy because I'd never noticed it before. One of those dust-ball dingle berries hanging off the bottom of the frame is going to plop right down in Magda's pea soup if I don't clean it soon. As soon as I regain the use of my hands, I'll get right to it.

How does dour, humorless Magda with her brown-tinted teeth and the profile of a bulldog have a boyfriend, while I, at almost twenty-four years old, which is almost thirty, which is almost dead, have been single forever?

She does have nice eyelashes. Very long.

If I don't meet someone soon I'm going to end up being so alone and desperate I'll say yes to the first psycho who likes my ankles and end up with someone like my high school boyfriend Sam.

The first time I tried to break up with him, ten minutes into our first date, he burst into tears and threatened to kill himself, which was weird since he was twenty-two and could drink legally, so he had it made. It was so flattering and horrific I ended up staying with him for four months. He tried to push me out of a moving car so many times for things like singing along with "that fag" David Bowie, I started jumping out at stoplights even if Dire Straits was on the radio, just to be safe. If I tried to go out with my age-appropriate, happy high school friends, he'd threaten to kill himself. Thankfully, like most failed stand-ups who live in their mothers' basements, his follow-through was horrible.

I'm guessing I was the only junior in my high school getting pushed out of a car by her twenty-two-year-old boyfriend. It was all so Tammy Lisa.

Last month, I found out that for the first eight days of my life, my name was Tammy Lisa. The adoption agency let my birth mother and birth father each give me a name for my original birth certificate. My birth father chose Tammy and my birth mother chose Lisa, so put it together and you've got Tammy "Get off me, Daddy, you're crushing my smokes" Lisa. My adoptive parents recrowned me "Lauren Huntington," but no matter how many country club sports they trained me in, they couldn't quite scrub all the coal dust off my neck.

Tammy Lisa lurks. I have to be very careful.

My back has stopped throbbing, and I could probably get up if I wanted to, but my head hurts. My headache could have less to do with a concussion and more to do with the gas leak in my apartment. Ever since I read Sylvia Plath's journals I've been paranoid that the gas heater in the corner of my bedroom is leaking, and I'm dying a slow, drawn-out version of her death.

You know what bothers me about the idea of death? It's so hard to look forward to, and I love planning. I guess I can add "go blind, go deaf, lose teeth, and start to shit myself" to my list of things to do.

One by one, you lose your senses as you age. The only thing that connects us to life is our senses. That's pretty deep. You see, my Buddhist boyfriend pot still treats me right. I'm going to get up really quickly and write that down in my journal. Then I'll lie right back down in case I have a concussion and shouldn't be moved.

You know what else this headache could be from? The giant zit on my forehead. It's morphed the entire shape of my head. I could barely get my hat on this morning. Or it could be my new vitamins. Besides the daily pot smoking I'm really trying to take care of myself.

It's getting dark out. Magda will be home in twenty minutes. If I get up now she may not believe me when I tell her that I fell. She might think it's just a big ruse to get out of dealing with the mound of cat hair she calls her living room.

You know when I peaked? Fifth grade. Words like "ugly" and "pretty" didn't matter to me. The ability to make my arms into the shape of a *Y* and an *M* and a *C* and an *A* as I sang along with the Village People gave me all the happiness I needed. As many days of the week as I could, I wore my purple satin disco pants and matching purple satin jacket that said STAR on the back, and under the word STAR, in case anyone found the yellow cursive stitching hard to read, was a giant yellow satin star. I strutted down the hallways of Grandview Elementary like they were the streets of Brooklyn and I was John Travolta in *Saturday Night Fever*.

Then puberty hit. I bought a DISCO SUCKS T-shirt and never wore purple satin again.

Well, Tammy Lisa, traumatic brain injury or not, get up off the floor. Tonight could be the night Magda plays squash; if I wait for her to get home, it could be hours. I'll leave her a note explaining about my accident. My head still feels a little sore, but I haven't felt this rested in a long time.

Magda calls me after I get back to my flat and yells at me for leaving early and not finishing my job. "I felt nauseous from the fall, Magda!" I sob to her. She is not moved. "Whatever. I wanted to fire you anyway." Her name alone should have given me a heads-up that she was going to be a cruel and awful master.

Before I smoke pot and watch *Oprah* (busy, busy), I should check the want ads section of the *Volkskrant* for any housekeeping jobs. Hey . . . what's this?

> The award-winning American-Amsterdam Theater Company, from Houston, Texas, is bringing their unique style of Raw Emotional Theater to Europe. Seeking special individuals who are risk-taking artists who demand artistic excellence to become full-time paid company members.

A full-time professional theater company is looking to hire company members? And they'll pay them? I've never seen anything like this in the want ads. In Amsterdam *or* back in Indiana, and believe me, I've looked. This is huge. Being a full-time paid member of a theater company is something that happens if you're a Barrymore or you graduate at the top in your class from Yale School of Drama, not by responding to a want ad in the back of a newspaper. But this is Holland. Everything is different. Being an actor here isn't something "special"—it's a common trade, like being a carpenter or a prostitute who specializes in eating bananas with her vagina.

The Dutch aren't big on the whole "special" thing. The whole premise of the country is "So what, big deal." Being famous is completely different here. As far as I can tell, the big dream for Dutch actors is getting a gig on the popular soap opera *Goede Tijden, Slechte Tijden* (Good Times, Bad Times). It's a tiny country, so the actors are famous to about four people.

Normally I wouldn't even try for something like this, but maybe they'll need someone to play soldier number four or interns to make coffee. They wouldn't have to pay me. I'll make sure to tell them that first thing. Don't pay me, and give me the shittiest parts.

I snuff out my joint (oops, where did that come from?) and call for an audition.

Apartment 1408. Somewhere in North Amsterdam where I've never been before.

Billie, a twentysomething guy in tight Wrangler jeans and cowboy boots, is leading me down a dark hallway. The apartment is full of things like glass butter dishes, ceramic swans, teacup collections, and musty old rugs. There are mysterious brown smears on the walls. I wouldn't be surprised to find a skeleton with a gray wig wearing a housecoat sitting on one of the kitchen chairs.

Billie has a crooked cowboy smile and a tight little sparkplug body. He's bursting with incredibly attractive, rugged Texas passion. I'll never get in this company. Good-looking people like to be around other good-looking people so they can feel free to say things like "You're beautiful, I'm beautiful, but I want so much more in my life," or "I know it sounds awful, but why do poor people have weird foreheads?" without feeling bad.

The artistic director is an ex–hand model turned genius theater director named Nico McMasters. She chose three of "her very best" actors to help her start the new company, and Billie is one of them. He is clearly in love with her. He tells me how working with Nico changed his entire life. Testing to see if he could ever be persuaded to love a clown, I ask him, "Before you met her, you were an armless hamster learning to paint with your feet, right?"

All I get is a quick "ha," and he's right back to Nico.

"Nico is kind of a god in Houston. Everyone wants to work with her, but it's really hard for her to find folks who can do 'the work.' She was feeling so limited by American audiences she had to get out."

I nod—"Oh god, I *get* it"—but the truth is I'm hardly listening because I'm trying to wrap my head around how tiny Wrangler jeans make men's butts look.

On the lumpy baby-poop-colored couch in the living room sit the other two chosen ones, a short, buff version of Paul Newman and a short, buff version of Jesus. They are also quite handsome and sexy. Either I need to move to Texas or Nico *is* a genius—whom, sadly, I won't be meeting today.

Nico wants "her boys" to make the final decision on who joins the company since they're the ones who understand "the work" and know what it takes to do "the work."

Let's hope that "the work" they keep referring to is stuff like memorizing lines and learning how to glue fake noses on and not mining kidneys from desperate illegal immigrants. I'm in the middle of answering buff Jesus's question, "If you could invite anyone to dinner, living or dead, who would it be?"

"Loudon Wainwright III, Oprah, Kurt Vonnegut, Walt Whitman, Sinead O'Connor, Abbie Hoffman, the Dalai Lama, Robert De Niro, Vincent van Gogh, Sylvia Plath—"

I'm about to say "and the guy who played Starsky on *Starsky and Hutch*" when I hear the distinct sound of a match being lit followed by a long exhale coming from behind a cracked door in the back of the room.

There's someone or something looming in the dark shadows.

It's that Nico lady. I'm sure of it.

I couldn't care less.

At this point I don't care if she's an alien kept in a jar. I've never been around so many good-looking heterosexual actors in one room. The theater boys I know scream "*South Pacific!*" just to celebrate being alive.

The monologue I've chosen to do for my audition is a self-written comedic piece entitled "Weight Watchers Group Leader." As Margie, the perky Weight Watchers leader, flaunting my tiny wrists in the faces of the obese housewives and encouraging them to pry their fillings out of their teeth before weigh-ins, I was heralded at North Central High School's "A Night with Repertory Theater" as "better than Carol Burnett by Kristin Chapman's stepmother." It's a sure thing.

Halfway through the monologue there's been nary a chuckle. Even when I'm all alone at home rehearsing I have to stop for laughs.

If they don't laugh at the motivational poem, I'll tell them the monologue was written by Wallace Shawn and go home.

Aaaaaaaannnnddd . . . nada.

Forget it.

These guys are just another group of pretentious Texas artists looking to change the face of European theater. Perhaps if I had set the Weight Watchers meeting in a concentration camp and the leader had a Polish accent they would have liked it. "Elsa lost five pounds! That means at eighty-eight pounds she's gone past her goal weight by forty pounds! Good for you, Elsa! Remember cockroaches are three points, ladies! They count!"

If I promise not to bring my dictionary and not to drink all Magda's orange juice again she'll hire me back.

"Thank you." Billie stands up and walks toward me with what seem to be tears in his eyes.

"That was amazing."

Buff Jesus tells me it's "very complicated stuff."

Buff Paul Newman can't believe I wrote it myself.

Apparently, without the laughs the entire piece becomes this deep examination of misogyny in America. And calorie counting.

Billie called this morning. I'm in. I cannot believe it. I'm an official company member of the Amsterdam-American Alliance Theater Company. The first thing I need to do is bow my head in gratitude and give thanks to the unseen forces that got me to this life-changing moment *where it turns out that I am better than all those schmucks who didn't make it in!* In your faces! I won! You lost! Find me a tailor in Amsterdam who works with purple satin; I'm making me a new suit the Bee Gees would kill for! Yes! Yes! Finally, yes! I am going to be a professional actor. Paid. With money!

My phone rings. It's my ex-boyfriend Hans. Buzzkill. Hans and I were together for almost two years. We've been broken up for a year. Every so often, he likes to show up at one of my housecleaning jobs and chase me home on his bike trying to kick my spokes, determined to make me suffer how "I made him suffer." The last time I saw him was when he came over to my apartment at three A.M., completely drunk, and accused me of having sex with strangers and never loving our pet rabbit, Liza. The next morning he sent me a Joni Mitchell tape to apologize.

He's calling to share with me the good news. He's going to be a company member of an exciting new . . . Texas . . . blah-blah . . . bigger buzzkill.

We both agree that we shouldn't mention to anyone that we've dated because we don't want it to get in the way of "the work." Mostly I don't want him complaining how hard it was to give me an orgasm in case I have a chance with any of the Texas boys.

Monday morning. First company meeting.

This is the funkiest group of artists I've ever seen in one place. It looks like a scene from a Fellini movie. People of all ages and pant lengths are running around the raw open space of the eighteenth-century canal house that is going to house the new theater. It's a gorgeous space. People from Texas have so much money!

With Hans safely on the other side of the room talking to an attractive blond woman with yellow paint splatters all over her face, I corner Billie to share with him my passion for life. "Thank god I got in this company. Not acting for me is like being a whale and taking in huge gusting breaths of air and not being allowed to blow it all out the top of my head." If I ever want to have sex again, perhaps I should stop using whale analogies.

Nico makes her entrance.

All twenty-five people in the room go completely silent. She didn't even have to go, "Shhhhhhh." It's like a lion sauntered in. Or a movie star. Or someone with a gun.

She is one tall, beautiful drink of lady water. Early thirties or late forties; I'm bad with ages. Miss Texas hair and dreamy blue eyes that look like they were painted on by the guy who designed the sixties Barbie face.

"Whoa, now. I love you guys already!" Nico says and laughs. We all laugh with her. I can't stop laughing. Right as I start to wonder if this is what an anxiety attack feels like, I look up and see Nico looking right at me. Immediately I feel a connection. She sees past my Michigan State sweatshirt and MC Hammer pants. (I'm the only one who took the "dress to move" note seriously.) She sees who I really am. What I'm capable of. Or maybe I look like a girl who goes to her hair salon. I get that a lot.

Nico steps to the side and introduces R. T. Thomas, a retired Hewlett-Packard businessman. He is "a dear old friend, whose financial commitment and passion for truth have made all of this possible." Amsterdam must be R.T.'s version of a Carnival cruise, because he's wearing shorts and a Hawaiian shirt unbuttoned halfway down his chest, which blesses the viewer with a glimpse of gray furry belly, and he has a camera around his neck. R.T. became a die-hard supporter of the theater after seeing Billie play the title role in *Jesus Christ Superstar* seventeen times. He tells us that he's very excited about what the future holds for this group of talented young people and excuses himself. "Gotta make hay while the sun shines."

Nico yells after him, "Careful you don't make too much hay

where the sun don't shine, my friend," and busts out in a "you gotta love this guy, right?" laugh.

Once R.T. is completely out of the building, the mood shifts. Nico takes a deep breath and makes a slow scan around the room.

"If y'all don't want to be here . . . if there is anything that is keeping you from being completely present in this room . . . go do it. I don't want y'all in here unless you are *here*. I'm serious. You won't be fired. Just go do whatever it is you need to do in order to be here with your full self. When you're done . . . come on back."

Nobody moves. I love it. Good stuff. This is how every moment of our lives should be lived.

"We looked for the bravest artists in the world. And we found y'all. The stakes could not be higher for us. That's the kind of work we do. High stakes. If it's not high stakes . . . If you're not on the edge of a cliff about to fall to your death, you're not doing 'the work.' Let me tell y'all something. Your fears are not that you are inadequate, but that you are powerful beyond all measure."

That's what Oprah says. Oh my god, Nico knows Oprah. This doesn't surprise me at all.

Now it's time for verbal contracts. She warns us that the work is going to be very personal. The contracts are vital for our un-blocking our creative selves. She has us repeat after her:

"I promise to be open, honest, and reactive
"I promise to maintain confidentiality
"I promise not to have sex with company members—"

Ohhhhh. That's why Billie was so nice to me. He knew about the contract. He knew he could dry hump me without needing to see it through.

You know what? This is exactly what I need.

Now I can be myself and not worry about if I had a chance with any of the Texas boys, which, considering the presence of our beautiful Italian set designer and the tall blond Dutch actress, was unlikely to happen anyway. I'm free to pretend that secretly everyone wants to have sex with me but they're contractually bound not to.

Nico pairs us up and puts me with Emile, a German playwright with very angular features and little tiny glasses perched on his nose that look like he'd stolen them off of a figurine of an old lady.

"We are going to practice being all knowing. Dipping into the collective unconscious. For the next thirty minutes you will be able to see into a person's soul. Not pretending to see into their soul but seeing into their soul."

I'm being paid for this?

"Look into your partner's eyes. Do not look away. You are going to be able to see into their soul. Every image that comes up needs to be shared. Don't think about it. Don't judge it. Say it. Don't hold anything back, and whatever you do, don't look away from their eyes."

I offer to look into Emile's soul first. I'm worried that I'm going to do it wrong. What if the only images that come up are about me? "I see me eating my breakfast. I see me eating my lunch." Perhaps I should have had a snack.

Emile takes off his glasses, and by golly if the images don't start coming to me so fast I can't keep up with them. "There's a house. And flames. People are screaming. Horses—yes, there are horses running out of barns. There are men praying, clergymen, wrapped in red flags, handing you babies to save. There's a food court in a mall—no, it's not a mall; there are women with torches. It's the French Revolution. Yes, the French Revolution . . ."

By the time it's Emile's turn to look into my soul I've seen the moon explode and entire empires crumble and I'm completely drained.

Emile needs his glasses to see into my soul. He puts them on, peers into my eyes for about thirty seconds, and says, "You look like Kathy Bates." Takes his glasses off and sits back in his chair, looking around the room to see what everyone else is doing.

I want a new partner. That is not what my soul looks like. That is what I look like when I don't put enough contouring blush on. If Emile can't at least pretend to be deep, there's no way he has what it takes. I wonder if I should alert Nico.

Every once in a while I catch Hans glaring at me. As skinny and pale and bald as he is, there's something about a six-foot-seven lapsed Catholic Dutchman glaring at you from across the room that's unsettling. He's constantly judging me as a madonna or a whore. It's like he knows I made out with that Dutch bartender last night. I also bought flowers, recognized the existence of synchronicity, and read an Allen Ginsberg poem. Why doesn't he sense that about me?

After a smoke break we jump into "wound work."

I have my journal and my pen poised to write down every word Nico says, so I'll do well on the test. Nico tells me to put the pen down because I'll remember what I need to remember. She doesn't know how much pot I smoke. Or I bet she does.

"Deep inside each of us is a wound where we carry the knowledge of our death. If we are brave enough to do the work, we will eventually be able to cut through all the layers of resistance inside of us and have full access to that wound."

I don't get it. Is she saying that inside of me at this moment I know that one day I will be drowning in darkness but I won't notice because I'll be a corpse rotting away as people I love live on? Ouch. Found it.

Nico starts rolling herself a cigarette. She's already so European. What's next? Neon orange shirts tucked into tight white jean shorts and hairy armpits?

"Touch that wound and you will cry like you have never cried and laugh like y'all have never laughed. I'm not gonna lie. It's a long road to get to this place. Not all of you are gonna be able to make it. But those who do, get ready, because the power that will be released onstage will be magnificent."

On our fifth smoke break, Nico walks over and puts her arm around me. "You didn't think you'd be here, did you, girlfriend? Let me tell you something. You are supposed to be here. I have no doubt and I cannot wait to see what you can do."

Uh-oh.

She's got high expectations for me.

Just like the 950 graduating seniors before I delivered the commencement speech at my high school graduation. At the audition I'd beaten out bright young speech team leaders with messages of hope and "Gandhi said unto Martin Luther King Jr."–type quotes simply because I had a lot of energy and didn't mind large groups of people looking at me. In fact, I preferred it.

From the podium I could see row after row of my fellow students filling up the floor of Market Square Arena, with big, hopeful smiles, hands poised over gown-covered thighs, ready to slap. "Oh, this is going to be funny," all their faces said. "That's the crazy girl I sit next to in algebra who pretends to smoke tampons like a cigar. Didn't she do that Weight Watchers monologue that Kristin Chapman's stepmom loved so much? Oh, we are gonna *laugh*."

Speeches like "Today I consider myself the luckiest man on the face of the earth" do well in large arenas meant for major sporting events, their impact made more powerful by the echoing and tinny reverb quality. Not so much with lines like "You know how *Grease* was a musical about a group of high school kids in the fifties. Well, maybe they'll have a musical about high school in the eighties and call it *Mousse*." By the time I got to my closing line, "Remember, whether you're flipping burgers at McDonald's"—don't make eye contact with Ron Gude . . . don't make eye contact with Ron Gude— "or you're the CEO of a big business, give it all you have," I was convinced I'd ruined graduation for 950 teenagers. As I stood on the podium, it all came back to them—"Wait a minute. That's not the crazy funny girl. That's the girl with the twenty-two-year-old stalker boyfriend who waits for her in the parking lot after school threatening to kill himself. That's the crazy *crazy* girl."

Nobody knows anything about my past here in Amsterdam. That's the beauty of living overseas. Today, I consider myself the luckiest manly girl on the face of the earth.

At the end of the day, Texas Jesus leads the whole company in Garth Brooks's "I've Got Friends in Low Places" around the electric piano he brought from Texas. Nothing like Garth Brooks to open up the primordial wound.

It has been two blissful weeks of singing, massaging, and visualizing winning Oscars and our deaths. The only turd in the punch bowl is Hans. He's convinced that I've broken the contract and am having sex with one of the Texas actors and continues to shoot me furious looks throughout the day. Sadly, he's wrong.

This morning Nico announced that the company is ready for the next level and she will be pairing people up to work on scenes. No performances yet. We're at least a year away from that. She's got a remarkable ability to sense what people need; where they are blocked; who's most likely to be killed by whom. Hans and I will be working together on a scene from the play *Danny and the Deep Blue Sea* by John Patrick Shanley.

Hans will be playing the role of Danny, a truck driver prone to violent outbursts whose nickname is the Animal. Nico would like me to play the role of Roberta, a divorced mother haunted by memories of an ugly sexual incident in her past. It's a real madcap comedy. Playing a victimized lady is a stretch for me and will require real acting skills. All Hans has to do is show up.

Twenty minutes into the first rehearsal and Hans, the man who cried tears of joy on our first date when I made him spaghetti, and who less than a month ago was throwing up into my trash can and asking me to marry him, has tried to strangle me twice. Nico doesn't believe in blocking, so whenever Hans gets a whim to put his hands around my throat, he throws in a few little flourishes of strangling and blames his wound. I get one line out and then spend the rest of the scene trying to dodge his lunges at me.

"I need a break," I say, and run toward the door. He runs right after me and grabs my arm to pull me back into the scene. "Stop! Curtain! Half time! Let go! Ow! Ow! Ow! Your nails are digging into me! That's me talking! Not the character—Sarah or—"

I can't remember my character's name. Stumbling out of the room I collapse in the hallway in tears, yelling "Stop it! I can't breathe! I can't breathe!" Hans is hunched over his backpack getting a drink of water.

"What are you talking about? Why can't you breathe? I'm not touching you!"

He suggests we take a break. I guess he needs to ice down his wrists so he can keep strangling me without getting carpal tunnel and make it through the rest of the rehearsal.

I scream one more "ow" and run to find Nico.

"Nico, I don't think Hans and I should be scene partners. He and I were once engaged to be married and now he's trying to kill me."

Nico was already smiling when she saw me limping toward her, checking my body for blood, and now she's full-on laughing. It's not a laughing-at-me laugh; more like an "Oh, humanity, aren't you delightful?" laugh.

"Girlfriend, what's Roberta's main characteristic?"

Roberta! That's her name. I'd only read the full script once and was focusing on our four-page scene, so to be honest I wasn't completely sure. "Compassion?"

Nico makes the "wrong answer" buzzer sound that they use in game shows.

"She's mistrustful of men. She's been hurt by a lot of men. It's all she's known."

God, she sounds awful.

Nico wants me to do homework before our next rehearsal. I hate homework. It gets in the way of pot smoking.

My homework is that for the next twenty-four hours I am to silently repeat the following sentence to myself: "He can't hurt me; I can hurt him." I still think that if she could have simply made "no strangling" a rule, that would solve all our problems.

The next day, here I am again, ten minutes into rehearsal with Hans on top of me with his hands around my throat.

That's it. I'm quitting.

"Did you do the homework I gave you?"

I tell her yes, but the truth is I made a few adjustments. Like changing "He can't hurt me; I can hurt him" to "He can't hurt me. Oh yes, he can, guard your solar plexus, he hates me."

Nico reaches out and puts her elegant hand-model hand on my shoulder.

"Lauren, the world is divided into two different kinds of people. The Okays and the Not Okays. There are those of us who know in the deepest core of their being that they are Okay and there are those of us who have had a few doozies thrown our way and know in the deepest core of our being that we are Not Okay. So, sister, which one do you think you are?"

Is that a rhetorical question?

New homework assignment: Silently chant "I'm okay. I'm okay.

I'm okay" to myself nonstop, starting now. Not "I'm the best" or "I deserve to have all my dreams come true" or "Jesus sent me"; just "I'm okay."

If I discover that I've stopped chanting it, no problem; start up again.

"I'm okay, I'm okay, I'm okay, I'm okay, I'm dumb. I'm okay. I can feel my fat butt shaking behind me. Oops. I'm okay."

The next day I feel completely different. Rehearsal begins as it always does—with Hans running at me with his hands up like Frankenstein, but today he suddenly stops a foot away from me. He looks disoriented for a moment, turns, and walks away. This happens three times in a row. Did Nico put him up to this? Are they trying to empower the Not Okay girl? Stop thinking that! Get back to your mantra, you fat, insecure cow! I mean, I'm okay, I'm okay, I'm okay.

Hans walks toward me and every time stops like he's hit a wall. He can't get near me. His confusion turns into anger. His years and years of being rejected by women can't be taken out on me, so he starts a fistfight with the only vulnerable person left in the room. Himself. With a primal scream, he grabs the front of his turtleneck with both hands and rips it off of his body, leaving only the collar around his neck, and crumples to the floor in sobs. He looks like a deranged priest.

Why is Nico wasting her time running a theater company? This "I'm okay" thing is a gold mine. Our troops need her. As well as bank tellers, teenage girls, junkies, and airplane pilots.

"I'm okay" is changing my entire life. My Dutch used to be limited to words like "yummy" or "clean the toilet," but suddenly my Dutch gets better and I can order stamps at the post office. Specific types of stamps like the ones for postcards even. My bike was stolen for the eighth time this month, and I convinced the junkie dragging it down the sidewalk to give it back to me. In

Dutch. All it took was a little calming of the "Shut up, shut up, you ignorant monkey" voice in my head.

A few days later, there is no scene rehearsal because it's all-company training day. We're in the middle of filling each other's compliment pots when Nico walks in. She looks like hell. Greasy hair stuck to her scalp. Mascara smeared.

"Y'all, this is the worst day of my entire life. I've been passing out all morning. Throwing up. Dizzy spells. You name it."

My god, she's dying. She gave us all she had and we sucked her dry. She's like the spider in *Charlotte's Web* who helped Wilbur the pig see how special he was. Just as I see that I'm "some pig," I'll have to carry on without her. I'll be back to being a plain old pig within a month.

Terrified, we all sit waiting for her to tell us what's going on, watching her roll a cigarette with shaky fingers. Nico's fingers are stained yellow from nicotine. I'd never noticed that before. I also had never noticed how important curling-iron use is for Nico's ability to maintain a "functioning human being" look.

Finally she speaks.

R.T., Hewlett-Packard moneyman, left the country.

"Y'all, he lost his mind. Had a complete mental collapse."

If she had known he was so unstable, she would have never gone into business with him. "R.T. had secrets and a dark side."

Nobody knows what to say besides "Oh shit."

She promises the Amsterdam-American Alliance Theater will live on. "I couldn't pay anyone, but you know I'd love for you all to continue the work. Especially the brave ones. Y'all know who y'all are."

She looks directly at me. I smile and wave at her. Perhaps not the most appropriate reaction.

Nico steps outside to give us a moment to discuss as a group what we'd like to do. I'm anxious to hear the Texas boys' take on all of this.

They know Nico and they know R.T. Has this sort of thing ever happened before? Is R.T. at the Cockring as we speak and all will be forgiven by the time he sobers up tomorrow? But I can't ask them because Nico motions for them to follow her outside. In times of crisis she likes to be wrapped in the warm blanket of hot Texas boys.

Once she's out of the room, Orla, a shy Danish dancer, famous for giving people what she referred to as "instinctual massages," stands up. "This is crazy bullshit. I'm going home," she says and walks out the door. After she's gone, the entire company votes to quit. They file out of the building in "the dream is dead" complete silence.

Nico stands right outside the front door, watching us leave, with a sad smile on her face. She thanks each member and apologizes as they pass her.

My hope was to quickly scurry by her without making eye contact, but I'm the last one out the door and she calls me over. Most of the company, including Hans, are unlocking their bikes, watching to see if I'm going to stop and talk to her. How can I not?

"You know what the worst part of all this is, girlfriend?"

That we've all quit our jobs, we've been working full-time for more than a month, we thought this was going to change our lives, and today was the day we were supposed to get our first paycheck?

"No, Nico, what's the worst part?"

"The worst part of all of this is that today was the day I was going to announce the first play of our season. *Burn This*, by Lanford Wilson, and you were gonna be in the cast. I've already booked the second stage at the main theater in town, the Stadsschouwburg. It was going to be a big ole deal."

This strikes me as an embarrassingly transparent tactic. A bit too "Oh, hey, don't go yet. I was just about to buy you a car. Guess you don't want a new car" for me.

Nico tells me not to tell the others but I was the only one of the new company members who understood wound work. "It's a rare gift, Ms. Thing. You've got direct access to that wound. You know who else does?"

A stabbing victim? I have no idea who else does and I don't care. This is a huge blow. I, too, would like to be wrapped in a warm blanket of Texas boys and need to know ASAP if our contracts are null and void so I can get to work on making that happen.

"Meryl Streep has direct access to her wound. Marlon Brando, Anthony Hopkins, all the great actors. Oh, Lauren, it breaks my heart. You would have made an amazing Anna. She's such an interesting character. Smart and tough but she won't let herself admit love—"

Okay. Here we go. Now Nico sees me as someone who can't be vulnerable—

"And she's the lead role."

Wait. Hold on, there. She's the lead?

You know, now that I take a moment to reflect, does anyone really know me? No. And do you know why? I simply can't let my guard down. Letting my guard down is tantamount to certain death. It's like I was born to play Anna.

I'm glad the others quit. Get rid of those greedy people who want to be paid. Gross.

The entire company quit except for the four Nico cast in *Burn This*.

Before I could have sex with Billie, R.T. stopped paying the Texas boys' rent and sent them one-way tickets back to Houston. It's not fair. My feet get cold when I watch TV. There must be Texas boy blankets all over Houston—why couldn't he leave one behind?

It's opening night. You'd think I was about to be on Broadway, I'm so out of my mind with opening-night jitters. I don't have to be at the theater for another two hours and I'm out of my mind. All two hundred seats have been sold. I'd throw up I'm so nervous, but I've been unable to eat. If I wasn't so busy being excited, I'd dry-heave. I'm pacing my flat in a purple silk robe I bought at H&M because I thought it seemed actress-y, going over my opening-night mantra "I am not too fat to be seen as a dancer. There are lots of fat dancers."

I'm a little sad rehearsals are over because they were beyond life-changing. Nico outdid herself. One of the male leads, Patrick, an actor from Canada, is convinced that Nico cured him of his diabetes with an "I don't have diabetes" mantra. Thanks to my "I'm Meryl Streep" mantra, as long as I don't look in a mirror I'm convinced I'm Meryl Streep. Every rehearsal ended with all of us saying "In the name of Nico." It started out as a joke but we've been doing it so much it's started to feel very much not like a joke. It's not a joke. The play is incredible and it's all because of our wound work. Our mantras. Our trust. The original company died, but as Nico always says, "You can't always get what you want, but you get what you need."

My phone rings.

It's Nico.

"Lauren, this is the worst day of my life."

Uh-oh. Wait. I thought the other day was the worst day of her life. Please tell me she hasn't already topped it.

"They're shutting us down."

Nico didn't get the rights to the play. She asked for them, but Lanford Wilson said no. He wants another theater in Amsterdam to premiere the show and has already given them the rights. Nico kept on rehearsing hoping Lanford would be too busy dusting his Tonys to notice. The theater got a letter at six thirty tonight from Lanford Wilson's people telling them to shut it down.

"Listen, girlfriend. We are all gonna meet at that café that sells hard-boiled eggs to talk about this."

She asks me if I'm okay. No, I'm not. I'm not okay.

The whole cast goes and Nico never shows up.

I've been in a deep depression for the last few weeks. I'm listening to a lot of Garth Brooks.

Hans has fallen in love with a Swedish girl and he never stalks me anymore.

The good news is that I got my work permit and have been doing room service at a five-star hotel. The medium-to-pathetic news is that a one-night stand with a bartender named Mark who speaks English like Borat—a lot of "Cool, man. Real cool. High five!"—has turned into a series of one-night stands.

Initially, I'd seen Mark as a distraction from all the Texas drama. He was very tall and handsome. In the months that we've been seeing each other, he's made it clear that he has a very strict policy of not seeing me during daylight hours, which at first I thought was very impressive. "He's got such strong boundaries," I told myself. "Plus, I have gigantic pores, so staying out of direct sunlight is a win-win!"

Last night, I lay there with my belly distended from hours of holding in gas listening to him describe the eyes of the only woman he'd ever loved as "specks of gold on a big green ball."

Finally, he got up to leave and when I started to stand up to see him to the door and slam it behind him, the pressure of me sitting up pushed out a fart that sounded like a piano being dragged across a wooden floor. I'd hoped he'd been too busy putting his socks on to hear it, but he must have, because as he walked out the door he told me, "Just so you know, I don't love you." Or maybe the fart had nothing to do with it.

Tammy Lisa is creeping back.

A few days later, the buzzer for my front door goes off. It's light out so I know it's not Mark. It's Nico. I can't believe it. She looks smaller, but again it could just be a curling-iron issue. Her voice is completely changed. Gone are the deep Texas drawl and the "y'alls."

I don't mean that suddenly she was like, "Haaay, get outta here—not for nothing—Sal from Long Island here," but it might as well have been that, because the change was so dramatic.

Weirdly, I forget that she is a liar who ruined all my dreams and am really happy to see her. She'd been such an important person in my life and then she'd vanished. I invite her up.

"I gotta stop trying to be some big guru changing everyone's lives and having all the answers," she says. "I gotta take care of myself. So I'm just going to take it easy. Eat hard-boiled eggs. Go on walks. Figure out how to make money since I'm illegal and dead broke. Maybe I'll babysit."

She wants time to take care of herself, figure out what she wants, and explore Amsterdam. And by the way, she's homeless.

"Come live with me!" I blurt it out and realize immediately that I don't want her to. If she's here I can't have Mark over. Or any guys. She knows me so well, she'll know when I'm stoned.

Oh, who cares? How many more stoned nights of holding in farts do I need?

She needs me, and I can help her. How could I pass up the chance to live with the person who had been my greatest teacher? The fact that I know about her one big screw-up of all time just makes me feels closer to her.

Get on in here, you flawed human being. *Oprah*'s on in twenty minutes!

So she moves in.

It's fun. Not to get maudlin, but I don't think I'd realized how lonely I'd been. Thank god I have somebody keeping me from lying on the floor for hours bemoaning my outcast state. Loneliness is so hard to sit through, and now I don't have to. We laugh and talk all the time. I feel awful admitting it, but since the company died she's gained quite a bit of weight. It's rare that I'm the skinny one in any group setting. Now I'm the skinny one first thing in the morning and throughout my whole day if I don't leave my apartment.

After a month, it's Nico's thirty-fifth birthday, and I'm taking her out for Mexican food. I come home after work at the Hotel Pulitzer, pumped to start celebrating, and she's lying on my bed—a fancy mattress on the floor. She bolts right up when I walk in. It's startling.

"HEY, GIRL, IT'S MY BIRTHDAY! MAN, WHAT A DAY!"

She's her HAPPY, laughing, shaking-yellow-fingers, rolling-cigarette-after-cigarette self. In fact, she's better than ever.

She's had yet another AMAZING MAGICAL DAY. There've been a lot of those lately. Every day when I come home from work, she's got another mind-blowing, life-changing, magical story to share. Crazy things happened to her and all she had to do was stand still. She didn't know why—they just did!

Old Dutch women would come running up to her on the street, flagging her down just to hand her a flower and thank her. "It's the power of loving thought, my friend. I'm telling ya!"

And dag nabbit if her birthday hadn't been yet *another* blessed day of miracles.

"I saw the most beautiful sunrise over the canal when I was doing my five A.M. workout this morning—"

"Five A.M.? What's your workout called? Lying on your back breathing like you're sleeping, because I never hear—"

"I swear to god, I've been doing it every morning. I have to. Keeps me sane. Hey, could you hand me that cake behind you?"

She's bought herself a cake for her birthday. I hand it to her and notice a tiny red gash on the inside of her palm where she's digging her thumbnail into her skin. I'd seen her do this before, a nervous habit but never to the point that she drew blood. Which is what she's done today.

"Oh my god, I almost forgot to tell you this. Unbelievable what happened today. Mind-blowing. You know how I've wanted to learn to speak Dutch? Well, last night before I went to bed I said a little prayer—'Help me learn Dutch.' Just decided to say it out loud to the universe. Didn't say, 'I know this is dumb but—' Just said it. Then today, I swear to god, this little Dutch girl comes right up to me, like she knows me, and starts just yammering away in Dutch to me, and, Lauren, I swear to god, I understood every single word she said. Now, she was five, so it wasn't real deep, but . . . Hey, could you hand me that fork right there?"

I hand her a fork. She takes it and says to me, in her same happy singsongy voice, "Okay, what you're about to see is something I've never let anyone see before. We're about to get real close real quick." And stabs her fork into the cake.

I watch her eat the entire cake, the whole time thinking, I don't think she's going to save me a piece. And she doesn't.

She keeps on chirping away, telling me the other crazy little funny things she saw all day—butterflies landing on her nose, newborn infants saying her name . . .

"Hey, girlfriend, could you hand me that bag on the floor?"

Against my better judgment I hand it to her and she pulls out five avocados. I hate avocados. Avocado is the one food that I'm allergic to, and people are always like, "Oops there's some avocado in the salad. Is that okay?" No, it's *not okay*! And whenever I say I hate avocados, people are like, "What! Well, what about guacamole? Do you like *guacamole*!" and I'm yacking. I'm sweating watching her.

She eats five of them. Should I bring up the Mexican dinner? Is she going to throw up? Turns out I didn't have to worry about bringing it up because she sees the time and yells, "Hey, time for Mexican food!"

At dinner, the party doesn't stop. She's ordering enchiladas! Loving her birthday! Singing "Happy Birthday" in Dutch. I'm scared. What's next? Is she just going to reach into her purse and pull out a gun? "HAPPY BIRTHDAY TO ME!" BAM!

Back at the apartment she turns off all the lights. There's no possible way she's not feeling a little ill. God knows I am.

"I'm tired of lying to people," she tells me. "Tired of saying things I don't mean. I've let so many people down in my life. My parents must be so exhausted. Been married three times. I've brought so many different lovers home with me over the years. White men, black men, old guys, young black women. I've made so many promises, started so many different lives, that I don't know who I am anymore. If I flew home tomorrow and showed up on their porch with my arm around a can of beans I was planning to marry and announced I was becoming an astronaut, they wouldn't bat an eye. Lord have mercy on my sad little soul stuck in this big old body, how I wish I was kidding."

Nico never talked about her past. All we usually talked about was how special I was going to be or how special she was going to be.

It's incredible and she's not done. She tells me secrets. Upsetting stories about her past that if I had heard from anyone else but her I would have judged as bat-shit crazy, but the truth from the source is a completely different truth.

Weird to think, but in my twenty-three years, I've never heard an adult, someone I look up to, admit to making a mistake. It's so comforting to know that all the intensely overwhelming emotions I feel all the time aren't reserved for me.

In the middle of me telling her about dating Sam, I stop myself. It's bad enough one person went through it—I suggest we eat some rice cakes and call it a night. Nico tells me to keep going and don't leave anything out. "Why not? I got at least two hours before this enchilada lets me get to sleep."

Friends my age didn't admit to the awful things from our past. Never. Who wanted to think about all that? I spent most of my time trying not to be found out. Being able to get out what I'd been carrying around for so long was, to put it mildly, so nice.

From that night on we refer to ourselves as BFFs.

Nico's parents fly her back to live with them in Houston. It's tough to be away from the one person on the earth who knows me. We're making little mini-cassette recordings for each other, just like *Felicity*. We call them "the BFF tapes." The best friends forever tapes. The recorder is plastered to my lips all the time. The tape that came in the mail today had an hour of an *Oprah* episode about "unsung heroes." Nico forgot she was recording and accidentally recorded the entire show. I'm glad she still sent it. It was like we were watching TV together.

The other side of the tape is the sounds of her driving around Houston in her VW bug, drinking Diet Coke and looking for an office job. "BFF, if you moved back to America you could be a movie star. I'm telling you."

Dreaming of being a movie star is so fifth grade. I was going to be Annie in the movie version of the Broadway hit musical *Annie*. "Will have braces removed if cast" was written at the top of my résumé. The part was my mine to lose. I was adopted. I'd perfected the screaming song technique that all good Annie wannabes had. The auditions required you to submit a headshot before you showed up in Chicago for the audition. My father took pictures of me in our backyard exuding more confidence and chutzpah than Judy Garland in her prime. "Sure it's a hard knock life, but look at me now!" with hand on the hip, jaunty head tilt, and big smile, screamed at the camera. I even went so far as to get out my special *Annie* purse I'd bought at the merchandise table when the Broadway touring company of *Annie* came to town, and stuck our white Persian cat,

Phantom (or maybe it was Diablo or Demon or Goblin; there were so many family cats with demonic creepy names, it's tough to be sure), in it for a few photos (and this was before carrying small animals in your purse was high fashion). I flung the purse and the tense-looking cat over my shoulder with a wink to the camera that said, "See ya on the set, girls!"

The auditions were held at the Hyatt Regency ballroom in Chicago. There were hundreds of girls, wealthy suburban girls dressed in exact replicas of Annie's signature red dress, putting my *Annie* cat-pee purse to shame. Other Annies did what they could with red T-shirts and burgundy shorts, Ronald McDonald curly red wigs slipping off their heads. The director, an old white man with poufy gray hair wearing a pink cardigan sweater, circled us up to sing "Tomorrow." He pointed at a girl and she sang. If he liked a girl he let her sing a few verses and then cut her off and pointed to the next girl in the circle to pick up the song wherever it was left off. To the right of me in the circle was Marissa, a tiny Jewish girl with naturally curly auburn hair and large boobs for an eleven-year-old. She sang an entire verse before she was cut off at the word "tomorrow." She didn't even get to finish the word. All she got to was "To—" and the director cut her off and pointed at me. This was it. This was my moment. I opened up my mouth—"MORROW!"—and was immediately cut off. That was it. My parents drove three hours to Chicago so I could scream "morrow" in a gay man's face, get in the car, and come right back home.

My dad suggested I focus on school and learn to type. All the girls in that room thought they were special. But they weren't. None of them. Including me. Especially me. Well, there was a delicate little boy who came dressed as Annie who had the best voice in my circle. He was certainly special, but he still wasn't any movie star.

Or was he? That was a long time ago. How do I know that little boy wasn't Neil Patrick Harris? Anything is possible.

Anything *is* possible. I'm okay now.

I'm going back to America. It's time. I decide to move to Seattle, a city where I know no one, because it seems like Amsterdam. Lots of rain, bikes, and "I like these shoes; they're comfortable" kind of people. And it's the only city where I was accepted for a theater internship.

Moving back is a lot of work. I can't hold a tape recorder to my mouth as I'm packing boxes. It doesn't leave enough room for the joint to be in there. I'd think about calling Nico up, but I was so busy surviving I'd have enough time for only a quick "Man, the portion sizes are big in America" before I needed to get to the bank to try to figure out how to get a checking account.

"Hey, BFF! I'm here! I'm in Seattle! I sold my car and bought a bike but Seattle is so full of hills, I end up walking around pushing my bike everywhere. This internship thing is good, but it's hard. People all seem more suspicious of the fact that I lived in Amsterdam than impressed. I'm so poor I've been going to a food bank. None of the other interns at the theater understand what my deal is. They all have girlfriends and husbands and houses and lives. They're clearly the Okays."

The next morning I want to tell Nico about how I smoked pot out of a bong the size of an eleven-year-old with a picture on the side of it of a skeleton dressed as Uncle Sam saying, "I want YOU," and how *Bride of Frankenstein* was on TV as I had sex with the lawn care guy who works on my block—but I can't find the tape recorder.

The lawn care guy's name is Greg. It's nice to have someone to smoke pot and watch old horror movies with. I'm not going to feel bad about spending night after night with someone who may have brain damage from excessive pot smoking, but I do hope I don't get in trouble for missing the last three internship meetings.

Tonight, I'm not staying at lawn care guy's house. Attempting to maintain the Euro lifestyle I'd grown accustomed to, I moved into a quaint little month-to-month studio that seemed artsy because it had a shared bathroom, "like an artist commune," but the place turned out to be an SRO that houses mostly male ex-convicts. It's not ideal, but I need some time alone.

There's always some surprise awaiting me when I open the door to my room. Cockroaches, a drunk man the landlord accidentally let into the wrong room slumped over on a chair, you name it. Tonight I open the door, and there she is, sitting in the dark. Nico. She'd used her Texas charm to get my landlord to let her into my room.

I cannot believe she's here. It's incredible to see my BFF here. Or it should be incredible, but I'm feeling slightly ambushed. I'd missed the tape she sent me that said she was going to take a road trip to Seattle to come see me. We laugh about the pile of dried throw up in the hallway. She tells me about a "god moment" she had right as she crossed the border of Arizona.

She thinks my voice sounds odd. I think her voice sounds odd.

I am a little worried she's mad at me for not sending any more tapes. I'd like to turn the lights on to make sure she's not sitting there with a horse's head on her lap or a loaded gun, but she won't let me.

In the dark, she starts making plans for day trips for us to take. Got to go see that mountain! Got to check out those fish throwers! Got to see this waterfall I heard about! We laugh about how I'd missed that she was coming to see me, but I'm fake laughing. Thanks to my wound work, it sounds real.

Most days, I stay at the theater filing plays for the artistic director, or watching him play video games on his computer. I have no idea what she's doing with her time and I don't want to know. It's going to be something huge and dramatic and I won't believe her and I don't know what she plans on doing here in Seattle. I'm working with a new theater company. And honestly, I don't really need a roommate. The only reason I'm staying at the lawn care guy's place every night is to give her room. My place is tiny.

Praying she's not home, I'm making a quick stop to pick up some clean clothes. She's not there. At all. Her stuff is gone. She's written me a note on the cover of a *People* magazine (I mean *The Atlantic Monthly*): "Gone to stay in a motel."

Sure, I'd avoided her completely and been deliberately unwelcoming, but I hadn't meant for her to just leave. I feel awful. And completely relieved.

Nico has also left me a message on my answering machine. Her voice is flat. "Why don't you meet me the Irish Lion at eight P.M.? We need to talk."

At 8:15 I'm standing outside the door of the Irish Lion wishing they served beer on the sidewalk. I'm a nervous wreck. Making eye contact with Nico is impossible. She seems very . . . okay. The nachos arrive. "I read your journal."

What? She read my journal? I'm trying to think of what I wrote about her. I'm sure I wrote something, but hey. Wait a minute. You can't read my journal. It doesn't matter what I wrote.

"Listen, girlfriend, something was going on with you and you weren't being honest with me."

"So you took it upon yourself to go into my private things and take what wasn't yours to have? Wow." Reading a person's journal is too far. You don't read a person's journal. The only thing I think I even wrote about Nico was something about how she annoyed me sometimes. Big deal. I may have mentioned how I think she could be a big old lesbian and was full of shit, but outside of that I think I mostly wrote about what I ate for lunch.

"You aren't yourself, Lauren. You're pulling yourself down and I'm not going to watch."

"That's a real deep insight, journal reader," I say to her and order another beer. I don't have to listen to a word she says.

Victims don't have to listen to perps.

"What happened to that little twenty-three-year-old who was working so hard to be okay?"

"Well, what happened to the American-Amsterdam Texas whatever it was called Theater Company? Blah-blah-blah. Big words coming out of a journal reader's face, Nico."

I'm about to tell her how sick I am of hearing about all her "good moments" and how amazing life is for her and how special she is, when she stands up and throws a twenty-dollar bill on the table. "I don't want to be friends with you anymore," she says, and walks out of the pub.

It's been almost five years since my ex–best friend and guru paid twenty dollars for four-dollar nachos and broke up with me. I've just started as a cast member for a local half-hour sketch comedy show in Seattle called *Almost Live!*

During the first year Nico was out of my life I tried to call her, but her phone was disconnected. I tried her parents' number and their number was disconnected too. Did she make her whole family move because she hated me so much? For a long time, it was tough knowing that the one person who knew me better than anyone else on the earth was out there cursing my name.

I'm sitting at my desk reading a book about doing yoga instead of writing jokes when my phone rings. I jump up and close my door. If a comedy writer overhears a serious conversation it can make them do crazy things like scream "cocksucker" as loud as they can or organize a group of writers to stand in front of you in their underwear to distract you.

"Hey, girlfriend, guess who this is!"

Nico. How on earth she got my work number is beyond me, but

I don't waste time finding out because I have too much I have to tell her. It was a year of hell after she walked out in Seattle, but since then it's been kind of incredible. All the skills she gave me, all that she taught me, helped me start writing plays, and it's been going so well. I got married. He's a bartender but not the gross kind. The sweet, loving kind. He's one of the Okays, Nico. And he says he loves me, and I believe him.

Soon after a producer from this TV show saw me in a play I wrote and now I'm a cast member of this show that's local but it's a big deal here and it should lead to other things. I get in trouble a lot for never writing for anyone but myself, which is embarrassing.

Nico started her own computer repair company, got married, bought a house, has a little boy, and could not be happier. "I'm no rock star. It suits me fine."

In Amsterdam, Nico had given me answers to help save me from myself, but all of that disappeared once I moved. The loneliness I felt in Amsterdam quadrupled in Seattle. I was so scared when I first moved here, and I didn't want her to see how badly I was coping. I didn't want her to see how awful the lawn care stoner guy was for me. I think she just had too much power in my life and I had to push her away so I could find out who I was on my own. The passing of time and being surrounded by comedians has helped me come to the understanding that we are all fundamentally alone. No matter how many times I think, oh, this is it, I'm okay, I'm home, I'm fooling myself, and within a month or a week or a year, I'm homeless again.

The main thing I have to tell her is how sorry I am for what happened when she showed up in Seattle but how ultimately it was a good thing that I was allowed to save myself.

Nico asks me what the hell I'm talking about.

"Listen, I did crazy stuff back then, so I wouldn't put it past me!" she says, and bursts out laughing.

Maybe she honestly doesn't remember. Or maybe she doesn't trust me enough to get back into it. Or maybe she's bat-shit crazy, which everyone knows is just another way of saying "incredibly gifted."

Before we hang up she makes me promise that if I'm ever in East Texas I have to look her up. Without hesitation, I make that promise, because the truth is she changed my life, and it's so good to hear the sound of her voice again. And it was also easy to make that promise because I'm fairly certain she mentioned at the beginning of the call that she lived in Tennessee.

Skin on Skin

During my first appointment with my gynecologist, Dr. Addis, he told me that he was required by law to ask if I'd like a nurse present during the exam. "Are you going to molest me?" I'd asked him. Without missing a beat he told me he wouldn't. "At least not *this* time." Our Abbott-and-Costello (if Abbott was on his back and Costello had a glove covered in K-Y jelly and was inserting a finger up Abbott's ass) relationship, which has developed over the years, would be considered by many women to be in poor taste. But I love it. His office is in Beverly Hills, so what do you expect? When my dirty artist friends shake their socialist fists at me for getting Pap smears on Rodeo Drive, I tell them it's the best place to get the diamonds that line the inside of my vagina shined—a service the Planned Parenthood clinic in Van Nuys, where I used to go, doesn't provide.

Finally, after ten years of Dr. Addis ending every exam with "Okay, see you next year and don't forget, have a baby!" I get to tell Dr. Addis the news he's been waiting for: I'm preggers. He bounces on his toes, claps his hands like an excited little birthday girl, and starts high-fiving me. "Yay! Yay! We're having a baby! I can't believe it!" It's a far bigger reaction than David's had been, which makes sense because my having a baby puts money in Dr. Addis's pocket and takes it out of David's. Poor David. At hearing my home pee-test results, David had eaten an entire log of Vermont goat cheese and lay on the bed itching his face all night.

Somehow, no matter how many times I've explained my situation, Dr. Addis never remembers that I'm in a relationship, so his high fives were followed with his feminist support of going it alone. "Good for you! You don't need no stinkin' men, right? Noooo, we don't need no stinkin' men." He kept repeating the "stinkin'" to get his Mexican accent right, when I have to tell him (again) I have a man. It's an easy thing to forget since I usually come alone to preserve our precious one-on-one time.

I've never had a baby, so my main question for Dr. Addis is if there's anything I should be doing to prepare myself. Like eating cotton balls and feathers to create a nest in my stomach.

"So how old are you now?"

The good doctor puts on a big show of not believing that I'm forty.

"No way! Forty! You're twenty-seven!"

He picks up my chart and makes a "Wowza!" face. "Hey, you are forty! Well, that's okay. Not a huge thing, just a higher chance of Down syndrome and miscarriage. Is your underwear off?"

"It is."

"Where were girls like you when I was sixteen?!"

He uses the same joke every year. "We'll talk more about babies after I do a breast exam."

I open my gown with a "Where're my beads?" Mardi Gras joke. I get nothing. In fact, I may have upset him. Usually he jumps right into kneading and poking around with a steady stream of chatter intended to distract me from the "Hey, that guy's touching my boob!" feeling, but today he just stares at my chest, lets out a long, sad sigh, and says, "Sucks to get old, huh? Yeah, I'm not having an easy time with it. You want to think you've done something with your life, but how do you really know?" My naked breasts have inspired a lot of different reactions over the years, but this is a first.

"The other day I realized that, geez, when my son is thirty I'm going to be seventy-six. If I'm lucky. Right? And I want to be there to see his life. That's all you hope for: just to be able to be there as long as you can. Okay, feels normal in there. Let's check out her sister over here."

It wasn't uncommon for him to wander into tricky topics for patient/doctor relations land. But knowing he loved expensive German cars, hated Obama, and dined with NRA-loving celebrities was tolerable compared to this existential hell he was pushing me into.

I try to change the subject and ask him if McCain is a nice man in person, but he doesn't hear me and switches over to my right breast.

"Yeah . . . you know what's funny about me? I know I'm going to die. I get it. That's why babies are born crying . . . because they get it too . . ."

At the end of the exam he snaps off his rubber gloves—"I can't believe we're going to have a baby!"—and tells me to start taking prenatal vitamins.

Before I got pregnant, I'd see a child and think, "Welcome to the earth, little spirit. Enjoy your journey—and what are you here to teach us?" Then I'd throw sand on their feet to make them grow. Now that I'm pregnant I see a baby and think, "Oh my god. His head is so flat." Kids are freaking me out. And so are the ones who make their heads flat, the *mothers*.

People keep assuming that I'm going to be this wacky mom type. They're assuming that my whole "I'm an asshole who can't do anything right!" is real, and I'm going to play that shtick right into motherhood. That's not really me. Yet when it comes to what kind of mother I'll be, I have no idea.

Will I be the mother who relishes the bond with my child to such an intense degree that I refuse to stop breastfeeding in public? Even on airplanes after the child unlatches himself to ask a flight attendant, "Hey, can I get a Pepsi with this? The whole can?"

Will I be the mother who is so sensitive and attuned to her baby's needs that instead of diapers I just wait for that certain twinkle in her eye that tells me it's time to hold her over the sink so she can pee?

Or will I be the fifties-style martini drinking mother—"The only reason I'm not holding my baby is because a pamphlet I read told me not to. Now hand me the olives."

"Oh, babies are fun. Don't get too deep about it." My sister Emily has just arrived from Indiana with my teenage niece, Kaitlin. They've never been to Los Angeles and are hoping to see the big attractions like Tori Spelling. Emily has two kids and is now a single mother. I've admired her tenacity as she's gotten out of a bad marriage and how she dedicates herself to her kids. At the moment, both Emily and Kaitlin are trying to convince me that having a baby is no big deal. I ask Kaitlin how she can know this at fifteen and she tells me that she's seen every episode of *I Didn't Know I Was Pregnant*. "Basically, you're just going to be standing in line at the bank thinking, man, I got to take a BM, and next thing you know you've got a baby in your sweatpants." Okay, so, sure, child birthing—outside of the money it would take to pay for the cleanup—is a breeze, but what about all the years after that? The birth was not my worry; it was everything else after that. Jack would be long gone by the time this kid was old enough to talk. The kid would have only elderly parents to entertain him. No brothers or sisters. But maybe that wasn't so bad. I have only two older sisters, Emily and Joyce, yet whenever I go home for holiday dinners at my parents' condo it still feels like a mob scene. This is exactly how my parents like it to feel. They tried to use the old "I'm tired of mowing the lawn" excuse when they sold the two-story, four-bedroom Colonial home we grew up in. Lawn care had nothing to do with it. Their dream retirement home was one that was just big enough for the two of them. "Well, we're out of chairs, guess you better go home." My parents love their cozy retirement condo. It's bright and sunny and it smells like dogs, vodka, and dusty Christmas candles—nothing like the house I grew up in.

The house I grew up in smelled like dried cat shit, microwaved Weight Watchers ravioli, and my middle sister, Joyce. My gritty sibling childhood memories all involve Joyce. Emily, with her long straight hair, like a red-haired Cher, tossed her cheerleading pom-poms in the back of her little yellow Datsun and took off to join a sorority, leaving me behind with Joyce, aka "the mean one."

My best friend in third grade would take one step into my house and start sniffing the air like a dog. She was picking up the scent of Merle Norman's Ice Blue eye shadow mixed with stamp collecting and cystic acne cream. "Joyce's here, isn't she?" Before I could answer, she'd suggest we play in the street, where it was safe.

She didn't want to witness the jail-cell violence that went on between my older sister and me, because it was ugly and raw, and because the warden who should have broken it up was an eighty-nine-pound ex-ballerina. My mother would sit licking rice crackers as my sister pinned my face down with her knee in the family room. Joyce would wait until my mouth was wide open, screaming into the carpet, and then she'd tell me, "Right where your mouth is, that's where the dog threw up last night. That's why it's still damp." Then she'd rug burn my face.

One sunny Hoosier spring day, as Joyce pretended to burn me

with her candy cigarettes, my mother's voice came screeching through the house. *"Joyce! Come to the kitchen!"* The *kitchen*. The kitchen is where we went to be told things like "Santa is dead." Or "You're adopted." Or "I've signed you up for Weight Watchers. At seven years old you'll be their youngest member. Congratulations."

Something was going down. Maybe somebody had died. I ate two cigarettes while I waited for Joyce to emerge.

Ten minutes later, the kitchen door flew open and Joyce came running full speed, heading directly toward me. My first thought was that my mother had given her a knife and directed her to kill me. "Go, run. Do it now before she suspects." But before she hit the shag carpet of the family room, my mother screamed, *"Lauren . . . come to the kitchen!"*

I kept a wide berth around Joyce as I ran toward the kitchen.

As soon as I'd climbed up on the kitchen stool, my mother began. "Listen, I don't care how much pain you put each other through physically, but I don't want you two hurting each other mentally. Those scars *never heal*, okay? So I want you to promise me that no matter how angry you get at your sister that you will *never, ever* tease her about not having any friends. That is off-limits. Okay?"

I couldn't believe what my mother was saying! Joyce had friends. There was Lori, her friend from middle school, who got her addicted to candy cigarettes, and her cat, Demon. If my mom really didn't think she had any, then why didn't she help get her some? Get some stamp-collecting types over here. Get her some acne medicine. Host a foster kid—do something. And, geez, if you say that about her, what do you say about . . . Oh no. I'm not sure why she chose that day to do this. We hadn't been fighting more than normal. Maybe it was my mom who thought these things about us and she was making a preemptive strike.

It took me about five seconds to run out of the kitchen and find

Joyce. She was waiting for me on the couch in the family room. As soon as she saw me, she stood up. I walked toward her. Neither of us spoke. She looked at me for the first time in my life like she maybe felt sorry for me. Sorry that I was the only adopted kid in the family, sorry that she'd turned me in every single time she even suspected I was doing something wrong. We'd been through a lot, but we were still sisters. We were still—

"You're fat," Joyce said.

"Well, you have no friends," I replied.

I waited for her to crumple, and to my horror she did. She fell to the floor, and while she was down there she picked up a piece of dried cat shit and hurled it at my head. I wish I could say she missed me, but she didn't. It hit my forehead. A direct hit.

Nowadays Joyce and I are golden. Her superpower of not caring what others think of her has led to a successful career in middle management. She laughs easily and you can forget to call her back for weeks and she never gets mad—all the best qualities in a sister.

After I share the story of growing up with sisters with my niece, Kaitlin, she tells me it's another example of why I need to make sure I have only one kid. "And you better hope it's a boy, because I'm the princess in this family, and I'm not going to be happy if there's another girl grandchild. I can't guarantee her safety."

Kaitlin is all about hip-hop, and coincidentally, the one part of her body that I'm getting to know during the first day of their visit is . . . her *hip*. That's the part of her body where she wears her Ritalin patch. If she doesn't wear her patch, according to Emily, she's moody.

Over the years, when I've complained to Emily that I don't believe in putting minors on drugs to alter their moods just to suit our comfort levels, my sister reminds me of my last trip home.

"Remember when Kaitlin screamed at me, 'Motherfucker, don't touch my yearbook!'? She wasn't wearing her patch that day."

Because the patch is like a giant piece of packing tape, my niece has decided to follow a pattern of (1) reapplying her lip gloss; (2) yanking her mini skirt down; (3) yanking at the hairs that have gotten stuck to the patch. The patch is a repository for every imaginable hair—cat hairs, sweater hairs . . . hairs that were blowing by in the wind.

Our first stop on "Lauren's Hollywood tour for visiting family" is the Rose Café in Venice for brunch. Light and airy and lovely and sunny. My niece and sister say nothing about how lovely the restaurant is, which makes me think they're mad there isn't a race car hanging from the ceiling. Kaitlin's been spending most of the meal hoping her friend will text her. She likes this one friend, she tells us, even though that friend is a real *cockblocker*. The word "cockblocker" is like a magic wand, tapping me on the forehead and, *poof*, turning me into a shocked granny. Clutching my heart, I ask her if she still has the finger puppets I'd given her for Christmas when she was three. "Or have you been using them as whimsical condoms?"

Then we go shopping. Kaitlin insists on being taken to Beverly Hills and then refuses to go into any of the stores. "I can't handle it. You don't know me. Once I decide I want something, I do whatever it takes to get it. If I walk into Chanel and see something I want and I can't get it, well, somebody could get hurt."

At the end of a long day, I take them to a café so I can watch my sister drink. We go to a place that I thought would have a Venice Beachy vacation feel but instead it's a complete date-rape sports bar.

As we stand at the hostess podium, my niece starts hiking her miniskirt up—or down (what's the difference, really?)—and ferociously weeding the stuck hairs out of her patch. She notices me watching her and tells me that "Mommy can bring one for you tomorrow . . . You'll love it. You're never hungry."

As soon as we sit down I realize that, yes, indeed, I've taken them to the wrong place. *Again.* The chairs are these odd plastic balls with no backs. We have to grip their sides with our thighs to prevent slipping off. My niece, who is absorbed in taking pictures of herself with her camera, doesn't seem to mind that she's sitting on an egg. I still want to make sure that they're comfortable and that they won't go back home and tell my dad that their vacation felt like they were just back at home—sitting on eggs in a sports bar, just like every afternoon.

"Are you guys okay? Do you want to sit in a booth?" Emily and Kaitlin share a look, but both insist they are comfortable. Without speaking, Emily opens up a pillbox. Kaitlin puts out her hand, and her mother pours about ten pills into her palm. Kaitlin throws them all in her mouth, swallows, then turns to me and speaks to me in the same tone that I'd used with her when I asked her not to scream "cockblocker" at breakfast. "Um, Aunt Lauren, can I give you some advice that's going to help you be a parent? You need to calm down. Right now. And stop caring about what people think all the time. You really need to relax . . . I'm not kidding. You're going to drive your kid crazy if you're like this all the time."

She gives her mom a sort of "*Now* I know what you mean about her" look.

I reach out and start patting her leg. Little staccato pats. I can't stop. The pats just keep going and going. Five minutes later, when her leg has gotten a little pink, I stop, take a deep breath, and get right in her face like a basketball coach. "I DON'T THINK THIS HAS ANYTHING TO DO WITH BEING A PARENT. YOU ARE MY GUEST AND I WANT TO MAKE SURE YOU

GUYS ARE COMFORTABLE. DO YOU WANT TO SIT IN A BOOTH OR NOT!?"

Either my screaming in her face was the most relaxing thing that has happened to her all day or else her Xanax has just kicked in, because her face lights up in a big smile and she says to me in this little baby girl voice, "Nooo . . . I like my egg!"

After Kaitlin and Emily fly back home, not only do I worry they didn't have a good time, but I miss them. According to Emily, they had a great time and Kaitlin is planning on moving to LA as soon as she graduates. I'm four months pregnant with a baby boy. I'd love if Kaitlin moved to Los Angeles. She could help me. Even if I heard "Bitch, I'll cut you" coming from the nursery, it would still be nice to have family around.

The best thing so far about being pregnant has been David. He is running around washing apples, fetching napkins, making salads, and telling me that a bigger butt is an exciting pregnancy bonus.

My face is covered in brown splotches, I throw up after every Fiber One toaster pastry, and I can't stop burping and shitting my pants. Perfect time to get my sex drive back! This morning David said, "You look so beautiful," which made me start laughing because I felt so gross. Then he said, "Whoa, watch those double chins."

We watched *So You Think You Can Dance* last night and he had one hand on my stomach the whole time. So he wouldn't miss a moment of gas. I've had people putting their hands on my stomach to feel kicks of the baby, and I'm fairly certain now that it's been gas bubbles bursting. I should just be honest and shout, "Oh my god, give me your hand . . . *gas!* You've got to feel it!"

Our French ultrasound lady sent us home from our last exam with a photo of the baby with his hand up over his head like he's waving. Whenever I pass by the photo on the refrigerator I wave back. It's exciting to see that he's going to be good on a parade float. I like this "growing a baby" thing. Why didn't I do it sooner? Oh, because I had no desire and was petrified of being so poor I'd have to learn to make a baby diaper out of car wash coupons.

When I told David that I wanted to stop our "Get off me now!" birth control method so we could try to get pregnant, he panicked. "Oh. Okay. Well, I don't know. I'm really busy, I've got a lot of stuff to do and things to take care of at these places with some people. Maybe in a few years when I have less stuff with people in places."

The timing did feel particularly cruel, but isn't freedom just another word for nothing left to lose? Besides, my ovaries were threatening to puff out dust clouds.

The real panic inducer for both of us was money. I had no idea how much money David actually had. He rinsed out and reused old ziplock baggies from the eighties to store the Altoids he bought in bulk from Costco in the nineties. I'd always assumed he was super-thrifty in order to support the teenage son who needed to be clothed, fed, and deloused, but he could have been an eccentric millionaire trying to keep me off the scent.

No matter. The baby idea was mine. I'd pay for it. I was the stable one, because we always knew what to expect when it came to me and money. Give me fifteen hundred dollars or fifty thousand (please give me that), and without fail, I'd still be three months away from being completely broke. My friends like to joke that I spend money like a rapper—if I suddenly had a lot of it I was buying iPads and gold teeth for all my moms.

After I promised to "feed it, wash it, put it to sleep, and find a way to pay for everything," David had said yes.

Once the decision was final, he was excited. According to him, kids were pretty fun up until age eleven. He told me that I had better hope that I'm a movie star by the time the kid turns eleven so I can afford boarding school.

David's only son, Jack, whom he'd raised alone since Jack's mother died, had just left for college. At a dinner party, I'd overheard David say to a young-looking dad type seated next to him, "That's it, man. I'm free. I'm gonna buy a tent and camping gear. I'm going to go on road trips. Learn to parasail. Maybe I'll jump in the ocean and just start swimming, because after eighteen years, I'm free!" He'd then thrown his head back and started laughing, tears of relief and joy running down his cheeks.

Here we are, five months later, pregnant at Jack's high school graduation. I love Jack but I hope nobody tells him that, because he'll try to borrow money from me. I'm so happy we're having a boy. It's cheaper and everyone keeps saying, "Boys love their mothers so much"—hard to enjoy when I think about Jack. Jack's mother died when he was eight. When that graduation procession music kicked in, I could have sobbed and pounded my chest. Instead I got teary and dabbed. There were a lot of families shouting back and forth at each other. "Can you believe it! It's a miracle. I thought the day would never come." It seemed like every kid at the school just barely graduated. Or maybe it was just our section—we were in the very last section of the arena because we got there late. All the parents sitting closer than us were shouting "Stanford! Thanks for asking. And you?"

The day after Jack's graduation, David left for his new job working on a salmon-fishing boat in Alaska. He's been gone now for three weeks. This morning I woke up and thought I felt something in my stomach. I'm like a giant who's swallowed a little person. It was just gas again, but this time it's sadness gas. I've heard nothing from David since he left. When he said it was remote I thought he was just trying to sound macho, like when he described the housing as "barracks." What if he made up the whole "Oh, I'm going to Alaska . . . no cell phone reception . . . I'll call when I can" and then I never hear from him again? My friends keep telling me that I'm worrying about David so much because of my hormones. I think it's more from the fact that I've eaten nothing but Fiber One toaster pastries since he left.

Yesterday, I was on an elevator going to my manager's office and Janice Dickinson got on. Right as I was thinking how she looks like Mick Jagger in the form of a tall, thin woman she turns to me and screams, "*Are you leaking yet?*" The two men on the elevator started pushing the buttons to get them off at the next floor as quickly as possible. I was so thrilled she was talking to me, I told her, "Now I am." And then: "No, I'm not, but other gross things are happening to me." To which she responded, "*No! You're beautiful! Do you hear me? You are beautiful.*" She had to get off the elevator, but not before turning again and screaming back at me, "*You are!*" Later that day, I got the news that Michael Jackson died and I saw the helicopters fly over me rushing to take him to the hospital. This is the surreal world I'm bringing a child into.

David is finally back from Alaska. It was a good season. Something to do with the massive global warming.

We went to our all-day birthing class yesterday. The teacher was blissed out of her mind on babies. She described the importance of skin-on-skin contact. "You're going to lay that baby on your chest, next to you, the yummiest baby you've ever seen, and you're going to just eat him up." It was a little cutesy for me. I feel about using "yummy" to describe something that isn't food the way other people do about "moist panties." David was taking copious notes while I scanned the room looking for people older than us. There weren't any.

We were by far the oldest in the room, I think. There was one abusive Dutchman who seemed somewhat old, but that may just be because he looked crabby. His wife kept having weepy break-downs that she claimed were about being scared of birth, but I think she was trying to give the class subtle hints to call the cops and get her out of her relationship. Next door to the class, the hospital was giving out flu shots to family members who worked for the hospital and it was like they were murdering children in the next room. There were SCREAMS OF TERROR, kids just screaming their heads off as our instructor taught us how to slow dance with each other to help the labor pains.

The birth is coming up. Today's doctor appointment lasted less than ten minutes. I walked in. I peed a teaspoon of pee into a cup. (It's getting harder and harder to do that—I asked the nurse if next time I could get seven or eight people to help me and she said, "How about a funnel?") The report was that he was "perfect." I'll be sure to use that against him when he's older: "You were sold to me as being *perfect*. What happened?"

I've been having trouble sleeping. I wake up in the middle of the night thinking about how we live on a dark planet with dark hor-rible people, a place where monkeys eat other monkeys' faces off. Sophie had to make a choice. John F. Kennedy Jr. crashed his plane, and the show *Intervention* will never run out of addicts to follow. If JFK Jr. could die, anyone could. The curse of the Kennedys. The curse of being born and knowing no matter how much money, power, or muscle tone you have, you will be a bad pilot. A baby is born into the cycle of suffering. It's going to have to face my death and its own death. Oh my god, what have I done? I just wanted something to hug and go on walks with and now suddenly every-body is dead. After a few days of nonstop death anxiety I have a breakthrough—an Oprah "aha" moment. There is a death here. A part of me is dying forever. It's what I want, but it is a death.

I've decided to spend the day with my friend Julie because she is my one friend who has not let having kids change her one single bit. Being around her is the comfort I need right now.

I go over to spend the afternoon at her house, and she's stand-ing in her kitchen trying to figure out how many Weight Watch-ers points are in a cosmo. "The glasses were minuscule, plus my husband kept taking sips from each drink with his big old horse mouth, so I'm rounding down . . . Fuck it. Ten. I'm saying ten." She says all of this while managing to also complain about her mother.

"She's selfish! Did I tell you about our trip to see her last week-end in New Hampshire? Oh my god. She was up all night playing her banjo! 'Five foot two, eyes of blue . . . could she, could she?' She's a kook! And she knew my kids needed to get to sleep but she had a contra-dancing concert to go to the next night, so she insisted on staying up late and practicing. I told her she was being loud and my kids needed to get some sleep, but she doesn't even care. She cares more about her sheep than she does her grandkids. All she cares about is her sheep and her banjo! And she's cheap. I know she's got money but she won't buy the kids new gifts. It's always something used. I'm sick of it. She's an insane person. She just spent all this money on some special electrical fence for her sheep."

By the time she gets to the word "sheep" her voice is so shrill I feel like my ears are going to start bleeding. And my nose. And maybe my feet.

"Yeah," I say, "the last time your mom was visiting for

Christmas and I came over to visit her, all she did was show me pictures of her sheep wearing wool sweaters that she made out of them."

Julie throws her head and back and screams, "Ahhhh! She should be showing you pictures of her grandkids—not her sheep." She starts shoveling what looks like homemade tapioca pudding into a coffee mug.

"I can't talk about her anymore. Okay, let's go get Annabelle and Henk out of the hot tub."

Annabelle and Henk are Julie's kids, and they are five and six years old. I didn't even know that they were home because I've been here for more than an hour and haven't heard them screaming and fighting like I normally do. I just assumed they were being driven around town by their seventeen-year-old live-in nanny from Yugoslavia who doesn't have a driver's license. Per usual.

There are no noises coming from the backyard, and I can't imagine that kids this age are just lying back in a hot tub, relaxing with their thoughts.

Julie must see the panic on my face because she hits my arm and says, "Take it easy. It's empty!"

It turns out that Julie wanted us to spend the day drinking wine ("Oh, come on, pretend you're a French mom!") and soaking in the hot tub ("Come on, pretend you're a Swiss mom! They do it all the time!"), so she drained the tub, but when she saw how filthy it was, she stripped her kids down, gave them each a sponge, and plopped them in the empty tub with a running hose, telling them to "Scrub, scrub, scrub!" before going inside to make herself a cocktail.

We get to the edge of the hot tub and peer in. Henk and Annabelle are naked, smeared with dirt, and sitting in about a foot of filthy black water while quietly chewing on their antiseptic sponges.

These are the kind of sponges they tell you not to clean your fish tank with or all the fish will die.

Julie hoses the kids down and then sends them inside to play. About a second after they're back in the house we hear a scream, one of definite physical pain. At eight months pregnant, I go running into the house full speed. I look behind me and assume I'll see Julie about to pass me or at least keeping up, but instead I discover her at the fridge, scooping more pudding into her mug. She sees me see her and says, "Oops!" and laughs and then follows me into the bedroom.

When we get to the bedroom, Annabelle is pulling on Henk's penis. Full weight, leaning back like she's water-skiing. Henk is freaking out, screaming. It's so horrifying I can't even speak.

Julie jumps in and ungrasps Annabelle's hand from poor Henk and scolds, "No, no, no!" with her mouth full of pudding.

"You guys, go put your clothes on, and if you want you can do your 'High School the Musical' show for us—we'll watch." Henk still has the hiccups from crying, but this cheers him up and suddenly he and his sister are back on. "He'll thank her later, I'm sure," Julie says after they run, hand in hand, out of the room.

As soon as Julie's sure the kids are in the living room rehearsing, she takes her one-hitter out of her pocket, packed and ready to go, and offers it to me. "Here, take a tiny hit. It makes their shows *so* much better. Otherwise, they can get really long."

I calmly explain to Julie that I'm pregnant and I've decided that I'm going to wait until my kid is born to start fucking him or her up. "Oh, come on," Julie says, "take a tiny hit. Pretend you're a Dutch mom!"

In the living room, there's no preshow excitement in the air. In fact, Annabelle and Henk are both just lounging on the couch. Still naked. I head toward the La-Z-Boy chair in the corner of the room, but Julie races over and beats me to it, leaving me to sit on the couch flanked by naked children.

Rocking in the La-Z-Boy while eating another mug of pudding starts to make Julie uncharacteristically self-reflective.

"When both the kids were first born, I talked on my cell phone all the time. I think that's why Annabelle has attachment issues. Poor Annabelle, she's all fucked up."

"Julie, she's right here."

"Oh, she didn't hear me." Julie waves me away and jumps up, gets a handful of pistachios and throws them in her mug, then flops back down in her chair.

"Yes, I did," Annabelle says.

I'm going to spend more time with her, I think. I'm going to look in her eyes. I look over my shoulder to start the resolution right now and discover Annabelle sitting on the couch with her feet up in the air, staring off into the distance as she puts a pistachio in her . . . crotch. She's doing it very innocently and absentmindedly. Just la-la-la. She doesn't even seem like she's aware she's doing it. I, on the other hand, notice.

"Julie . . . Julie!" I'm trying to get Julie's attention without shaming the child.

Finally Julie sees what's going on, looks slightly embarrassed, and says, "Oh, gross. Annabelle, stop!"

She then starts talking about how important making eye contact with your baby is.

"I know it sounds dumb, but you have to try and remind yourself, if you can, to look your baby in the eyes. Believe it or not, it makes a difference. I didn't do any of that stuff, the skin on skin after they were born . . . none of it. I really regret it. I do."

For a moment Julie looks like she's going to cry. I might join her. When someone with seemingly no self-awareness suddenly becomes aware, it's painful. I feel as if she were in a coma for years and we all just assumed she had no idea what was going on around her, but it turns out she heard us talking shit about her the entire time.

I'm about to tell her, "I'm sure it's going to be okay; you can make it right!" when I notice a little hand feeling around on my face. At first I don't know what's going on, but then a pistachio is suddenly being shoved into my mouth. I clamp my lips shut, but Annabelle's little fingers manage to push the nut in through the side of my mouth. Annabelle, Henk, and Julie shriek with laughter.

Welcome to the earth, little spirits; thank you for teaching me that underwear and shame are key to a happy houseguest. I'll try to remember this after my child is born, which will be happening never. This pregnancy is endless. I'm going to be pregnant my entire life.

That was quick. Less than twenty minutes ago I had a baby. I'd suggested the name Kareer Killer but we decided on Leo. It's amazing, and if I weren't so nauseous, I'd be crying tears of joy. I have to do the skin-to-skin contact—putting Leo on my naked chest—that the birthing classes went on and on about, ASAP; otherwise he'll get a learning disorder or never learn to love unless it's a woman (or man, fingers crossed) swaddled in a hospital-issued baby blanket.

David rips open my hospital gown and lays Leo's little body on my chest right as a wave of nausea hits me so hard that I'm forced to hand him right back. After a few deep breaths I feel like I can probably hold Leo without yacking on him so I turn to tell David this and am met with a sight that I cannot make any sense of. I literally cannot figure out what I'm seeing. David is sitting in a chair in the corner of the recovery room with his shirt off and Leo is on his chest. There's a young blond nurse pinching David's nipple and directing it toward Leo's mouth. The nausea comes back with such force I can't speak. I just lie there watching the bizarre first moments of Leo's life.

David claims the nurse acted of her own accord. She saw him trying to give skin-on-skin contact (like the classes told us to do) and assumed that we were doing some hippie bonding moment, so she jumped in and was trying to support whatever it was we were about. The nurse says that she walked in and was shocked to find a half-naked man in the corner holding Leo. When she told David she was going to give me the baby to nurse, David said, "I'll do it," and she thought, "Okay, dirty hippies, whatever you want."

The first night after Leo's birth I'm not able to sleep. I'm anxious that he's starving. I'm starving him to death. I'm killing him. He's not able to latch on for breastfeeding and it's going to give him brain damage. Are all of his organs formed? They haven't told me that yet. His heart could be riddled with holes. One of his eyes is loose. It's rolling around too much. I need a Sharpie so I can connect the moles on his back and see if they spell out "666." I can't catch my breath. This isn't some postnatal hormonal anxiety attack. This is THE TRUTH coming through.

The next morning, I wake up to Leo crying to be nursed. I sit up in bed, ready for the anxiety again, but it isn't there. While I nurse I stare at Leo and wait for it to return, but it has vanished. Leo with his wispy brown hair and big eyes that are looking deeply at the world, yet I have no idea what he's seeing. They remind me of the eyes of a whale. At first I'm relieved, and I want to guarantee the anxiety won't return by going online and getting a month's supply of Xanax for Leo and me. But maybe it's a good thing. If I can face the existential angst of being alive, I think I'll be a better mother. Yes, a few dark nights of the soul are a good thing, a necessary thing, and I shouldn't spend my valuable time trying to escape them by brushing them off as hormonal or shutting them down with some online black market Xanax from India. Especially because my niece, Kaitlin, will be coming to visit again next month and she could hook me up with handfuls of the real stuff for free.

Dirty Laundry

I'm nine months pregnant, sitting in Dr. Addis's office listening to him make arrangements with Cedars-Sinai to do an emergency C-section for seven thirty tonight.

According to Dr. Addis I have a medical condition that pregnant ladies can get called "preeclampsia," which means I have crazy-high blood pressure, and if the baby doesn't get out of me soon awful things could happen. I could have a seizure. Or explode. That's not even the worst part. The worst part is that Dr. Addis is insisting we "call a mother" to set up some help for after we get home with the baby.

"You'll be recovering from a major surgery; you're going to need help," Dr. Addis tells us as he's writing down instructions to get to the hospital. "I'd offer to come over and help but I'm playing golf next week with one of my patients' husbands."

No, no, no. We don't need any help. David and I are old; we can handle it. I don't want any family members around those first few days we're back home. Not even my favorite ones. Those first few days at home as a new little family are going to be so intimate.

There's going to be a lot of snuggling on the couch with baby

Leo, taking turns singing "You Are My Sunshine" to him, and kissing each other as tears of joy rain down on Leo's new little mushy head. As a *Glamour*-magazine-diagnosed codependent, I'm not a good host in the best of circumstances. You throw a baby in the mix and the first time one of our mothers is wading around in ankle-deep dirty bathwater because our drain doesn't work, I'll be a wreck.

To be honest, I'm not convinced that I even have preeclampsia. I don't feel sick at all. It is true that when I take my socks off it looks like the bottom part of my leg has been sewn on. I like to say I look swollen up like an abandoned dead body, but that bothers most people and I'm trying to replace it with "bloated with the blessing of a baby."

I wouldn't be surprised if what I was really suffering from was a condition called "My Beverly Hills gyno has a dinner reservation at Nobu for eight P.M. so let's get this going." On the bright side, I'm going to have a baby tonight. David grabs my hand and I try to smile at him, but my face is so bloated I have to put my fingers in the sides of my mouth and pull up.

Nobody is more excited about my C-section than Ronda, my surgery prep nurse from Saint Louis. "You are going to *love* a C-section. Keeps your vagina nice and tight." I love Ronda. She's an older African American lady with long gray braids who laughs without smiling and walks so slowly it's like she's standing still. Ronda's hooking me up to a magnesium drip telling me a story about how she walked in on her aunt giving her uncle a blow job when she was a little kid. "It really messed me up for a long time. She was the churchgoing auntie, you know what I'm saying?" Sure, I know what she's saying, but what's the magnesium for?

"So you don't have a seizure, honey."

Oh god, this birth is all medical-emergency-like. I really was hoping for it to be more born-in-a-tub-with-dolphins-like. At first I'd been high-fiving Ronda about getting to skip out on missing labor—but now as my insides are starting to feel like they are on fire from the magnesium, I can't believe I'm never going to experience what it's like to go through labor. If I don't go through the excruciating pain of childbirth, how will I increase my capacity for suffering? Labor serves a purpose. It's nature's way of preparing you for motherhood and learning how to shit the bed in front of people.

Rhonda thinks I'm crazy for feeling this. "How you get that baby here has nothing to do with the kind of mother you're going to be—and I'm telling you, you're gonna be cracking walnuts with that vagina."

At seven thirty P.M., curtain time for theater lovers, Dr. Addis sliced me open, and a license plate, a stripper shoe, and a baby boy fell out. Leo is here. The bliss I feel is unreal and perfect.

I'm no longer in the cute little maternity recovery room with rocking chairs and comfy flowered-print couches for the visiting family members. I'm in a straight-up hospital room with Leo lying in an Ikea-looking container next to me and David sitting on the single metal chair in the corner. A nurse who looks like she's fourteen years old but is wearing a lot of makeup to pass as nineteen walks in and mumbles something about "getting me to the bathroom."

This getting-to-the-bathroom thing is not as much fun as she made it sound. I try to stand up but I can't remain on my feet without holding on to her for dear life. In the bathroom she lowers me down onto the toilet, tells me to "let her know when I'm all done," and turns around and faces the bathroom wall to give me a sense of privacy even though she is standing right next to me.

I pretend to knock on an imaginary door to alert the nurse that I'm done peeing. "Knock-knock-knock!" She grabs a spray bottle that's on the sink, turns around, and without any warning she aims it between my legs and starts aggressively squirting at me with this "I'm gonna get it!" focus. Like it was bug spray and she'd just seen a wolf spider.

She pulls a pair of gauze medical underwear on me, and I start crying for all the people in the world who have to have their crotches spray-bottled clean. For the morbidly obese, Thai sex workers, and the elderly.

She drags me back to the bed and I start sobbing on her shoulder.

Back in my bed with Leo finally on my chest, there's one thing I am certain of—there's no way David and I will be able to handle taking care of Leo with just the two of us. Dr. Addis was right. We are going to have to ask one of our mothers to fly out and help us before David's milk starts coming in.

The problem is that I'm adopted, so I have two mothers and that means I have to choose which one to ask. If I ask my birth mother first, and she says yes, which she may, I worry that my adopted mother will think that I asked my birth mother first—because I will have. I've known Diane, my birth mother, since I was nineteen years old. My adopted mother actually did the search to find her, yet I still find myself trying not to show too much enthusiasm for Diane. Whenever my mother asks me how Diane is doing, I say something like, "Well, you know, give that lady a baked good, a Long Island iced tea, and a dog pillow to pass out on, and she's happy." And my mom will laugh and shake her head, like, "Oh, that's Diane."

Diane helped take care of three of her grandchildren who were born this year. Or maybe she just brought Chanel lipstick to the mothers right after they had their babies. I can't remember what form her post-birth care took.

But I can't ask Diane because my mother is the first mother, like Queen Elizabeth, and must be consulted first.

I make the call to tell my mother that she won the help-me-to-the-bathroom sweepstakes, but it turns out that she can't come because, sadly, she hurt her knee. I'm fairly certain that after I've regaled her with tales of medical underwear, spray-bottle cleaning, and the challenge of inverted-nipple breastfeedings, she picked up a letter opener and stabbed herself in the kneecap.

So, the real winner is Diane, who might turn out to be the better match anyway. Once she gets past her maternal urge to shove the baby in a pile of dirty laundry and go out dancing (I assume that's what she did the day after I was born), she'll have a much easier time staying in our tiny apartment because she, unlike mother number one, doesn't mind sleeping on couches. Actually, she's probably the best choice since her other three are grown and have all been having babies recently.

David wants to know why we're not even considering his mother, who lives in Brooklyn, but then agrees that she tends to choke a lot and that could be nerve-racking. Whenever I bring up her choking habit, David tells me how beautiful she used to be and how refined and well-bred she is, as if this explains it, like she was bred with a small, ladylike esophagus that makes eating a whole lamb chop unimaginable. Besides, the F train doesn't stop in LA so she's off the list.

One call to Diane and it's set; she's going to fly out and help us for a week after we get home. "I vacuum and I do laundry," she said. I didn't care if all she did was fluff pillows. I needed her to spritz me clean once in a while and give me her emotional support. I wanted someone I didn't have to fake new parental bliss around, and Diane was perfect; she didn't fake anything. In fact, the last time she flew across the country to see one of my solo shows, she came backstage afterward, walked right past me, collapsed on a couch, and announced, "Man, that was tough to stay awake through." Later she apologized and blamed the pitcher of margaritas she'd had before the show.

My friend Gay Jay (I don't actually call him Gay Jay anymore after Chinese Lesbian Kristin yelled at me to stop) has stopped by the hospital under the guise of seeing the new baby, but I've known him since seventh grade. What's really brought him here is the opportunity to see me vulnerable. He would have paid good money to catch the breakdown-in-the-bathroom scene. He's being patient, though, and diligently oohing and aahing over Leo, though I can tell it's boring for him. He tries to get some action started by poking me about motherhood ("Are you excited about being humorless, sincere, and chasing cars you think drive too fast with a rolling pin?"), but I'm too worn-out to take the bait. He asks me to save my Percocets and is about to leave when I mention Diane's visit.

"*Oh my god!* You are going to ask the woman who gave you up as a baby to come and help you with *your* baby? When she sees Leo she's going to see the face of the baby she gave away and have a major flashback. This is beyond profound."

"Should I hire a documentary film crew?" I ask, knowing that Diane is not going to have painful emotional flashbacks about my birth.

She's a probation officer by trade, and though she tends to talk in a baby voice, say words like "otay," and dress in pink overalls and bright purple clogs like a giant toddler or Rosie O'Donnell playing a handi-capable adult, she's tough. She's moved past the moments of my birth and giving me up long ago. She's not what I would call unemotional. She's empathetic, easy to talk to—has all the traits of a good person—but she doesn't indulge emotions or wallow in regrets. Years after we first met we were picking up some dinner, a box of white zin and American cheese, at a Denver Safeway when she spotted a giant salami in the meat section. She picked it up, waved it wistfully in front of her face—"Oh man, I knew this guy. I miss him"—and threw it back on the stack. That was as close to expressing regret as I ever saw her.

The lactation specialist shows up. Jay can't get out of the room fast enough. He tells me how he hopes I don't plan on losing the eighty pounds I've gained because he's never seen me looking so radiant and dewy, shields his eyes, and runs out, but not before letting me know that he thinks I'm being incredibly naïve about Diane. "Just get ready."

Diane and I have known each other since I was nineteen. Our reunion, though life changing, wasn't the hysterical emotional scene I'd been led to believe it would be from all the dramatic reunions I'd been watching on *Oprah* since seventh grade. When there is a reunion on the talk shows, adults run to their long-lost mothers or grandmothers or kindergarten teachers like they are hostages that have just been freed after thirty years of captivity.

There was one *Oprah* where a middle-aged, somewhat odd woman—let's just call her "Florida Cracky"—had been separated from her twin sister through the magic of the Florida foster care system and hadn't seen her since she was three years old. I didn't even like the woman. But when her sister came onstage and they saw each other for the first time I was howling with sobs on the couch. It turned out, of course, that even though they hadn't been raised with each other, they were *exactly* alike, the only difference being one drew her eyebrows on with a Sharpie and the other one went natural. It didn't matter what the details were about the people or the situations—it could be a father meeting a daughter for the first time, a fireman meeting the toddler he freed from a sewer, or the cast of *Happy Days*—any reunion of any type left me sobbing.

Yet when it came time for me to meet Diane, the last thing I wanted was a big dramatic scene. On the plane from Indianapolis to Denver, sitting next to my mother, Sharon, I tried to remember if I'd ever seen a show where the long-lost child calmly walked up to his or her birth parent and just shook hands. "Hello." "Hello."

I knew that when it came to life's big moments you could never predict how you were going to act, much less how others would. My adoptive mother is an ex-ballerina who is obsessed with table manners and tucked-in shirts. She's not one for big displays of emotion. My worry was that she would think that Diane expected a big show and she'd turn all Liza Minnelli on me, with manic hand gestures, tears, and fake laughter.

The entire flight I was shoving doughnuts in my mouth but was completely unable to swallow them. Crumbs just went flying out of my mouth like I was Cookie Monster. Right before we landed, I was complaining of starving and then I threw up. At nineteen years old I couldn't identify that I was overwhelmed with nerves. When I couldn't find my seat belt and my mother pointed out that I was sitting on it, I screamed, *"No, you are!"*

My biggest fear had been that Diane would be a seven-hundred-pound shut-in covered in dirty washcloths who collected Cabbage Patch dolls that she gave the same name she'd given me after I was born—Tammy Lisa. Now that I was walking off the airplane about to see for the first time the woman who birthed me, my fear was that she'd sob into my hair or give me a long, lingering hug. And it would be in front of my mother and all the strangers in the airport and I was sure that everyone would be watching to see how I reacted, waiting for me to crumble. Thanks to the Thorazine that my body seems to naturally produce to help me survive, I shuffled off the plane and then stood there, stone-faced, as my mother and Diane hugged and cried.

Diane was nothing like I'd pictured. Five foot three inches. Short brown shiny hair, sparkly green eyes, and a huge toothy grin. I watched her and my mother whisper to each other, both giddy with nerves but without any big hand gestures or fainting spells, and I realized that I'd never expected her to be so young, pretty, and happy looking. I guess I'd thought that the loss of me would have left her blind in one eye or at least a little grumpy. After Diane and my mother had their moment, Diane turned to me, smiled, and with a quick squeeze of my arm, said, "We'll have a lot of time to catch up." Then she turned around, and I watched my butt walk to the baggage claim.

Since the big reunion, I'd visited Diane every year or so and even went so far as moving to Colorado to be closer to her for a time. Diane seemed to instinctually get who I was and how I was feeling without any words being exchanged. She always happened to be there for major life events. Well, she missed that *one*, but otherwise. We went through 9/11 together. She was in New York for the September 10 Off-Broadway premiere of *Homecoming*, the play I wrote about my mom's search for Diane after she had adopted me. "Kind of makes you want to drop acid and have sex with strangers" was the first thing she said after we found each other the afternoon of 9/11 on the Upper West Side. I saw Diane and her kids every year and sometimes more if she flew out to see me in New York or Los Angeles. In the final moment of *Homecoming*, the Lauren character hears the sound of her birth mother's voice on the phone for the first time, Aretha Franklin's "Think" fades up, and the lights go to black. Audiences would leave the theater happy that I'd found my African American mother. The reason I didn't bring Diane into the play as a character was because she was so perfect and fun it didn't seem fair to other adopted folks whose reunions ended in tears and gunshots in front of Cinnabon. Over the years, I've seen her foibles, but ultimately she's been my Aretha Franklin fantasy birth mama.

David has just arrived at our apartment with Diane after picking her up from the airport.

Diane flops down on the couch next to me.

"Man, those C-sections are the way to go," she says, looking at Leo's head. "He's not as ugly as some of my other grandkids were when they were first born. Don't tell the others I said that."

Diane has decided that her grandma name is going to be Bubs. "He's a heroin addict turned police informant on *The Wire*. He's my favorite character. Full disclosure, his real name is Bubbles but that sounds like a stripper name. And since my breast reduction surgery I can't in good conscience call myself that."

She leans over Leo's face and shouts at him like he's deaf.

"Hey, Buddy! Check it out! Bubs is here! I'm your Bubs!"

David laughs and I nod and open my mouth like I'm laughing, but no sound comes out.

I am trying to hide my tears. She's the first family member to meet Leo. She didn't have to run in slow motion with her arms outstretched and tears streaming down her face, but I would have liked the moment to have a teeny bit more emotional weight to it.

Now Diane's wandering around the apartment in a flowing paisley print dress and a cheerful pair of ankle socks covered in rainbow horses that she loves but rarely gets to wear because her judge won't let her wear them in court. She's "here to help" and is looking for any cloth surface that can be vacuumed or laundered as she tells me stories about her job.

"Well, my murderer is having a hard time because he murdered again."

As a probation officer, Diane can't walk through a Walmart in southern Indiana without having to nod at someone or give a little shout of encouragement. "Hey, Jeanie, you're not getting your foot caught in air-conditioner vents anymore, I hope. Watch out for those."

I love her probation stories and I'm listening, but I'm also struggling to get Leo latched on to breastfeed.

Diane notices this, stops for a second, gives me a "You're a natural" thumbs-up, and keeps talking.

"So, his cellmate offered to help him kill his stepmother and his grandmother. Now, my murderer at least has some motivation for killing them because they were his family. But the other guy, now, he's just pure evil."

She lets out a huge exhausted sigh. "Ahhhh! Oh man, I need a baked good." She grabs her strawberry-shaped purse and heads out the front door.

"I'll be right back, honey. And *this* time I mean it."

True to her word, Diane's been putting her special helping skill to use and doing a lot of laundry. I have to grip on to my pants when she passes by me: "I'm still wearing these . . . they're not dirty."

David has confessed that he thinks that Diane is more worried about her baked goods and getting to bed early than helping us. Maybe after three babies and four grandkids, babies can't compete with turtle brownies. No, she's had four babies. I'm always forgetting to include myself.

Diane's three little "ones she kept" from another marriage didn't know anything about me. They were six, nine, and eleven. To break it to them, Diane took them out to Chuck E. Cheese's and told them they were celebrating and that she had a big surprise for them. At the end of the night, she had a cake and balloons brought out. "Okay, guess what we're celebrating!" Before they could start throwing out ideas, she made the big announcement: "You have an older sister! And she's coming to visit! On Wednesday at four P.M.!" They had no idea how this was possible; they just thought, "Cake . . . balloons . . . *good*," and they celebrated.

On the day we met, they ran up the driveway after their bus dropped them off like they were being chased. They were pushing each other out of the way, dropping their school papers as they ran. And then, when they got to the door, they all just stopped and stared at me. Saying nothing. They surrounded me and looked at my toes for an hour. They marveled at the skills I'd picked up during my nineteen-year adventure away from them—"She's going to brush her teeth! Mom, get in here. You got to see this."

My birth father, Rob, had a harder time with my adoption and felt a lot more shame around the whole thing. After Diane got pregnant, he was kicked off his high school baseball team and sent back to the hills of West Virginia, where he could get away with that sort of thing. When Rob broke the news to his kids, who, like Diane's, were little and had no idea about me, he sat them down in their bedroom and shut the door. "A long time ago, I made a mistake," he said. "Well, that mistake is back. She'll be here next Thursday." For years after we first met, I'd sit on the couch and wave to them. "Hi, I'm the mistake."

Diane's positive PR campaign has played a large part in why I've felt a part of her family from the very beginning. They are the only humans I've been around where I don't feel a separate "me," just a clump of "us."

Having Diane around gets me thinking about family. I realize that I've been telling this dreary little story to myself for all these years about how I've never really had my own family. I've been a visitor in all sorts of families but never felt like I had my own. Now that Leo is born, I see how untrue that is. All of those families are his families. And they were mine, too. Are mine. How amazing to go from "I have no family" to "Wake the fuck up—you have five! Six if you count the gay boys." I don't care if she never vacuums another napkin; I'm so grateful she's here.

It's four A.M. Leo and I are the only ones awake. Oh my god, there's a baby in my arms. How do any babies survive for more than a week? They're so frail and helpless. Look at him. I need to shove him back in so he's safe in my belly again. Or buy him a shell. Leo's squirms are familiar to me; he moves the same way in my arms as he did in my stomach. How on earth did my mother jump right into taking care of an eight-day-old newborn she'd just met? I can't imagine. I've asked her what those first few days were like and she told me, "Oh, fine. You ate and slept and went to the bathroom. Like a baby." This was the same sort of midwestern pragmatic answer she used when I asked her why after having two daughters of her own already she'd chosen to adopt me: "Well, I had so many girl clothes . . ." Apparently Goodwill didn't do home pickups at that time and it was just as easy for her to adopt a baby.

I'm sure my mom wasn't up in the middle of the night, like I am, feeling terrible that she'd invited a sweet tiny baby to an awkward party with shitty parking where everyone's parting gift is some form of cancer.

The next morning, Diane goes to pick up twelve-dollar scones for everybody at our local coffee shop, which, after two days in town, she refers to as *her* coffee shop. She shows up three hours later with a bag of dried-out scones and a giant green leaf that she claims to have found on the sidewalk but later confesses to ripping off a tree in our neighbor's yard. She says it looks like the kind of leaf you could put a baby on and float him down a river.

"Not that I ever thought of that before," she cracks, and then says she wants to take a picture of Leo lying on the leaf.

Normally, I love her abandonment jokes, but I'm still queasy from last night. I don't want to tell David about it because I don't want him to lose his mind in the nothingness and the terror since he still gets so much joy from online Scrabble. Diane, on the other hand, has been through a lot in her life. Divorce, death, and murdering murderers—she can handle it.

As Diane rummages through our toxic cleaning agents to find something to clean the leaf off, I share with her all the graphic images of reality that I, thanks to being a new mother, now understand—the cycle of suffering, John F. Kennedy Jr.'s plane going down, and the end of time as we know it.

Diane thinks she remembers that Danza, my half sister, had something like this happen to her after her first baby was born. "You should ask her. I'm just not as deep as you guys. Parenting wasn't that heavy for me. Maybe because I had no idea what the hell I was doing."

I reminded Diane about the reunion story as evidence of how untrue that is.

Diane smiles and gives me a little loving squirt with the Windex she's holding in her hand. "That's sweet, honey, but I don't know what you're talking about."

"It's really my favorite story."

"What is?"

"How you took Danza, Justin, and Kenneth to Chuck E. Cheese's. There were balloons tied to all their chairs and a big cake comes out. You were like, 'Okay, guess what we're celebrating! You have a big sister and she's back! She'll be here on Wednesday!' If you had done things any differently it would have changed everything. It's all about the spin you put on things."

Diane is scowling. It's the scowl she has on her face when she's thinking. Or hungry.

"I hate to tell you this, but that never happened. I'm not sure where you got that from. Listen, what's going to stress you out more: if I lay him on a dirty leaf or one covered in Windex?"

I've told that story since the day I met Diane. It's how I describe the essence of who she is to people. She's just forgotten.

"No way have I made up that entire story. Where would I have gotten that from?"

"I don't know, sweetie, but it's a wonderful story, so I think you should keep telling it."

"Is any of it true?"

"I don't think so. I think what I did was just tell the kids that I'd gotten pregnant in high school and that I'd given up the baby for adoption and now that baby was nineteen and she found us and was coming to visit. See, your story is better." Diane walks over and takes Leo out of my arms. "Okay, race fans; let's go put this baby on a leaf."

Two years later, Leo and I are in Bloomington, Indiana, visiting family while David is away working for the summer, trying to make big money as a salmon fisherman in Alaska. We're staying with my half sister, Danza, who was named for the great Tony Danza, not because Diane was particularly fond of his *Who's the Boss?* work, but because she just liked how it sounded. "Or maybe I was a big fan of his. I can't remember. Who cares? Just be glad you don't have a brother named Fonzie."

All of Diane's kids live in the Bloomington area, and when there's a big event, like our visit, Diane shoves her third husband into their little sports car and drives the hour from their house to see the family.

Since (one of the twelve of my avid followers) Diane's trip right after Leo was born, she's been an avid follower of my baby blog, *Wigs on a Baby*. Once in a while we'll talk on the phone for a quick check-in. I still had this feeling that I'd been blinded by who I needed her to be and had no idea who she really was.

All the things that I'd loved about her suddenly seemed suspect. For instance, over the years I've watched Diane chat up people who most of society would run from. You could wheel up a headless torso on a gurney and Diane would chat away with it like they were old school buddies. Adults with severe cerebral palsy who can communicate only by blinking can chat for hours with Diane simply because she isn't scared of humanity in all its forms. I've always loved this about her, but it leaves me with a "well, she likes everybody" insecurity. In fact, if she was due for a coffee and a baked good, she might not have been able to determine who was standing in front of her, much less cared. We were making plans for my upcoming visit over the phone and I tried to share this fear with her. Her response was "What are you, adopted or something?" That was it.

People talk about genetics versus nurturing, but within six weeks of being Leo's mother I realized that what makes a mother is being there. The hours alone with him in the middle of the night. Feeding him. Loving him. Feeling that old "you and me against the world" Helen Reddy bond. The hell of knowing I will worry about his safety for the rest of his life. That is a mother.

All these years I've had an ongoing "it's a hard-knock life in the orphanage" shtick about how my mother didn't get me. How Sharon didn't understand who I really was. "I can't laugh without her screaming 'Seizure!' at me and shoving a stick in my mouth." I'd tell my friends that the picnic table in our backyard was "the adopted table," where my family had requested I take all my meals.

Now that I'm a mother, it makes perfect sense how my mother

worried that a note in my adoption file had fallen out that had warned, "At age twelve her arms will fall off due to a rare West Virginia genetic mutation," and she'd never know for sure if there was something seriously wrong with me. Leo's my biological son, I knew my medical history, and I still worried after he was born that he was blind in one eye and had half a kidney.

Right after Diane arrives at Danza's she announces that her cat, Tiny Tim, is sick.

"We're putting him to sleep before I go to England. It would cost a lot of money to keep him alive, and I don't want to be worried about him on my trip, so I'm just gonna get rid of him and get a new one when I get back. Kind of like I did with you."

A dry smile is on my face and I give her a "good one" slow nod. Diane once told me that the reason she was able to hand me over after I was born was because they drugged her up. "It's what they did back then so girls could go through with it. I've had haircuts that were more stressful."

What if all those adoption extremists are right and I'll never be able to attach to another human being? If my dad put his arm around me in front of other people—or in private, for that matter— I thought he was just trying to hold me still so someone could punch me in the stomach. Not that he'd ever done anything like that, but sometimes physical contact with people made me fear the worst. When the Snuggle fabric softener commercial came on, the giggly baby voice of Snuggle Bear was too vulnerable and needy and it would make me punch the couch pillows. That may not have been specific to an abandonment issue. The sound of that bear's voice made most non–mentally ill people want to blame everything that was wrong in their lives on him.

I'd hoped all of my misgivings about Diane had more to do with hormones than with Diane herself, but if anything she's gone from "casual I don't give a shit" land to "aggressive I don't give a shit" land.

I don't hate her; I just see her more clearly now that I've been a mother for two years.

Danza and Diane are upstairs plugging in curling irons, getting ready to go to a Paul Simon concert. It's one P.M. Danza feels horrible that the only person who isn't going is "the adopted one." The whole clan is going and they don't have a ticket for me. When I made my plans to visit, Danza had asked me if she should buy me one, and I'd said I'd rather save my money for wine and online gambling. I'd imagined that I'd use the free night to visit with one of my brothers or cousins in the area whom I don't always get time with, but it turned out that *everyone* in the family was going. I'm wandering around Danza's big house enjoying her homemaking skills, making mental notes on how to best organize batteries and ribbons, trying to fight back a little of the "which one of these is not like the other" feelings. I stop in the kitchen to make a cup of coffee and hear the familiar sound of Diane's husband, Randy, snapping photos of me.

Randy is a photographer for an Indiana paper and has the photojournalist's gift of not being at all affected by people not wanting their picture taken. He instructs me to "get that coffee mug like you were just doing. That was pretty funny. You have a funny way of doing it," and stands an inch away from me snapping my picture.

During my visits, Randy will always take the opportunity to ask me a series of questions about Hollywood. Things he assumes I must know about, like, "Is Lindsay Lohan starting to regret doing some of that stupid stuff she's done?" Or, "Why does Pamela Anderson like looking like that?" It can be endearing, how he thinks there are twenty people in Hollywood and I know all of them, but then, in the next breath, he'll ask me, "Lauren, can you understand anything those black people are saying on *The Wire*? CAN YOU, Lauren?"

"Hey, Lauren, how do you deal with paparazzi always chasing you and taking your picture without you knowing it? That's gotta be tough."

"I hate to break it to you, Randy; nobody wants my picture but you."

This kills him and he collapses into laughter and then pops right up and starts to take more photos.

Right as I'm thinking how wonderful it would be to be upstairs with Diane and Danza getting ready for the concert, Randy offers me his ticket.

"Come on, Lauren. How many times will you get to sit by your foster mom at a Paul Simon concert? I mean, come on."

The whole family has tried to explain to Randy that Diane is not my foster mom or half mom or stepmother; she is my birth mom. Randy married Diane only ten years ago and has a hard time keeping it all straight. In the end, I just tell him that Diane is my Guatemalan plumber.

"Listen, I don't care about Paul Simon and honestly I don't want to go," he says. "I'd rather stay here and read and watch some basketball."

"Are you sure, Randy?" I ask his camera lens. He puts it down so I can see his face.

"Oh yeah, it's the chance of a lifetime—see Paul Simon with your stepmom, come on."

I run upstairs to announce the good news.

"Randy just gave me his ticket! I'm going!"

"He did what?"

"He gave me his ticket . . ."

Danza looks like she's going to cry and yells to Diane, who is lying down in the next room.

"Why is he doing that, Mom? He's the one who said it was his dream to go, and I got it all arranged and— Mom, Randy gave Lauren his ticket!"

"He did *what*?"

It turns out that the Paul Simon ticket was Randy's birthday present. The family chipped in and bought the ticket and were going to take him to dinner beforehand. The entire evening was to be his birthday celebration.

"He offered it to me . . . I swear." This is the sentence I have to repeat all night long every time a new family member or close family friend joins up with us. It's like I stole a birthday present from a sweet, confused man. I'm an entitled selfish monster . . . who's been a lifelong fan of Paul Simon and is going to his concert!

Diane and I sit down in our seats. We are in the last row of the concert hall. The very last row. We turn around and there's a wall behind us.

Paul is pretty great. He looks exactly the same as he did when he was banging Garfunkel, I mean playing with Garfunkel, but with white hair, like he'd gone to makeup and told them, "Make me look like an old-man version of Paul Simon."

He plays the first few notes of "Kodachrome" and Diane is up on her feet, dancing. The entire theater is seated politely. Nobody is moving, much less dancing. "All right, this is cool! We can do whatever we want!" Diane says and waves her hand in the air and shouts out a *woooo*.

She's the only one in the entire place besides Paul's band who is standing. Even the ushers are sitting on the steps. I try to make her sit down and she turns around and asks the wall if we're blocking its view and keeps going. "We're in the back row so who gives a shit!"

Diane starts dancing with her arms above her head, swinging her hips like the child of the sixties she is. She gets worn out before the song is over and sits back down, grabs my head, brings my ear to her mouth, and yells over the music, *"Man, how much am I wishing I'd worn a bra right now."*

Paul, I call him, now that we've spent a couple of hours together, is playing what he claims is going to be the last song of the night, "Mother and Child Reunion."

"On this strange and mournful day . . . Is only a motion away."

Diane reaches over and grabs my hand. It's nice for a moment, but then my hand gets sweaty, so I wriggle free. She grabs me back. We repeat this until finally I'm full-on struggling to get my hand away.

Nobody ever holds my hand. David will grab my hand for a moment and then immediately get exhausted and let go.

Diane pins my hand down and won't let me pull away, like an orderly in a hospital trying to calm a mental patient. By the time the song is over, all the struggle stops and now I'm just holding hands with her.

Holding hands is good shit. I will hold hands with my son longer than he wants me to. I will hold on because it feels so good to have someone hold you longer than you want. You let go but they still have you. It's why you hold someone's hand when they are dying. No words, just a presence. I start crying and this time I know it's not hormonal. Thank god for Randy's birthday present.

The topic in Danza's minivan after the concert is which song was everyone's favorite.

"Lauren and I vote for 'Mother and Child Reunion,'" Diane yells from the back of the van, where we're sitting.

"Little known fact: People think that that song is about a dog he loved but it's actually about his favorite dish at a Chinese restaurant in Brooklyn that closed down." Thank you, Justin. Justin's my half brother, Diane's oldest son. When I first met him he had a mullet and a rattail. Of course, I had blue eye shadow up to my eyebrows and a bad perm, so who I am to talk? Nowadays he's a disgruntled lawyer.

Danza's father-in-law, who is also a lawyer, jumps right in. "Actually, Justin, it was the restaurant itself that added the dish to their menu in honor of Paul, their favorite customer. The song itself is about the death of a dog."

Don, Diane's second husband, is in the van too. He insists that the song is about the Korean War.

By the time we've dropped everyone off at his or her car or home, the song might as well have been about a meatball finding tomato sauce.

The next morning Diane knocks on my bedroom door and asks me if I want to go with her to *her* coffee shop.

"I thought your coffee shop was the one by me," I say.

"That's my coffee shop in Santa Monica. This is my one in Bloomington. You coming or not?"

We pull into the parking lot and I'm about to jump out when she stops me.

"There is something I was thinking that maybe would be good for you to hear. Since you and your mother found me, I've never wanted you to think that the moment that you were born was in any way horrible or that your adoption was an awful ordeal. The last thing I wanted was for you to feel burdened or worried about me. But you know what? Maybe you need to know how painful it was. I'm realizing as you get older that maybe it would have helped you to know that giving you up for adoption was the most painful thing I've gone through in my life. Maybe the one thing I kept from you was the exact thing you needed to know—that you were not an easy baby to give up. Anyway, I just thought it would be nice for you to know that and I wish I'd told you earlier."

If anyone would have asked me if I needed to hear what she just told me I would have said no, but that's because my need to hear it was so completely buried. Before I met Diane, I'd thought that out of necessity for my birth mother to move on, I'd been born unloved. Adopted by a family that had to love me but didn't know what exactly they were getting. I didn't feel incredibly valued, but everyone I knew felt that way, so why make a big Macy's Thanksgiving Day parade out of it? But if I were really honest, I had to admit that there were times I felt like a random clump of a human that had to be assigned to someone in order to be cared about. When awful things happened to me, I never thought anyone would care all that much.

It mattered to me more than I could have imagined to know that I wasn't an easy baby to dump.

She rummages around in her purse and pulls out an old wadded-up Starbucks napkin and offers it to me to wipe my tears off my face and blow my nose.

Diane reaches over and grabs my hand. "And hey, kid, I need to tell you something else."

By the way she's staring out the window at the coffee shop, I take a guess that what she wants to tell me is something about how if they only have one piece of lemon pound cake, she's not sharing. But I'm wrong.

"I don't give a shit about the pound cake; it's all about the coffee cake at this place. If there's only one piece of that left, hands off. It's mine."

Horny Patty

I'm fourteen weeks pregnant at an artists' retreat in Florida.

Most of my time is spent wandering around taking in all the natural beauty that the state has to offer. I've seen a turtle, an armadillo, and a bunch of drunk guys with no shirts buying honey buns at the 7-Eleven, when I should be writing. I remind myself that only moneymaking projects are allowed at this retreat, so I can squirrel away like a good waspy rodent for the long winter months when I won't be able to perform because I'll be too fat, and I won't be able to write because I'll be too distracted about being too fat.

I'm here for only three weeks and I need to conceive, start, and finish an Oscar-winning screenplay, maybe something like *Juno* but with Aboriginal transsexual people; a web series that can be shot in a minivan, pay nothing to the actors, and be developed into a lucrative TV pilot starring all men; and a new theater piece about how having a baby is going to end my career. The theater piece may have to wait, because there's no money in theater.

Too bad, because the only thing I'm remotely inspired to do is the theater piece. The source material is endless here. None of the fifteen artists who were already here when I arrived have kids. None. They are accomplished professional artists. Most of them are professors at fancy liberal colleges who are on salary. There was one woman with kids, a Brazilian sculptor, but she broke her ankle after the second day and had to go home. Joseph, a sixty-two-year-old Pulitzer Prize–winning composer from New Haven, whose only child is his opera—"a spoiled little obnoxious girl who I will drown before the end of this week unless she kills me first"—broke the news to me at breakfast. I'd been saving a seat for her at my table so that she could tell me all about how having a baby affects your career.

A few breakfasts later Joseph told me that the pain of missing her baby was so intense "it snapped her bones."

I said that I'd heard that she'd gotten drunk and fallen down some stairs.

"Same thing," he said. "Pass the flaxseed spread."

The best part of the day is when all the artists gather after dinner in the "Fellowship Hall" to sit on dirty couches, drink red wine, and shit talk whichever artist was dumb enough to stay in and work that night. That was the key to being respected here— showing up. There have been several transitions of artists coming and going. New ones arrived on Monday night. One of the new arrivals, an intense and dramatic playwright from Seattle named Tonia, very pale, with flapper-style jet-black hair, who is what I imagine Virginia Woolf must have been like, notices that I'm drinking only a half glass of red wine. I tell her I'm pregnant and she gasps. I thought maybe she'd recognized my giant glass as the centerpiece filled with floating candles from the night before, and maybe she did, but it wasn't about that.

"I had dreams once," she tells me in a voice that sounds like an old-timey radio performance. "They all died. There are file cabinets full of my plays, but that's all over now. You cannot be an artist and a mother—I don't care what they say; they lie. You know why they lie? They lie because they want to lure you over to the other side. They say, 'Have a baby. I did! And, why, I've never been happier.' Lies. Believe me; the serpent draws blood along with milk!"

Applause would have been an appropriate response to her performance, but I was too dizzy to slap my hands together. If I can't tour and perform and experience the world outside of myself to write about—if I'm always here with Leo—I'll go crazy.

My career is being in the world. Walking around being traumatized every five minutes and making a two-hour show about it. It's an embarrassing way to make a living, but if I didn't do that, I'm fairly sure I'd develop an addiction to engine cleaner or vaping saffron or something. It wouldn't be the addiction that would kill me. It would be the fact that I couldn't write a story about it because the baby would be a part of the story and writers can't write about their kids because it's not their story to tell. You can't tell sex stories or curse or make fun of their fathers or talk about anal (that's a type of foot cream, baby). Fuck.

All the artists in the meeting hall are nodding in agreement with Tonia, or nodding off from red wine, except for the married writing team from San Diego, Carla and Paul. Thankfully Carla and Paul had brought in a new batch of folks who didn't have metaphorical "stretch marks on their souls," but real ones on their bodies.

"That's a bunch of cuckoo-bird yak-yak," Carla, the wife, a ball-buster, no-makeup, no-nonsense lady originally from Mississippi, tells me. According to her, kids focus your time and generally make everything better. "Children are happy if you are happy," Paul, who's either Russian or just extremely exhausted, adds. "And if you are getting paid to do what you love to do, they'll be happy." I watch him get up to get some scotch tape to hold in the lenses of glasses that keep falling out whenever he isn't sitting completely still.

Their advice to me is to continue to tour, but take David with me. I love that idea because it's essentially who we are—carny show folk. David had directed one of my theater shows in the past; now he could direct all of them. Run the lights with the baby strapped on his chest while I performed. We could combine our finances, throw the baby in the back of the wagon, and hit the road. They love their life. "It's not conventional, but our kids are growing up with parents who get to do what they love, and more importantly we all get to be together." They had dropped their kids off with a relative and were enjoying what they referred to as a rare romantic work getaway.

Finally, I found my role models.

Role models who fought like George and Martha from *Who's Afraid of Virginia Woolf?* every single day of their retreat.

"I don't know what page we are on! Do I look like MapQuest?!" The sound of their stressed-out marriage became a part of the retreat's swampy soundscape. Every night after Fellowship Hall, the artists would retire to their studios and drift off to sleep to the sounds of gators grunting, insects chirping, and Carla screaming at Paul, "Why are you so fucking crabby? What's your problem? Go home if you're in such a bad mood!" Yeah, Paul! If you can't sit there and be screamed at with a little better attitude, go home.

Back at home, I'm driving to Nate 'n Al deli in Beverly Hills when Allen, my agent, calls me with an audition. Thank god. I accomplished absolutely nothing during the retreat. That's not true. I memorized an e.e. cummings poem and learned how to play the chorus from David Bowie's "Space Oddity" on a ukulele. Not exactly powerful skills for the workforce.

As many women's magazines go on about working mothers and

having it all, I have noticed that on airplanes when I pass through business class on the way back to the Septic Tank Section, it is still dominated by white men in suits. And rappers with their moms.

Only celebrities are allowed to be pregnant and still work. They can afford nannies, and entire film shoots are scheduled around their pregnancies. Pregnant ladies in Hollywood are like spiders. The Hollywood studios scream when they see a spider and want to get rid of it, but then a good producer reminds them that spiders are vital to the system. They serve a purpose. The ones who serve a purpose are A-list famous ones. Talented ones. The bit players don't serve a purpose. They don't bring money into the studios or sell tickets. A pregnant Anne Heche is a spider. An alien spider but still a spider. A pregnant me is more like a flea. They will crush me between their fingernail and their forefinger and my career will be over.

Without my career I'm nothing. I'm just a stack of bones covered with skin on a big rock hurtling toward my death.

"Okay, what are the details?" I make "mmm-hmmm" noises as Allen talks, so he thinks I'm writing it all down instead of speeding down the 10 toward creamed herring and street parking I can't afford.

It's for an HBO show called *Hung*, a comedy about a down-and-out high school baseball coach who, thanks to his special talent of having a large penis, becomes a gigolo. They would like to see me for the character of Horny Patty.

Horny Patty sounds like a sexy bombshell type. I, however, am, as I've mentioned, pregnant. My face is covered in brown splotches, and I can't stop burping and shitting my pants.

"The casting people said just go in with no makeup and nerdy. Think lonely odd girl in the office who masturbates at her desk and goes to SeaWorld by herself."

He assures me that they want a "real" person and to play it "real." They always say that. They said that when I auditioned for *Desperate Housewives* for "a shut-in who marries prison inmates." The waiting room was a sea of tall, leggy models wearing tight mini-sundresses and high-heeled sandals. They all had so much makeup on they looked embalmed. I was wearing a full-length denim skirt and an oversize Mickey Mouse sleep shirt. Before I'd left the house David had begged me to put on more makeup and detangle the back of my hair.

"David, she's a shut-in! Why would she brush her hair?"

"It's a network show. Those are the parts that you have to add a 'that you want to fuck' at the end of every description," David said.

"Really? So if the character is a ninety-year-old Native American in a coma and it's network, then it's a ninety-year-old Native American 'that you'd like to fuck'?"

Turns out, David should have been a manager.

My real manager assures me that this is different; it's HBO.

"Just making sure it's actually a part that I could get."

"Listen, Weeds, you were invited to the party. When you're invited to the party, you go."

I'm about to ask him if he stole that line from the Dalai Lama when he gives me a quick, "Sounds good, Weeds," and hangs up.

Of course I'll audition. I have to. Everybody keeps telling me how babies are magic, so maybe I'll get a good parking spot.

On the way to the audition I call Allen to ask if there's anything else I should know before I go in today. Anything that may throw me off, like "Bill Clinton will be in the room" or "The casting woman has no eyebrows."

"Her name is Horny Patty," Allen says. "How many more details do you need?"

The waiting room is crammed full of women. It's clear that we are all here for the same part. It's also clear that some of them have taken the "that you'd want to fuck" note to apply for network *or* cable. There's an actress with amazing posture who came dressed as "nerdy porn girl." She's got thick black glasses on with tape wrapped around the nose and double Ds that the Lord gave her after she paid him a mighty sum.

The energy in the room is pretty heavy. All the actresses look so miserable. They're all deeply focused on inhabiting the character of Horny Patty. It's a room full of Daniel Day-Lewises. Or maybe they're just miserable. To break up the tension, or undermine the competition, I cross my fingers, shut my eyes, and shout, "GOD, I HOPE I GET THIS!" as I walk in. Nobody laughs. Usually I save my jokes for after the audition when I close the door, yell, "I GOT IT!" and then burst into fake sobs and run out of the room.

In the corner of the room I spot an actress I see at every audition, Emma.

She and I are always up for the same "crazy lesbian ballbuster" parts. To prove that I see her as a human and not just someone there to steal my health insurance, I tell her I like her outfit. She pulls out the sales tag still attached to the collar and says, "Nordstrom's. I put panty liners in my pits so I don't ruin it." She shoves the tags back in. She tells me how she's been thinking about designing a T-shirt that reads I HATE MYSELF on the front for when she first walks in to audition and then I'M SORRY on the back for when she leaves.

Emma is sure that she won't get the part. "I know how this bullshit works. Someone like Juliette Lewis or Octavia Spencer probably already has the part. They're just killing time until she signs her contract."

Usually I'm the manic wreck in the corner at an audition,

pretending to go over my lines, but what I'm really doing is chanting "dead body in a casket . . . dead body in a casket," trying to convince myself how unimportant booking a commercial for Gas-X is in the grand scheme of things. If it's a film role, "dead body in a casket" isn't graphic enough and I have to add images of eyelids sewn shut and a botched embalming.

Today feels different. Emma goes on and on about her diet and hair regime with her sweat-soaked panty liner peeking out of the top of her blouse, and I'm able to do what the Buddhists have been yelling at me to do for years: observe the world around me without feeling any attachment to it.

Did somebody slip a Xanax into my Red Bull?

It's so calming to know that in my always-uncertain life, one thing is for certain—a baby is coming.

I mean, come on. What's it all about at the end of it all? I've had a good career. I was on *The Daily Show*. I was fired from *The Daily Show*, but that doesn't mean I don't still have the luggage they gave me for Christmas. Eddie Murphy said I reminded him of Ruth Gordon. His body double told me later he meant Ruth Buzzi, but I think I'll go with the real Eddie on that one.

If I don't get this job—in fact, if I never work in this town again—the baby is still coming. We could move to Corydon, Indiana, and live with my birth mother, Diane. She's always letting me know that when I decide I'm done with the Hollywood thing, a simple small-town life is waiting for me. I'll go back to waiting tables.

I loved waiting tables for the same reason I love giving blow jobs: You get to put on a little show. Corydon is a small southern Indiana town. Small towns are so completely foreign to me, and I love foreign things. I thrive on being completely out of my element and chronically constipated from unfamiliar foods. The Corydon Ponderosa has an all-you-can-eat steak night. The waitresses chew gum and say things like, "Y'all ready for another steak?" There's a pharmacy with an old-timey lunch counter and soda fountain in the town square called Butt Drugs. Diane knows the Butt family and could get me a job working the lunch counter. Retired farmers sit at the counter sipping on two-dollar cups of coffee and talking about the good old days. The waitresses wear T-shirts that say I HEART BUTT DRUGS. Why wouldn't I want to work there?

The casting door opens up and this time a spunky-looking blond lady with a blowout sticks her head out and calls me in.

Sometimes I'll get notes during the audition like "remember you *love* him. He's your husband! He's Jim Belushi!" Or I'll walk into the room for an audition and the producers will literally shake their heads: "No." Sometimes they nod: "Yes." The blond blowout lady, who must be one of the writers or maybe a producer, explains to me again how Horny Patty is in her head—obsessing about sex. She's living in her isolated world of animal shows and SeaWorld. She doesn't have to love Jim Belushi. Or anyone, really. Just sex. I may have a shot at getting this part.

"You look hilarious," the blond lady with a blowout says and points to my faded black skirt from the Gap. "That skirt is so bad. I love the stains. The dirty hair, perfect." I don't mention that these are my normal clothes and I washed my hair this morning.

It was so effortless for me to inhabit this sad horny lady that I walk out feeling . . . good. The blond blowout comes running after me, grabs my shoulders, and stares into my eyes. Maybe she's looking to see if I have the soul of Horny Patty.

"You're okay with nudity, right?"

I tell her the same thing I tell the guy at the liquor store—"*Sure!*" (Whenever a creepy guy asks me to show him my tits, I do it. I don't want any trouble.)

On the drive home from the audition, Allen calls me. "They want to double-check that you're okay with nudity."

Absolutely, I tell him. No problem. Nudity is not a big thing for me. I'm an actress. Nudity is the given and the honor of the trade. Like a high-class hooker or a crack-house hooker. I'm a professional.

The next afternoon my phone rings. It's Allen. "It's between you and two other girls. They really want to be sure you're okay with full nudity."

Yes! Yes! Yes! They could have asked me if I was okay living in a tree trunk for a year and having a micropenis and the answer would have been "YES!"

Please god, let me get this job. I can't move to some small conservative Hoosier town and wait tables. The only gay people in small towns like that are married to women, have awful taste in music, and direct the church choir. Diane told me that the one black family in Corydon has the last name Black. I'd never be able to tell if people were being overtly racist when they said things like, "Oh well, he's a Black." I'll double-check when I get home, but I'm fairly sure you can buy I HEART BUTT DRUGS T-shirts online. If my career comes to a grinding halt because of this baby, I'll lose my mind. Or maybe I won't. I'm sure if you asked a dancer what she'd do if she lost her legs she'd say the same thing.

The calls keep coming—"So there's a chance you're getting this. Stay tuned."

The next morning at ten, Allen calls again. "Amazing news. Weeds, you got it."

Quick question: They didn't mean *naked*, did they?

I'd like to be jumping up in the air, punching the walls, and yelling "I GOT IT!" but the joy of getting the part is a little murky.

I can't be naked. They don't want me to be naked. Nobody wants to see me naked.

"Yes, full boobs, butt, and stomach. I don't think your lady hump, though," Allen tells me.

Oh good, so my parents can still watch it.

Allen assumes I'm being insecure because of my ten-pound pregnancy weight gain. "But don't your boobs get bigger? It's perfect!"

"No . . . it's not. They're not. There's a problem."

"You're a robot and taking off your clothes reveals your hidden control box?"

"Close. I have an inverted nipple."

Long pause.

"What does that mean?"

"You know. It means that it doesn't cut glass. The turkey's never ready. Tokyo can't tune in."

Once I run out of analogies for erect nipples two hours later, I have to get medical. "It's like an innie belly button. Except cleaner. And don't pity me. I've lived my life as normally as I could."

The boyfriends of my past would give it a quick "Okay, what do you do here?" glance, give it a nice "meet-ya, meet-ya" squeeze, and move on. I don't usually have to bring it up because nobody but David ever sees it and he politely looks away to save it any embarrassment. Once I jogged by a guy in New York City, and he looked at my chest and said, "One?"

"I wouldn't worry about it." Allen congratulates himself and hangs up.

I can't stop worrying about.

I've seen dead bodies on TV but never an inverted nipple. Actors have been recast for far less serious infractions. An actress friend of mine was fired after Kelsey Grammer didn't think she seemed excited to meet him. When they see my nipple, they're going to recast the part. I'll never have enough money to get my kid a haircut. Or Botox or whatever the new hot trend is when he turns two.

I shave down everything I can find. I shave my bathmat.

At the table read, a red-haired actress who's playing an office worker in the episode sits next to me, sees what part I'm playing, shrugs her shoulders, and laughs. "Ugly girls. At least we're work-ing, right?"

I say, "You said it, sister! So true!"

"Square peg," "mildly masculine," "not as cute as her friend"—those I can live with. But "ugly"? I'm sure she didn't mean to call me ugly when she said "ugly." What she meant to say was "At least we're working because we're so lucky to have anything positive happen in our lives besides winning the spelling bee." I lost the spelling bee. So now I'm back to just being ugly.

There are two fears that I've always had about being a woman—one is that I am ugly, disgusting, and smelling like a maxipad and the other one is that once I turn forty and have a baby I'll never work again.

All the confidence that I accidentally had when I walked into the room has been bled out of me. I'm going to get fired at the table read. Not for being ugly. I may have been hired for that. It took me a year to recover after being fired from *The Daily Show*. Jon was named man of the year by all of humanity, and I couldn't understand how someone didn't like me. As if my entire career was based on being liked.

A tall, ruggedly handsome man in a plaid shirt and no shoes walks into the room. It's Thomas Jane, the lead actor. God, I hope he likes me.

"Dead body in a casket, dead body in a casket . . ."

For a moment I wish I could run to the bathroom to put some makeup on, but it's too late.

He looks my way.

"Hi. I'm Horny Patty," I say and give him a little wave. Pretty ballsy move for an ugly girl.

Maybe I should tell him how much I'm looking forward to work-ing with him. That will sound like I'm looking forward to having a sex scene with him. Maybe he wants to hear that. Maybe he doesn't.

Maybe I should get up, walk over, and quickly disabuse him of some of the misconceptions about inverted nipples. No, leave him alone. If he's anything like Jon Stewart, the only inverted nipple he wants to discuss is his own. Or Elizabeth Warren's.

Thomas says, "Hi, Horny Patty" back to me and the entire room bursts out laughing. Doesn't seem quite fair, since I was the first to use my name in a dry, casual way, but it's still kind of a thrill.

The blond blowout lady, who is indeed one of the writers, comes up and does that thing where she grabs my shoulders and stares at my face again. "You have too much makeup on."

"It's just Carmex on my lips."

"Wipe it off."

"Should I go in the parking lot and throw some rocks at my face?" I suggest.

She squints her eyes, contemplating. "No. Not yet."

I want to bring up the inverted nipple so that maybe they can rewrite the scene, but I can't get myself to bring up nipples just yet.

Walking onto the Paramount lot the day of the shoot I'm completely focused on my character. Like Marlon Brando. "Just play the scene, don't worry about the nipples. Just play the scene, don't worry about the nipples."

A production assistant tells me one of the other actresses had her first sex scene the day before and brought her manager, her best friend, and two different sponsors from two different twelve-step programs for support. She drank two glasses of wine and still was a nervous wreck.

"When she took her robe off and stood there naked in front of everyone, did she have like a giant hair patch on her lower back or anything like that?" I ask the PA hopefully.

"No, she's gorgeous. I mean, like, drop-dead hot, perfect body, but she was still nervous."

The "body makeup specialist" is a lady from Argentina. She

must be used to dealing with pre–sex scene jitters. She's very professional. In order for her to spray me down I need to stand completely naked with my arms and legs spread.

"Do you pretend you're icing a cake sometimes?" I ask.

"No problem."

"Have you ever accidentally spanked someone?"

"No problem."

The process ends with her putting a sticker over my pubic area that is held in place by a long stringlike sticker that is attached to it and goes up my butt. Not into my anus but like a string bikini. That's all I will be wearing for my nude scene, and it's all I'm wearing when there's a knock on the door. It's the blowout lady writer. I put a robe on so I can save the big reveal.

The Argentine makeup lady points to my nipple. "Problem." I'm not sure why it's a problem for her. Did she want me to breast-feed her? She'd seemed so sensitive to my naked-lady comfort level a few moments ago, and now she's going to get me fired. I'm changing her name from "No Problem Makeup Lady" to "Problem-Making Makeup Lady."

Blowout ignores her, walks up to me, and practically talks inside my mouth she's so close.

"Feeling okay? You okay?"

This is the time to tell her. I can tell her. So I do.

"What does that mean?"

"It's like an innie belly button."

She wants to know if it's ever come out. I tell her no.

There's another long pause while she stares at my face. She's thinking. She claps her hands. "I love it! I'm gonna write some new lines."

Out the door she goes. Hey, this could work out! Finally this freak show is going to get me some perks. More lines!

Ten minutes later there's another knock on the door.

"Didn't work out. But be sure to check the new script pages on your table, had to cut some of your lines. Have fun today."

They escort me to the set like a dead man walking. I make my way through the gauntlet. As I pass, people turn their backs, look down at their shoes, and make the sign of the cross. It's a closed set, meaning no visitors or press. Or anyone who doesn't have to be there. Everyone is instructed to give me personal space and not ogle, which I appreciate, but as I sit on the edge of the bed waiting for Thomas Jane, I make an announcement: "Listen, everybody, I have an inverted nipple, please don't pity me." I hear one lone "HA!" that I think got whoever fired since right after that it was very, very quiet. Now it's out. I've told people. The hardest part of my role is the monologue, and I don't shoot that until tomorrow, so all I really have to do is look like I'm having sex and not think about the nipple.

The smell of a cigar fills the studio. Thomas Jane has arrived. He's on the phone arguing with his wife about child care. He puts his cigar out in a coffee cup, which is the costume people's cue to run in and grab my robe. He—TJ—drops his robe. All of my fears about the horror my inverted nipple was going to cause disappear when I see TJ naked. He's incredibly sexy. He's so sexy he should be an actor.

"Okay, funny lady, let's go."

He calls me "funny lady," which is exactly what you want before you're about to be naked and having sex with someone on camera. "Okay, funny lady, lie down."

He forgot his sticker. Must have gotten stuck to his robe.

Thomas fluffs himself—not in a "sexual fluff" way but more of an "unsticking sweaty balls from sides of thighs" way—and mounts me. He grabs my legs and slams into me so quickly and so rapidly that my sticker gets jammed up my butt.

Hysterically giddy laughter ensues. I'm hanging upside down off the bed and I can't stop laughing. Between takes I'm laughing. I'm having such a good time that it's embarrassing for the crew. It's easy to enjoy it because Thomas doesn't talk to me at all. He's in his own world. And it's helpful. My character on *True Blood* raped a guy and I had to straddle him for hours. We talked about his condo and his life back home in Australia, about his family and so on, and I felt very caught up in how he was doing. It made it hard to fake rape him.

The camerawoman comes up to me when we're done shooting. "I was worried he's pounding so hard he'll hurt the baby." The baby. That's right. There's a baby. Oh god. I'm going to have a son. How will I explain this? Actually, I know exactly how I will explain it. I'll tell him how the part was one of the many thousands of jobs that I did to take care of him, to put food on the table and books in his hands. It's got a bit of an "I was stripping to get through school" vibe, but hopefully that won't matter when he's enjoying his invisible braces and college education.

Leo was born a month ago. David has been such an amazing help, running around washing apples, fetching napkins, and making salads.

After the birth, we decided that he should be the stay-at-home dad. "You have more earning potential," he said to me. I haven't worked at all since my Horny Patty sex scene.

I'll never work again. I'll try to work, but I'll always be thinking about Leo. Worrying about him. My friend Gay Jay recently turned down a job in New York because he simply became unhinged when he was away from his family. A job would have to be *life-changing* to get him to make that sacrifice. It wasn't even a hard decision. He simply didn't want to go. He was talking about his dogs but I understood the comparison; he did breastfeed them.

How on earth will I be able to be touring and gone all the time? It won't work. It's all I've done since I was twenty-five years old. It's not even work, what I do, because I love it so much. I used to say it's all that I lived for. This little baby with his wandering eye is all I want to look at, hold, and eat. I'd eat him if I could.

I'm struggling to breastfeed Leo when the phone rings. My inverted nipple did come out, right after Leo was born, just like the old ladies at the breastfeeding store the Pump Station told me it would. It doesn't matter, though. I offer it up; he takes a look at it and turns away: "Oh, that's okay. Suddenly I'm not hungry."

It's Allen.

"Hey, Weeds, good news. They want you back for more Horny Patty."

"There's a little problem."

"I can't talk about your inverted nipple right now. I'm in the middle of a meeting and I'm driving and I'm at the airport Skyping with a client."

"No, no. Not that. Could you tell the producers that I'm about thirty pounds heavier than when I shot the first season? I can't be fully naked. I'm not being falsely modest. I'm overweight and it would be such a statement to see me naked on TV that it would be distracting. My inverted nipple is nothing. It's my freakish breast sizes. There's the one gigantic breast that Leo likes and the ex–inverted nipple one that he's neglected to such a degree that it's atrophied away like a little mini limb."

After he stops gagging, he says he's going to call them and see what they say.

He hangs up and calls me right back.

"I told them and they said 'perfect.'" God bless Blowout Lady.

My lips are Vaselined. My hair frizzed. Tonia was wrong. Damn, it feels good to work. On my way out of the makeup trailer I see my friend Emma, whom I haven't seen since the audition. She's been cast as one of the gigolo's female clients.

"Hey, Emma, how are you?"

She takes one look at me and smiles an ugly girls' "Hey, at least we're working, huh?" smile and walks away.

I'm working. This is the character. Thank god for character actors. Thank god for this part. I'm bringing home the bacon, frying it up in a pan.

It's a nude scene again. Of course.

The director has heard I'm concerned about full nudity. She calls me to the set and takes a break from shooting a scene to talk to me. After a long speech about how giving birth to twins, understanding women's relationships to their complicated post-birth bodies, and a documentary she made about eating disorders, she pushes her baseball cap back on her head and takes a loud slurp of her coffee. "Okay, let's see what we're working with. Open your robe."

I open up my robe. "Oh god, they look like breastfeeding boobs. COVER 'EM!" She yells this over her shoulder and a pit crew from the Indy 500 runs up and gets to work.

The head of the crew is a very sweet young girl from Michigan named Kate. She's the youngest girl in a Catholic family of thirteen kids. "I can't even believe you had a baby!" She puts me in a teddy to make sure that my stomach is covered up. "Not that you need it!" The director tells her to make sure the teddy is taped to my boobs so that they don't fall out. As she tapes me up I stare at the ceiling and take deep breaths. Do men go through this? Do they worry about saggy balls? At least my big saggy boobs are keeping a person alive. Saggy balls don't.

"Uh-oh!" Kate says, very cheerful. "Uh-oh!"

I look down to see what's "uh-oh." Milk is pouring out of me. My boobs are spurting like I've cut an artery.

There's a knock on my door. "Hey, Horny! Feeling sexy?"

Things are starting to feel surreal.

It's time to shoot the scene. Thomas Jane gives me a quick glance. "I just had a baby." He walks away to find a coffee cup to put his cigar out in. "It wasn't yours!" I yell after him.

We get the "Okay, let's go" cue to take off our robes. Thomas takes his off and this time he's wearing a little sock on his stuff. He must have gotten in trouble for not wearing one. I imagine the producer telling him, "Tie this tea bag around your penis or you'll be fined. Bark once if you understand me."

Horny Patty is supposed to be on top and "humping the shit out of him." I can't. At all. My hips won't hump. I can't get any sex beat going. They are completely stiff.

It hadn't dawned on me to warm them up. Oh, how I'd judged the porno people I saw when I first moved to LA. They'd be in the gym, standing in front of the mirror wearing pink spandex and just humping the air. I feel like I weigh five hundred pounds. Thomas looks angry. He's not used to reality like this. He's married to Patricia Arquette. He slaps my hips and tries to get me going. "Come on!"

Leaning down, I whisper, "My hips hurt. I just had a baby."

My hips will not move and I'm slowing down. Getting tired.

I lean down again. "I'm glad all of this is being recorded for all of digital eternity." I'm being paid to do this. It's bizarre but not the worst way to pay for diapers. For a moment, I worry that my muscles are going to simply give out, but they don't. I wind myself up, and, in the sage words of a redneck comedian, I git 'er done.

Finally, the director calls "cut" and they throw a robe over me. Thomas starts to leave but turns around and comes back to say something to me. I'm worried he's going to yell at me for squishing him.

"Uhm. Congratulations."

"On getting through the scene without lactating on you?"

"On your baby. Boy or girl?"

"Boy."

"That's great. Okay. Well, see you later, funny lady."

And he did see me later. Horny Patty came back for multiple episodes. For months after the show aired I got emails from fans: "Dear Horny Patty, you sure have big titties. You have one big old cow tittie and one small little cow tittie. Why is that? Keep up the good work."

Babies really are magic.

Serial Killer Blues

Today is the first day of the rest of my life.
Carpe diem.

Be here *now*.

I keep repeating these things to myself, but nothing's working. Today still feels like the last eighty-eight million mornings on the playground. Boring. I'm glad Leo is having fun going up and down the slide. Up and down the slide. Up and . . . Wait, maybe he's going to . . . No, there he goes, down the slide.

It's the same cliques as always on the playground. The Euro moms dominate the sandbox, the Santa Monica moms are in the west corner under the oak tree, and the Spanish-speaking nannies in hospital scrubs (which I really hope was their idea and not their employers') are sitting on the benches.

The redheaded dad from Chicago is pointing out to me how one of the ladders on the climbing structure is wood and the other is rope. "That one, do you see it? It's wood. All wood. The other one, not the wood one but the one next to it, it's rope. I didn't realize that until yesterday." I want to scream, "YOU DIDN'T?!" in his face, but I don't want to ruin Leo's reputation, so I point toward the sky. "What's that?" I ask and walk away to see what sort of soup the Euro moms are feeding their kids for breakfast today.

By the time I stroll over, they're finishing up breakfast and watching their kids play with handmade felt dolls that look alarmingly like Aunt Jemima. I invite myself to sit down next to the German woman with braids on both sides of her head. Not cool Björk-like braids, more like heavy eighties Princess Leia braids that could tip her over and bury half her head in the sand. The way she dresses Drajum, her two-year-old boy, in scratchy old-man suits makes me think she may be the dark comic of the group, so I lean over to her and say, "I think the only people that playgrounds are fun for are pedophiles."

My life has been exhausting and surprisingly isolating since Leo turned one. It's like being a sober buddy for a drunk celebrity who's fallen off the wagon, like if a movie studio assigned me to follow Charlie Sheen around and try to prevent him from getting into trouble. It's also so much more isolating than I thought it was going to be. I assumed I'd gather a little posse on the playground and we'd be sharing secrets and mimosas, but it's so boring. The last thing I want to talk about is kids. Yet it's all everyone talks about. The book publisher who warned me about writing a book about motherhood was right. She said, "Unless you're a zany drinking mom doing crystal meth and using diapers to sop up their spilled tequila shots, nobody really wants to hear moms tell stories about their kids."

Finally, a middle-aged mom parks her Winnebago-size stroller next to me and gives me a big crazy smile. She needs to talk. I can tell. Her hair is giant frazzled bed head; her blouse has coffee stains down the front and is completely misbuttoned. I like her. She comes right up to me—"Well, I've had a morning!"—and starts hysterically laughing. Pressing her for details, I get different variations of

the same response—"Put it this way. It's been quite a morning!"
"What a morning! Can I go back to bed yet?!"—followed by the
same unhinged laughter. Something is clearly going on with her.
What is it? Her husband dragged her by her hair because she didn't
feed the dog? She can't trust her sister with her foster children? She's
in the middle of a bipolar manic episode and all she wants to do is
paint rocks by the swing set? I need details.

"Let's just say, it's been a MORNING!"

Nothing. I get nothing.

Carpe diem, Leo. Let's go home.

Leo's naptime. Time to check Facebook for some action

If friend requests show up on my Facebook page, I hit the *Sure!*
button and toss them on the stack like a fat man's licked-clean
chicken bones. I collect friends like a Santa Monica housewife collects Adderall, like a hoarder collects toenail clippings and adult
diapers, like a child collects wishes and raisins. My point is, I don't
give it a lot of thought.

"Facebook is for friends and Twitter is for fans," a stranger
once wrote on my Facebook page. I didn't like to be reprimanded
in front of all my fake friends by a woman I've met only three
times. (Actually, I can remember meeting her only one time, but
it was at Martha Plimpton's house for a political event and since a
celebrity was involved, I bumped it up to three.) Having family
and friends all mixed together works for me for the same reason
New York City does: It's never boring and there's great people
watching.

So it isn't a huge violation of my personal space bubble when I
notice a message from a name that's completely unfamiliar to me
in my inbox.

Scott Bauer writes: "I want you to write my life story."

I write back: "I'M IN!"

He responds immediately: "This is amazing. Thank you so much. It's a story with a lot of ups and downs but laughter, too. I know you're the right person for it. Thank you so much."

I was kidding! He might as well have written me a message that said:

> "Build me a bridge to the stars.
>
> "Mouth kiss,
>
> "Your friend you've never met—Scott"

A life story is a huge undertaking, especially for someone who doesn't write about anyone but herself. Unless he's four years old or just wants a little pamphlet to hand out at his funeral, who's got that kind of time? His glib "and you're welcome to have been chosen" tone isn't helping either.

I may have another John Harris on my hands.

In the years that I've had a Facebook page, I've really had trouble with only one guy, John from Houston, Texas. Nobody was as excited about my pregnancy as John. He was the first to comment and he just couldn't get over it. "FANTASTIC NEWS! IT'S HAPPENING!" He got along well with my other half-stranger friends and struck up conversations, saying things like "You guys, I'm really feeling she's going to have a boy. What do you think?" He was such a constant presence and supporter in my life that after a while I forgot that I had no idea who the hell he was. His profile picture showed a guy with a large moustache, poufy black wig hair, and sunglasses covering half of his face. Not only did it look like he was wearing a disguise; it looked like the photo was taken either by a surveillance camera or by the cops on a stakeout in the early seventies. He had five friends and none of them were mutual. His name had sounded mildly familiar. He was either the insurance guy my sister went to high school with or the dude in Florida who sent me his book he wrote about managing money that had a cartoon of a frog using an ATM machine on the cover. Having John on my feed hadn't really mattered to me until a friend of mine died and I posted that I was "mourning the loss of Seattle's own Jose Hernandez. Sad day." John was the first to comment: "Seattle via MEXICO more likely!" I couldn't delete and block him fast enough. Since then I've tried to be a little more careful, but it's still not a big surprise that I've never really noticed Scott.

Before I write him back and see if he'd be interested in a new kidney, I should check his Facebook page to make sure he isn't a Seattle lesbian fan who goes by the name of Scott trying to get my attention.

The first post I read says, "I've been sobbing all night. The pain is unbelievable. I love you all so much—so much. So grateful to have had you in my life . . ." Within the first ten seconds of reading his posts it's very clear that he is a dying man. His post "I'm a dying man" clued me in.

"Goodbye, Anne, you've been a wonderful friend. Nobody better."

"They say there's no hope, but I'm not giving up."

It's hard to piece together any details about what he has—oh, wait—

"Cancer, ouch."

Yes, ouch indeed.

There are several posts asking if anyone knows the singer/

songwriter Jewel because he wants her to write a song for his friend Ben, who's been giving him rides to his doctor appointments. I wonder what stage of his illness he is in. Hospital? Hospice? Living in a car with a shotgun and a bottle of Jack? A few "Scott what exactly is going on with you?" posts have popped up, but he never responds, which is odd because he's such an energetic responder. If someone merely "liked" one of his posts he'd respond: "Thanks, Paul! Can't listen to The Smiths without thinking of you, my friend!"

Why couldn't he be more like my sweet friend Andrea? When she was dying of cancer she posted pictures of the lasagna they served in the hospital and her little baby-chick head as her hair grew back. Her suffering was polite. It was implied.

The thought of anyone witnessing me in real pain, even something minor, like nausea, scares me. The last time I had the flu, I sat at a dinner party, pouring sweat, and finally ran out of the house to throw up in the front seat of my car into a plastic bag. The sack had a hole in the bottom so I threw up directly onto my lap and had to change from a party dress to workout clothes that I had in my trunk. I walked back into the party wearing high heels and bleach-stained hiking shorts yet still wouldn't admit to having any trouble. I'm aware that having a mild stomach bug doesn't really compare to terminal cancer, but it was simply a very foreign concept to me to let people know about personal pain without jokes, metaphors, or the possibilities of movie deals.

Come on. The guy should be able to post whatever he wants. Who am I to say how someone should suffer, how he should face his own death? There is no doubt in my mind that when—and not if, but when—I get cancer I'll be running naked through the streets: "WHY ME!? WHY NOT YOU!? AHHHH!"

Ultimately, I guess he just wants someone to listen to him. That I can do.

Outside of watching Leo go up and down on the slide, my schedule is pretty open. Yet I still felt like since I didn't know him I had to set a boundary. I needed to be cautious. Even hospice workers don't just hand over their pearls.

I write, "Hey, Scott, sounds like, based on your Facebook page, that you're in the middle of a tough time, and I'd be honored to help you out. If you are able, why don't we start with you writing out some details about your life growing up, earliest memories, etc."

"Hello there!"

Again, his response is immediate. He must be in the hospital with nothing to do but be on his computer. Poor guy.

"Well, Lauren, this is going to be a long journey but we're going to do it together. I trust you. It's going to be fun, and there's a part of the story that needs to be told that's been a secret for a long time but it's time to get it out."

Shut the front door. Did he say "secret"? What a coincidence, because I have a secret too, and it's that *I love secrets.*

I switch to instant messaging.

"Hey, Scott, if talking is easier for you we could set up a time for you to dictate to me over the phone for an hour a week. You let me know what would be best for you."

"Sounds great! Thanks again, Lauren. Really."

Wait. I don't want him to go before he tells me what this *secret* is. Of course, I don't want him to think I'm some cheap sensationalist. I need to be subtle, so I type

"How are you today? Oh, and hey, when you say secret,
what do you mean exactly?"

He writes back: "I've done some crazy stuff in my life. But it's been a wonderful life. Had my ups and downs like anybody. I killed nine people and want to tell the story."

I slam my computer shut, jump up from my chair, run into the bathroom, shout, "HE JUST TOLD ME HE KILLED NINE PEOPLE!" run back and open my computer, and type:

"That's a lot."

Wait, he doesn't mean he *killed* nine people. He probably managed a McDonald's or was a producer for Marilyn Manson or wrote reality television. He metaphorically killed people and he can't shake the guilt.

Once I stop running around the apartment in circles I want to respond more but cannot think what to say, so I tell him that he shouldn't be hard on himself. We all regret things we've done.

"Yeah. Thanks. It was 4 in Seattle and 5 in Portland. But
• that was a long time ago. I'm not a bad guy."

"Of course not!"

He tells me the killings were through the FBI and that it's time for him to tell his story. He thinks that keeping the secret of the murders is what gave him cancer.

"If anything would give you gas, that sure would!" I type.

Scott and I must have been a part of the same social circle in Seattle, because we have more than a dozen friends in common.

Many of them have been the ones writing the "Sending prayers!" and "You'll pull through this, Scott!" posts on his page.

I'm going to send a group message to all of them to see if they have any insights into what's going on with this Scott fellow.

I'm not going to mention the killing part yet. There is no way to word it without coming off as lurid.

I worry that if I send anything that comes off sounding like "You guys! He says he killed 9 people! WTF?! Is he nuts?!" I'll get a response like "Yes, Lauren. That's right. On good days he claims to be Maya Angelou and on bad days he's a killer for the FBI. Dementia is a side effect of his rare brain cancer. If you think this is entertaining, I'm sorry that you're missing out on his tremors and partial paralysis. They're a real hoot."

I'll just ask people if they are good friends with him, and I'll wait to see if the killing stuff comes up naturally before I ask if anyone knows if he had a killer-y nickname. Like Charles in Charge or Officer Friendly.

The next day, I'm checking my phone constantly on the playground. The Euro moms offer to share their lentil soup and I don't even care. I'm dying to know what my friends know about Scott.

All of the responses are the same. Nobody seems to know him, yet everyone has one uncertain fact about him. "I think he got hit by a car once" or "I think he fell off a building one time." .

Brady is the closest of the mutual friends Scott and I have. He directed some shows of mine back in the day. I text him: "Hey, Brady, I have a question for you—you know Scott Bauer, right? He sent me an email asking me to write his life story for him. I know he's sick, so I was willing to but he just told me he killed nine people. Do you know exactly what is going on with him?"

"Hey Buddy, saw your message. Don't know him that well. Seems like he's pretty sick. I think he was in some

> accident involving a moving van. Wild about the killing
> part."

"Wild"—that's it? Brady was obviously the wrong person to ask. He's a big stoner. Nothing riles him. Or maybe he has a day job and is too busy to care. But come on! How can you hear about anyone claiming to kill even one person and not care?

My friend Elizabeth who runs a dance company in Seattle sends me a long response. I'm trying to read it while I push Leo on the swings. Elizabeth recently went through a pretty brutal bout of cancer. Everyone has cancer these days. I blame Facebook. She didn't really know him either and couldn't remember why she was even Facebook friends with him, but she has a theory—

I hear a female voice: "We're next for the swing!" I give a quick "You got it!" and keep reading.

Elizabeth suggests that the cancer could be in his brain, causing some delusion.

Oh man, I knew it. I'm sure that's what's happening.

I send a direct message to Scott asking him what sort of cancer he has. He writes back with an answer, but it's such a complicated name I can't even sound it out. A line is forming for the swings. I grab Leo out of his seat with a quick, "Sorry, buddy, time to go!"

A nanny in hospital scrubs holding a newborn asks me if I'm okay as I run out of the playground with Leo. "Oh . . . I've had a MORNING!" I say and run back to the apartment to look up what kind of cancer it is.

I go back to Scott's message so I can cut and paste the name of his cancer.

But the message has been deleted.

That night I get a message from a guy I used to wait tables with. He's the first to claim Scott as a close friend.

"Listen, he's a good friend of mine and I have to tell you,
it doesn't surprise me that he's saying he killed people.
I'm sure he has. He's that kind of guy."

He's *that* kind of guy. That's it? How can he be so casual? Are
his other friends ex–Khmer Rouge and Scott seems quirky in
comparison?

I used to think that my artist friends in Seattle were a bunch of
harmless carny folk whose idea of living outside the box was walking backward as they crossed the street or never going to the dentist.
Who knew they were running with such a dangerous crowd?

"Hey, Scott, quick question, does anyone know about
this?"

"Those that I am close to know. Like parents, siblings, a
couple of friends. I want to make the book truthful and
honest in hopes of helping others. I want the story to be
told with the trauma part but also with humor. :)"

It has been three days since Scott entered my life, and I can think
of nothing else. "What would you do if someone told you that they
had killed nine people?" has replaced "How much sand can a kid
eat before it becomes a medical emergency?" as my opener in all
social situations.

Moo Moo Musica is a music class for babies taught by free-
spirited yoga people in Venice that Leo loves. Today we're singing
"Five Little Ducks," about a group of baby ducks that go missing
one at a time. First there are five, then four, then three, then two,
then one . . . and then there are none. I get chills.

During the break, all of the moms are caught up in the Scott story. The oldest mom in the class, a woman in her midfifties, leans over during the next song and tells me that I have to go to the police, immediately. "You're an accomplice now," she tells me. She's singing loudly and off key—"Quack, quack, quack, and all the little ducks come waddling back"—right at my face and has a tiny little cowboy hat on her head.

She just made it even more exciting.

The only person I don't want to tell is David because he's always giving me a hard time for being too open with strangers. But he's my husband; I don't want to keep secrets from him. Plus, there's nobody else left that I see in the course of my day to tell.

After demanding to "see a picture of this guy," David declares him a "lonely drunk." Nobody should be vilified based on the red color and bulbous size of his nose, so I defend Scott. "I don't know, David. I think that this is what would happen to a killer for the FBI who lives with the secret for so long. Getting cancer, dying slowly. That is exactly the kind of scenario that would lead to this kind of death." David points out the idiotic logic in my theory. "So cancer wards are just full of lying serial killers?" He's right. According to my logic, the Race for the Cure breast cancer 5K should be changed to Race for the Killers.

David insists that I cut off all contact with Scott. "You're a mother now, Lauren. You can't let random crazy people into your life. And let's say he's telling the truth. Do you want to be number ten?"

I lie and tell David that I will stop contacting him. Scott hasn't told me how or why he killed those nine people. I can't stop now. *That* would be crazy.

That night, I can't sleep. Scott killed those people. Why would someone lie about something so huge that you could get into so much trouble for? Right before you die, why would you tell such a huge lie? Why did he tell *me*? I can't keep a secret. Everyone knows that. I'm the worst. The worst! People I hardly know will be mid-story at a party—"so I was trapped in the tops of the trees eating gum to stay alive and I"—but as soon as they spot me they clam up. "Tell you later. Here comes Lauren." Nobody tells me anything anymore.

I've been blabbing about Scott all over the place. I've told too many people.

David's right. I'm going to be number ten.

I've started making copies of all my correspondence with Scott. There's a good chance I'll be asked to testify in court at his murder trial. Or after he sues the TV network that I sell his story to for slander.

I open my laptop and type

> "Is this a secret? I know you said it is but I should let
> you know that if you tell me, I'm not great with secrets.
> It's no secret that I'm not great with secrets! So before
> I turn your very personal story into a musical, what are
> your thoughts about that? I know you wanted to write
> about it—but could I? Not saying I'm going to. I just
> want to let you know that I use my life as fodder a lot."

I type "Don't want to make you mad!" but delete it.

> "I don't care about me right now. You can write about it
> if you want. I will give you the info. You can do with it
> what you like. Yes, you can use my name. I will be fine."

I try to decide if his message has a bit of a "go ahead and enjoy yourself, you'll be dead by the morning" ring to it. But maybe he's resigned to it all because he's dying. I'm the one making a big deal out of this when he's facing something far larger and I need to grow up and stop sensationalizing the fact that he's a dying serial killer. He's also a person. Did I learn nothing from *Dead Man Walking?* Before we say good-bye, we set a time for our first phone conversation.

Scott's voice on the phone is earnest. And sweet. He's very sweet. The conversation starts with "tears of gratitude in his eyes" followed by a copious amount of thank-yous. Scott grew up in Missouri doing theater at his church. It was there he was bitten by the old acting bug and started getting involved with community theater. It's hard for me to stay focused as he slowly recounts his youth to me.

"I just loved how children's theater could touch ordinary people's lives."

Sure, I think, but not as much as murdering them.

We've been on the phone for more than forty-five minutes, and I've written down the words "theater," "church," and "killer!" on my notepad. He's talked about his high school years, his "pretty nice school and really cool friends," and about a book he'd received in the mail just that day, *Adventures of Frog and Toad.*

"So simple, but so heart wrenching for me. It made me realize what I'd really love for you to help me write—after we finish my life story—are children's stories."

He thinks the books should be about love. "And maybe we could find an angle on bullying since it's such a big thing in schools right now."

Oh my god . . . GET TO THE STABBY PART.

Not one time during his ninety-minute monologue has he mentioned his illness or the killing. If I have one note for him so far on his life story, it's "You may want to add in a mass killing to sort of punch it up a bit."

I thought I'd be hearing sounds of hospital machines or family members tucking in his sheets. But he's standing outside a mall waiting for his girlfriend to get done shopping. "She's done shopping, so I have to go."

None of this, as odd as it is, deters me from wanting to talk to him again. It's made me hungrier for the truth.

For the next week, we email daily. I realize that all I want to hear about is the killing stuff. I should respect a sick man. This is wrong. It's been good for Leo, though. Now instead of trying to pry him away the playground after twenty minutes I'm happy to stay for hours and hours.

I fess up to Scott: "I feel guilty about this, Scott. I have to admit that I can't move on past the killing stuff. Why did you tell me that that happened?"

"It's true."

"Oh, okay. Just checking."

How does anyone ever really know that someone is telling the truth? People make up shit all the time. They swear to god on their grandmother's dead body to be telling the truth. I've accidentally lied at least seven times since I woke up. It's so easy to lie. You just open up your mouth and start saying whatever the hell feels good to say.

If they don't lie to anyone else, you're the only one who has the info. They can say, "I didn't say that." It's their word against yours.

Sometimes people find out the truth behind lies and it rattles their entire life. "I never loved your mother." "We lived on Indian burial grounds." "The cat didn't run away . . ."

He's lying. He must be.

A brother is listed as a "family member" on Facebook. I email and I use my expired *Daily Show* credentials—"I'm a reporter for a cable news show"—to look like some sort of legitimate journalist. I tell him that I'm working with Scott on his life story but am confused as to what I am supposed to do with the information that he had killed nine people.

His brother responds, "Yeah, he keeps saying that." It's a long and very cordial email. It ends with "Cancer is the least of his troubles."

"WHAT? WHAT DO YOU MEAN? IS HE LYING? HE DOESN'T HAVE CANCER BUT HE IS A KILLER?" I never hear back from him and he erases our correspondence.

As I'm freaking out, I hear a super-cheerful tune, "The Bear Went Over the Mountain." Leo has become obsessed with a tiny plastic keyboard that has only five piano keys on it. The only song you could play if you really wanted to would be the *Jaws* shark-attack song. The rest of the toy keyboard plays prerecorded songs. There's a light-jazz version of "The Bear Went Over the Mountain" that Leo loves. He hits the button and scrambles to get up on his feet so he can dance to it. He moves like an eighty-five-year-old black man getting the spirit. The song is only six seconds long . . . "The bear went over the mountain—the bear goes over the mountain . . . yeah!" As soon it's over, he plops down on the ground, hits the button, and hurries to his feet. By the time he can stand up, there's only a few seconds of the song left. It breaks my heart to see him trying so hard to get up to dance. He could do it forever, and I could watch forever.

I snap back to my murderer. What did his brother mean "Cancer is the least of his troubles"? I break down and ask David. "It means he's lying about everything and is just a lonely drunk who has your attention!" I'm starting to agree with David. Except that I would add "who killed nine people" at the end of the thought.

David asks me if I'm still talking to Scott directly.

"Oh god, no! He's crazy," I tell him. David doesn't believe me.

"He wanted your attention, and look, he got it. You're taking dumb risks."

I remind David that I once was a volunteer in our nation's most violent jail, LA County. I know how to handle myself.

"You gave our home address to a gang member."

That was true. I had done that. My quick "that was a joke address" after I'd given her the cross streets had saved our lives.

David gives me a sad look and leaves the apartment. I have no idea where David is going. He could be going out to rob a bank.

He walks back into the apartment and says, "You are the only person I know who can be friends with a serial killer and not think it's a horrible thing."

"You know why?" I tell him. "It's because I'm aware of life and its complications and want to accept it all."

Scott was clearly unstable. Maybe the 654 people I told the story to were right and I needed to put an end to all of this.

Just one last question.

> "Hey, Scott. Yeah, it is hot here. But it's hard to complain when it's 120 degrees in Palm Springs, right? Anyway, my life is starting to get pretty busy over here so I need to get down to it. Why aren't you scared of prosecution?"

> "Hey, Lauren. I just looked up Palm Springs weather and you were right. It's 120 there. That is hot."

> "Why aren't you scared of prosecution?'

Long pause.

"Why aren't you scared of prosecution, Scott?"

"Listen, Lauren, they can't do anything now. Hey, I've been thinking that what I'd like to work on is turning my life story into a solo show. Are you down?"

"If you end up doing a solo show about the killings— what do you think is going to happen to you? Will it be the first time people are finding out? I'm a little confused as to why you brought up the killings and now never want to talk about it?"

An even longer pause.

"You know, Scott—I'm a little haunted and freaked-out by you telling me that you've killed these people. I'm trying to figure out if what you've told me is true and what I'm supposed to do with this information. Do you want me not to tell a soul? Do you want me to write about it? Get your story out there now? Later? I'm confused as to what the goal of this is and how I'm involved. I'm just so confused. You killed them—with a gun? Who does the FBI want dead? Couldn't you get in trouble for this now? Help me with this if you can. Hope I'm not making you mad. I don't want you to kill me! JK"

Before I shut my computer for the night Scott sends me his most killer-y message yet:

"You are good. I am good."

On the way to do my daily check of Scott's Facebook page, I notice a lot of posts about my friend Andrea. Today is the one-year anniversary of her death. Once I'm on her Facebook page, I start reading all her old posts. Six months before she died it looked like her cancer was in remission. "God, how I used to dread the monotony of the playground," she wrote. Andrea had twin boys who were four years old at the time of her death. "What a boring wasteland it's always seemed to me. But after all the treatments and procedures I've been through this past year I cannot tell you how wonderful it is to stand on that playground watching my boys play for hours on end. Oh, the bliss of plotlessness."

The next morning there's an email from Scott with details about the commitment he'd like from me during the run of his yet unwritten one-man show.

"I'd expect you to be there for the rehearsals and opening night. Don't feel obligated to stay for the entire run if it's a theater not near to you. But it would be nice to have you there closing night.

"I'll start it at the Seattle Rep, I'd say the second stage but I think this story is much more of a main-stage production."

This is the final straw. Not his delusions or demands or lies but the fact he thought he'd be able to get on the Seattle Rep main-stage with a solo show. I'd tried for ten years to get that gig and it was impossible. I've never believed that I could be on the Seattle Mainstage. If they offered to let me perform in the lobby I'd be thrilled. His delusion feels like confidence. I'm a little envious of it, but mostly I'm annoyed.

I push my chair away from the desk and calmly walk down the

hallway to organize Leo's pajama drawer into stacks of winter, summer, and separates.

Before I go to bed I'm on Facebook, and for the first time since Scott contacted me I don't go to Scott's page.

An instant message comes up from him—

> "I have some other details that I haven't told you yet
> because I wanted to see if I could trust you. Are you in
> or not?"

You know what I could go for right now? A chubby one-and-a-half-year-old falling to the light-jazz melody of "The Bear Went Over the Mountain."

> "Scott, I'm really busy. I don't have time right now. Good
> luck to you."

I hold my breath waiting for him to yell at me for being a self-serving, self-absorbed asshole. Or for the sound of a gunshot from the apartment window that faces my office. "FUCK YOU, NUMBER TEN!" BAM!

But all I get is—

> "Bye"

Good. The next time I go looking for some excitement, if there is a next time, I want to find a less bossy killer.

The next morning I'm back at the playground with all the usual suspects.

The Euro moms, the Santa Monica moms, the Spanish-speaking nannies, and the redheaded dad. The German mom's braided buns have migrated to the top of her head, but outside of that it's same old, same old.

Leo runs over to join the Euro kids in the sandbox and I follow. An English woman in a large floppy sunhat, aka Oscar's mother, says good morning to me. The other four mothers give nods and grunts of hello.

"Guess what?" I ask the ladies. Oscar's mother stands up, brushes herself off, and comes closer. She remembers me.

What crazy story am I going to tell? What gossip am I going to spread? The other mothers sense something good is coming and gather around me. My reputation precedes me.

"Leo loves mango. I learned how to cut a mango years ago from a guy who's from Suriname. You peel it in strips but you don't peel it all the way off because he taught me that there's a way to use the peel as a handle that you can hold as you slice the meat of the mango."

Oscar's mother takes off her glasses so I can see her eyes. Trying to let me know that I don't have to hold back. I can tell the real story. Let it rip. She's listening. She's with me.

"Leo ate an entire mango yesterday. No, actually, it was almost a whole mango. He dropped a piece of it. I'm going to buy more mangos today. They were on sale at Whole Foods. Three for five dollars. I don't know if that's a good deal, but today is Mango Monday and that's what I'm going to do . . ."

The sunglasses are back on; she's backing away from me. They all are. The entire Euro mom pack is backing away from me, looking for a sippy cup to wash off, a diaper bag to rearrange, anything but the graphic details of Mango Monday. I'll save my story about Leo watching ants crawl up a fence post for tomorrow.

Strippery Slope

I'm waiting in line for a coffee in Portland. It's my first trip to the city and I'm here doing my show *Bust* at Portland Center Stage. I'm trying to butter up my barista so David will be impressed by how quickly I've gotten to know the neighborhood when I get treated like a regular when we come in together tomorrow.

"My husband and I are trying to figure out a date night, which must sound so middle-aged to you." At the word "husband," my sullen, shark-eyed barista looks up from steaming milk, as if he's trying to imagine who would have ended up with me.

"Sorry, I think I gave you the wrong impression, but I have horrible news: I'm *taken*," I say. He turns around and walks into the back room. He does that a lot when I come in. "I better not hear a gunshot!" I yell after him. He comes right back out. "That's not at all funny," he says. I forgot I was in Portland, where it rains constantly, so suicide jokes don't go over as big as they do in Tahiti, where they kill.

Usually, our version of date night is "You go out on Wednesday night and I'll go out on Thursday. See ya Friday. Everybody wins!"

David's getting ready to go work in Alaska for the summer, so we need to at least pretend that we want to do something together. I tell the barista, "I want to get out of the Pearl District and do something really Portland."

"Go to a strip club."

A strip club. Oh, that's so Portland barista. I knew he was going to say something like "Make beer out of the yeast in your pubic hair" or "Ride a tricycle down a mountain naked." I might have been on board with those suggestions, but I can't do the strip club thing. I can't have a casual conversation with naked women dancing in front of me while I give little nods of "nice" as I sip my vodka tonic. Yet I'm so flattered that he thought I wasn't too old and square to handle such a thing, so it sucks that I react by bursting out in nervous laughter. "Oh no, no, no! Oh gosh. Think I'll skip that one. I'd rather tuck my one-dollar bills in your tip jar!"

The girl behind me in line, a pale young chick with pink hair, nose rings, and black eyeliner so thick it makes her eyes look like little pin holes for the light to spill out of her face, sticks her head in the conversation. "Just so you know, I go to strip clubs all the time. I always really enjoy myself. In fact, the girl I got a lap dance from last night just Facebook friended me."

My barista and she share a "right on" moment before he turns back to me. "I'm not sure what you're picturing but it's different here. Everyone goes."

"Everyone goes? Oh really? Everyone?! So it's just the Applebee's of Portland."

The pale chick lends her wisdom. "He's right, everybody does go. Last week there was a blind guy at the strip club I go to. My friends and I figured out that he probably goes for the smells."

After I'm able to stop yelling "Ew!" I ask her what smells she's talking about.

"Butthole and vagina?"

"Ew!" she yells back. "No! The smells of baby powder, god." She turns her back to me.

The barista says his mom's book club meets in a strip club. "If I were you, I'd take your husband to Mary's. It's a good one to start with. It's right around the corner from here. Mary's isn't even a strip club; it's just a bar that *happens* to have a stripper."

Oh ho, ho . . . very clever.

I'm willing to go a lot of places with David. I'll see London; I'll see France. But I'm not sure if I'm ready to go with him to see a girl without her underpants. (But with sexy talk like that I don't see how I'll be able to avoid it!) He would enjoy it, I'm sure, as most men, I think, would, but I'm old-fashioned and think that strip clubs are private activities to be done in a drunken haze and dripping with shame. I've been to a strip club once, and as with most situations that involve fake breasts, it was traumatizing. The only reason I even went was because I had a coupon. (Same reason I tried lotion toilet paper and with the same results: a life lesson about what a person's crotch area really requires for happiness that I vowed never to repeat.)

The details on my first strip club experience are hazy because it was so long ago and so much alcohol was involved. Like all my racy stories, it was back in my twenties during a trip to Vegas that my boyfriend at the time, Mathew, and I took with another couple, Meagan and Russell. Our first night in Vegas, Meagan stepped out of Circus Circus's mirrored elevator in her tight black dress, oversize sunglasses, and shiny blue wig, lit a cigarette, and said, "Remember . . . we aren't here to see the show. We *are* the show." Russell, in his vintage suit and fedora, would grab her around her waist and say, "Come on, baby. Let's make this playground swing!" Her legs were "gams" or "getaway sticks," and she was always "baby" or "doll."

Russell and Meagan thrived in Vegas. Mathew was a bartender, so he fit in with all the posing and martini drinking. I, on the other hand, wore overalls for most of our Vegas vacation. Meagan offered me one of her wigs to wear to cheer me up, but they just made me look mentally ill.

The first hour walking around in Vegas left me completely depressed. Dino and Frankie must have hired people to walk ahead of them and throw blankets over the dying senior citizens hooked up to oxygen gambling away their social security. Who could feel sexy or powerful in this sad town of sadness? Russell and Meagan, that's who. Meagan's always had a killer body that was known among the restaurant staff as "Meagan's killer body." Her cleavage was heaving and her ass went badonkadonk-donk. I'd brought a blue fuzzy dress that I referred to as my "Cookie Monster dress" that I could have worn, but I decided not to because I didn't want to look like I was trying to be pretty—in case I failed. My outfit wasn't without its sex appeal. If Mathew stood close enough to me he could look right down into my overalls and see the side of my leg, but only if I'd forgotten to snap all the buttons shut.

An hour later, I needed something to numb out the insecurity of showing up for our sexy couples' weekend looking like a loco-motive engineer and I became a full-blown gambling addict look-ing to cut a kidney out of a Chinese tourist to sell on the black market to feed the nickel slots. We were in line for dinner, and I lied and said I had to use the restroom so I could play the Wheel of Fortune slot machine. "I'm gonna surprise everyone and come back with a thousand dollars in nickels! Because I'm a winner. A WINNER!"

But instead of coming back from the "bathroom" covered in diamonds and with a Cadillac, I came back with not a cent to my name and the shakes. At the all-you-can-eat buffet, I obsessed about how I could get back to the slots. "Don't forget to make a trip to the nacho station!" the waitress said to us. Mathew, Russell, and Meagan enjoyed the coincidental train reference. I pretended to laugh with the others while I sat staring at the four-dollar tip that had been left on the table next to ours.

The waitress had my number and quickly snatched up the tip. After dinner, we were going to go see Marty "Hello Dere!" Allen. Marty was an old-school Vegas comedian whom none of us had heard of, but we had a coupon for the show and wanted to hear him say "Hello Dere!" at least once. Meagan sat down at a quarter slot machine to play while the guys went to buy cigarettes. She took a quarter out of her pocket and told me to make a wish and ask my guardian angels to bless it. I'm not as into the angel thing as she is, so I just opted to scream, "Put it in! Put it in!" like a seventeen-year-old virgin boy on prom night. She put it in and hit a five-hundred-dollar jackpot. She immediately insisted we divide it up among the four of us so we all could keep gambling. She was sexy and magnanimous, just like Ms. Indiana State Fair. When the guys returned with the cigarettes, jackpot sirens were going off, a crowd had formed, and I was laughing hysterically, jumping up and down and shoveling quarters into plastic buckets. "MEAGAN WON BUT SHE WANTS TO SHARE WITH US! SHE WANTS TO! OH GOD. LOOK AT IT ALL THOSE SHINY COINS! HA-HA-HA! JUST LOOK AT THEM!" Both Mathew and Russell refused to take Meagan's money. Mathew put his hand on my shoulder and said in a calm, low voice, "Lauren, Meagan won." I shook him off and kept shoveling. "SHE WANTS TO SHARE! SHE WANTS TO! SHE SAID SO!" When I heard Russell say something about how Meagan should save the money to help her pay rent when she got back and how it was nice she wanted to share but it really wasn't fair, we didn't need to gamble to have fun, I stopped shoveling.

The jackpot sirens stopped going off and I could hear the echo of the sound of my pouring my buckets of quarters back into Meagan's bucket in my shriveling soul.

That was my addiction bottom. It wasn't as grim as most—I wasn't blowing guys in the floor-model toolshed at the local Home Depot—but by the end of my first day in Vegas, I was staggering down the streets in my overalls, screaming for Jesus.

We hadn't even gotten to the strip club yet. That happened on our second night. We drank as many free drinks as we could and went to the strip club. Going with Mathew to a strip club made me jumpy. What if he snapped and an unacknowledged shadowy lust was released and he started having sex with the nearest ATM? Or he developed an immediate and lifelong addiction to strip clubs? As a recent gambling addict, you would have thought my heart went out to a possible fellow addict, but instead the thought depressed the bejeezus out of me. The night held the possibility of being our last one together. No, no. Don't make it too heavy. Lighten up. This is what you do when you're in your twenties.

As soon as we walked into the place I remember thinking, "Oh, this is fine. It's just girls with fake boobs walking around on a bar. That's all. We're all in this together!" But you know what they say: It's all fun and games until someone gets titties in the face.

I didn't really want titties in my face because I'd seen a few men get the service already and you had to sit there with everyone at the bar watching, your hands down at your sides like a dork while you got slapped by boobs. Meagan had kept her Vegas cool since we arrived and had not once sobbed in a bathroom stall, while I'd done it twice. Once after the embarrassing jackpot thing, and once after I saw a lady who looked just like my grandma Irene throwing up outside of a casino. Meagan was an ex-cheerleader from Orange County who was on acid the night she was voted homecoming queen. She wore blue wigs and made out with girls in hot tubs. She popped pills in her mouth and only after she'd swallowed them would she ask, "What was that?" I was an ex-kleptomaniac from Indiana with short dirty blond hair who was trying not to smoke so much pot since it tended to make me eat bread out of the trash.

When the stripper leaned down and asked if we were here with our boyfriends, Meagan yelled back, "*Yes.*"

"So do you guys want titties in your face or something?"

I started to yell back "Okay" but only got as far as "O-" before I was getting the shit beat out of me by these huge fake boobs. It hurt. It was like getting punched in the face by somebody who was mad at me. It felt like my jaw was out of whack. I handed her my dollar and thanked her. When I looked over at Meagan, she looked completely shocked.

The stripper asked Meagan if she wanted titties in her face. Meagan politely declined. "No, thank you, but you can have my dollar anyway. And have a really good night. I know it's gotta be tough sometimes." The stripper thanked Meagan for being so cool and turned to me to see if there was anything else I wanted done.

Meagan and I joined the guys back in our booth, and nobody would make eye contact with me. Back in our hotel room I asked Mathew if what I'd done was at all sexy. He turned to me with a sad smile. "It was funny. I will say that." I took off my overalls and went to bed.

It has been almost twenty years since I've had titties in my face.

I suggest to David that we go to a strip club and, shockingly, he is open to the idea. The entire walk to Mary's it's gushing rain down on us, but we don't care. We are giddy with pre-stripper anticipation. I tell him the "titties in the face" story and we laugh and laugh. He makes me promise to do it again but this time "punch her back!" Ha! Ha! "Hope they take coupons!" Ha-ha!

This is going to be fun because, thank god, I'm married to a feminist man who truly loves women. I'm not worried about him losing his mind over the hot young stripper bodies. His women crushes are Lauren Hutton and Jane Fonda. Not the 1970s versions of these women, but the versions of them in their seventies. Usually a handsome man such as himself would have to meditate naked in the woods for months eating nothing but one grain of rice and one drop of rain in order to obtain the level of enlightenment that would allow him to not only see the beauty of older women but crave that beauty. We are going as a couple to enjoy the beauty and skill of the art of stripping.

There's Mary's! With its classic old-timey bar sign. We open the door, take one step inside, and BAM! VAGINA! It's right there. As soon as you open the door it's a naked girl right there. I mean *right* there. I turn around and try to run out like cat in a bath, scrambling to get David to let me pass. "It's *right* there . . . It's too quick! Too quick! I need to ease into it. I need a hallway or some naked pictures." David pushes me back in. I knew it. He's already manic with desire. Pushing and shoving to get a glimpse of a naked lady like some pervy dirty monkey. "Lauren, come on, it's raining. Go in." Or he's trying not to get soaked.

It's early, so except for the two red-faced frustrated men my dad's age sitting on their hands watching a twenty-two-year-old naked girl dance, the place is empty. I grab David's hand. "Okay, here we go. This is happening. We're doing this. One-two-three and *go*. Walk, walk, walk, *just go in*, WALK!" I take the very first seat I see, which is in the front row at the same table as my dad.

"Lauren, let's move back a little," David suggests.

I scream back, "*Why can't I ever do what I want to do!*"

David just leans down and whispers calmly in my ear. "I think you'll be more comfortable farther back."

It felt very odd to be coming into a strip club as a female. As the thing that the old guys were paying money to look at. I told David that I had the urge to announce, "Look! More holes coming in! More holes!"

David tells me that I don't have to worry. Nobody wants my holes. My holes are bossy. Fair enough.

The last thing I'd want him to think about me was that I'm some school mom who doesn't enjoy a skeevy strip club once in a while. Hopefully he'll be able to ignore my actions and my words and see me as a woman who is not insecure.

The bartender comes over and asks if we want something to drink. She's a she. And she's acting so calm. Like she's just . . . at her job. I try to give her a secret "Let me know if you are being held here against your will" look and order eight glasses of wine.

Waiting for my first glass of wine, I keep asking David, "Is this fun? How am I supposed to have fun? How do I enjoy this? What am I supposed to do?" David worries that if I don't calm down soon it's going to look like he's dragged me there against my will.

I don't want to ruin David's night, so I yell a quick *"I've not been kidnapped."*

After my ninth glass of wine, I start to calm down and am able to get myself to look at the stripper. She's nothing like I pictured her. Nothing! Not to sound cruel, but she's dorky. Very long waisted, with a flat chest. A cowboy hat on her head, her hair in pigtails, she's not dancing to the heavy metal music that's playing as much as walking to it. She's got her hands on her hips and is just walking side to side to the music. There's a lot of nodding and winking. The sexy moments come when she crouches down, nods with a big smile, winks—"ta-da!"—and pops back up with a big fake laugh. She's like a musical theater stripper. Completely unsexy. I can handle this! It's hilarious.

David and I are laughing hysterically. "Go get your gun, Annie, go get it!" But then something horrible happens. Her song ends and she leaves. No, come back, Annie, don't get your gun!

The next stripper comes out, and she's gorgeous. Muscular, tattooed, short black hair, very confident—and why should she *not* be? She struts out, picks out her music, jumps up on the pole, and slowly spins down.

David has stopped laughing and has suddenly gotten very serious. He leans in to me. "Now, this is interesting. I mean she's clearly a dancer. So interesting how each of the girls approaches it. Very different body type. She holds her power in a different blah-blah-blah." Oh yes, Doctor, what is your scientific analysis? Mmm-hmmm. Hmmm. Hmmm.

This was it. This was why I'd been so nervous about coming to a strip bar with him.

My worst nightmare was that I'd have to sit next to David while he pretended not to be attracted to a twenty-year-old naked girl with a body that I've never had and it's not like I'm *going* to ever have. "Just wait, I'll be fifty soon, honey! It's coming! My saggy-boobed, covered-in-moles body is just around the corner!"

I think I can safely say that for most of our relationship, when it came to sex I'd always been a real "yes man." Up for anything. Put me in, coach. Glad to be invited to the party. You get the picture. I'd started our relationship with weight issues and the standard "I hate everything about my fat ass, face, and fat-ass body" self-loathing. His full-on love for every part of my body changed how I saw myself. His sexiness made me sexy. He infected me with sexy. My weight fluctuations, which would make me nuts, didn't bother him at all. I could tell they really didn't. He wasn't just saying that to keep the peace. Honestly, I think he enjoyed when I gained weight so he could pretend he was with a different woman.

Recently, I've been feeling a bit more clunky when it comes to busting a sexy move. The other night I tried to get undressed all slow and stripper-like and my shirt hadn't gotten even halfway off before David spotted something on my back and said, "Lauren! What's that mark? It that from your bra? Has that always been there? I don't think it has. Here, come with me, I want to show you what I see in the mirror." It all ended with me struggling to get a good look at what he saw. He was pushing my neck around and contorting my body so I could look at it.

David is also very taken by the music that the stripper has chosen to dance to. "Oh my god, this is Van Morrison's 'Into the Mystic.' You know that's the song I want played at my funeral, right?"

Are there any other details about your funeral you'd like to go over? Because *now seems like a good time.*

Perhaps I'm not evolved enough. Not sophisticated enough for strip clubs with my husband. I wish I could put my finger on the cause of this rush of adrenaline it's giving me. Is it knowing that David, if he so desired, could be with a woman like that? Some young beautiful women like old guys. Is it that cliché of how men get rugged and handsome as they age and women just get bitter as they watch them getting more and more rugged and handsome? Who knows? I don't want to spend the last half of my life talking about getting old and telling young girls how lucky they are to have fat in their faces. Dear lord, let me be wiser and let me get out of this strip club before I start pretending I love strip clubs and start making plans for my dad's eightieth birthday party.

The next day when I tell people about how I went to the strip club and it was just men my dad's age sitting on their hands struggling not to masturbate while a twenty-two-year-old naked girl danced, people are shocked and disgusted.

"Oh my god! Which strip club did you go to?" Every single person assured me that I went to the wrong one. "You have to go to mine. You'll love it. It's totally different. There are pirates . . ."

#Grateful

I loved David's apartment from the moment I met him. The scent of jasmine outside his Santa Monica complex was so pungent that the first time I smelled it I thought it was fake, and I checked around me to see if I was standing in front of the laundry room smelling someone's jasmine-scented Tide detergent. The plants with stems covered in brown fur that curled up like monkeys' tails and the cactuses covered in giant yellow blossoms were so exotic I took photos of them to send back home to my folks in Indiana, with a note saying, "Look, Mom, it's like Hawaii!" Once, when I was waiting in my car to pick up David for a date, I shot a video of the impossibly tall palm trees that lined the street as they swayed in the wind, thinking that if I ever opened my own spa I would play the video on a loop in the waiting room to relax people.

David had been drawn to the classic Southern California sixties-motel style of the building. He chose the apartment for its proximity to good schools for his first son. "I was willing to sleep on the couch for the rest of my life to make sure that Jack got into a good school," he told me when we were first dating.

The only minor knock on the place was the lack of views. The windows on the back side of the apartment faced the dirty white wall of the building next door, and the front windows looked out on "the Party Building," mostly occupied by UCLA grads. David and I both kept odd working hours and would get confused about what day of the week it was, but thanks to the loud techno music and a drunk girl yelling, "It's Friday night, woo-hooo!" we always knew when it was Friday.

In the very early days of our relationship, one of the Party Building's tenants would hang his wet suit outside on his balcony, and every time I'd open the blinds, I'd see the wet suit swinging in the wind and would think someone had hanged himself. The best thing that ever happened to the Party Building was the Chinese family that moved in for a few months. The grandfather did stretches on the balcony in his black socks and shorts. Sadly, by the time I moved in, a year and half after David and I started dating, the Chinese family had moved, and our view was of a Russian lady in a nightgown watering a single geranium three times a day.

None of that mattered to me. As E. M. Forster wrote in *A Room with a View*, the only perfect view is the view of the sky overhead, so if you can't have that, why even get picky about it?

David and I would sit on the front steps of the apartment after I first moved in and say things to each other like "I don't care about making money; I care about creating art" without laughing. Earnest and intense, we both loved historical documentaries, modern art, and going to music concerts where we were almost always the oldest ones in the audience.

From the get-go we were emotionally competitive. This sounded awful to most of my stable friends, but not for David and me. We were actors. Emotions were what we talked about, analyzed, and indulged every day of our lives, whether we were getting paid or not. It's what we got off on. Not the small stuff. Not the happy moments. We're not going to bother with the light stuff, comparing who laughed the longest or whose bliss blew our minds the hardest. When a weight lifter is looking to win the heart of another weight lifter, does he or she bench-press a folding chair or does the weight lifter bench-press a small pickup truck? It was all about who had endured more, who had suffered more in his or her life. David was a widower who grew up in the seventies in the roughest area of Brooklyn. He won that contest like he won my heart: easily and with a lot of monologues and wild hand gestures.

After Jack would go to sleep, we'd lie in bed listening to folky country ladies singing about life and loss, and it was never "Boy, that Patty Griffin writes some beautiful songs"; it was "Patty Griffin is trying to kill us. We can't listen to 'When It Don't Come Easy' anymore tonight because our hearts will explode. I'm not kidding; Patty Griffin wants us dead."

We were both drama school kids, but David went to Juilliard. He was trained to feel emotions that the back row of the balcony could see.

If I was "super-tired," David was so exhausted he was worried he was going to have a seizure and he'd stumble into the bedroom holding on to furniture and bumping into doorframes.

Comparing who had seen more shit go down, been through more dark nights of the soul, lost everything he or she had ever loved, and therefore was the deeper, more profoundly *feeling* human being, was our form of foreplay.

As an adult, I've always lived in tiny spaces. The house I grew up in seems like a mansion compared to all the places I've lived in since I moved out at eighteen.

Around the time Jack turned fifteen, the walls began to close in around us. Most of the apartment could be seen from the living room. If I needed one of them I never had to yell. I'd just say in a normal voice, "Jack?" I'd hear a "Yeah" that sounded like he was standing right behind me. It didn't matter if the bedroom doors were open or closed. Like Santa Claus, I always knew when Jack was sleeping and I knew when he was awake and I left the apartment when he was acting "bad" because it made me uncomfortable.

By the time he and his first girlfriend started having sex, we could have been living in a flight hangar and it would have felt stifling.

We came close to having enough money to move once, and we spent it on a new mattress. Another time it looked doable and I had a cancerous mole removed instead. Moving is reserved for millionaires and army people.

Eventually Jack moved to Boston to go to college. We had a baby, repainted, and added a screen door. Our apartment has contracted and doubled in size like a mini universe. Or me during my first year of college.

Nothing makes the apartment feel more like a mother's womb than standing in line for forty-five minutes at LAX waiting for a taxi. I've just returned from a trip to Boise. Why did I tell David that I didn't care if he picked me up from the airport? He should have known that everything I say is a lie or a test. (David used to love picking me up from the airport. He'd arrive early with a bottle of water and an energy bar from Trader Joe's in case I was hungry.) It's sad not seeing his tall, handsome figure waving his arms up above his head in a crowd of five people, yelling "Lauren! Lauren! Over here! I'm here!" when I'm standing right in front of him. I felt unclaimed. Like luggage. Not seeing Leo as I walk into baggage claim is even worse. He's gotten to be such an expert at airport reunions in the past year. As soon as he spots me he'll scream, "Mama!" and run to me like I just got off a plane from North Korea.

David must be exhausted after being with Leo all alone for four days.

It makes sense to take a taxi. My plane landed at eight A.M. from Boise. Plus, I've been gone for only four days.

David's a stay-at-home dad now. We decided to do the classic role-reversal thing, so now we're surviving on my salary, and he complains that I never tell him he looks pretty anymore.

For an ambitious Juilliard graduate whose greatest joys had come from his film and theater projects, it can't be easy. I'd worried that after a few months of full-time apartment-husband work he wouldn't be able to handle it. Things would start falling apart. He'd start collecting guns and shooting at passing cars. Or the arrival of the new Juilliard newsletter would set him off on a drinking binge and the whole neighborhood would watch as he stumbled down the middle of the street shooting out windshields and shouting at Eddie the mailman, "I coulda been somebody!"

But since day one he's been adamant about how much he loves it and is constantly telling me, "I love it. I love my life. I love being with Leo. I love my bike rides. I love living in Santa Monica. I love beer." I was okay that beer made the list and I didn't. My take is that he should do whatever he needs to do to make himself happy because I am so grateful for what he's doing.

I just hope he's as okay as he says he is. We're not young lovers, wooing each other with our tales of suffering anymore. Once we ran out of stories from our pasts to share, our tales of suffering started to feel like blancing rather than flirting. I suppose this is all perfectly normal with a toddler in the house. David's hitting his midlife crisis at the same moment Leo is hitting his toddler years. Nobody kills the sexy vibe of a sports car like a toddler, which is too bad because nobody appreciates sports cars more than a toddler.

I need new topics.

Things are so much better with David and me since Leo was born. We get along better. It's not as much fun to fight in front of a kid. Especially if you can't smoke, and I quit years ago.

David will still try to start fights now, but it's usually over such random things it's easy for me not to get sucked in. "You *never* want to go to Costco! That's the kind of person you are!" When I ask him what he's going on about, he'll admit that he doesn't actually know; he just wanted to yell.

As I move up the taxi line, I resolve not to take anything personally when I get home since I figure David will be stressed-out. Unless he starts talking about my mama being so fat that when she sits around the house she sits *around* the house. Nobody talks shit about my mama.

Once we get to our street, I tell the taxi driver to drop me off in front of the "pinkish peach building. That one. No, the one that's kind of like the skin-tone crayon color back when crayons were made by white supremacists." Why can I never figure out what color our building is? He says, "You mean the tan one?" and drives me right to it.

The cactus in front of the house has a 7-Eleven hot dog wrapper stuck to it. The monkey-tail plants have started to look less exotic and more like the tails of monkeys being kept in concrete cages in bad zoos. All the grass in front is dead. It's a little embarrassing. It's the most dilapidated building on the block next to the New Age philosophy center whose roof is caving in.

It's always hard to come back to the apartment after I've spent time with friends who live in houses. In Boise everyone has a house. I think they may actually be free there. My house envy has the tendency to become painful and ridiculous if I don't watch it. I need to watch it. I've watched *Dateline* specials on serial killers and I find myself envying them for their basements.

When I start to complain about the apartment, David hears it as "Why can't you be rich?" I don't mean it that way. What I mean is "Why can't *I* be rich?"

If I were able to complain without David taking it personally, I'd say my main complaint about the apartment is that it's sunless. It's true that the California sun beats down on us daily, and it is sometimes nice to be in a sunless apartment, but not always. I could buy a sunbed to help perk me up when I'm at home, but we'd have to get rid of the kitchen to make room.

I'm not complaining. It's a wonderful home. Leo's first home. Visitors are always telling us how they love the "homey feel" of our apartment, which to me always sounds like it has a lot of books and is dusty, but I appreciate the sentiment.

Besides, what is it that David always tells me? Don't judge someone's insides based on their outsides? My family is inside there.

It's one A.M. and my heart is racing. A loud scream has jolted me awake. It sounds like someone being murdered. Three screams later, I realize they're sex screams.

David sleeps pretty heavily, but I feel him stirring in the bed. "He thinks he's a dog," he says and gives a sleepy laugh.

"What?"

David leans over and whispers into my face, "Leo's having a dream about being a dog."

"He's not barking, David. It's from the—" David is already back asleep.

"AAH! AAH! AAH! AAH! AAH!"

It's the Florida newlyweds. The ones whose beat-up Saturn is being held together by Ron Paul stickers. When they moved in, I misread the stickers and announced to David, "Guess what. The couple moving into the apartment next door? They're big Ron Paul supporters."

I don't think the newlyweds have any idea how thin the walls of this building are. The whole building is like a series of bathroom stalls where you can hear everything that's going on next to you and see everyone's feet. I've been shushing Leo since he was born, and I practically smothered him when he was a baby so his cries wouldn't bother anyone, but here she is, screaming at the top of her lungs.

"AHHHHHH!"

This will make a great Facebook post. I hate Facebook. All those Lucky Ladies: "Hot-air balloon, champagne breakfast surprise from the world's best husband! I'm one LUCKY LADY!" "Whose husband surprised them with two tickets to Pink! Uhm . . . mine did! I'm one LUCKY LADY!" "10 years of laughter and happiness together that I never thought was possible . . . I'm one LUCKY LADY!"

"AH! OH! OHHHHH! AAH!"

How is David sleeping through all of this? This could be hot. Like being in a sex club but without the cover charge. Actually, I hope David doesn't wake up. I'd have to unbutton my nightgown and untie my bonnet. He must have doubled up his melatonin. Sexy stuff, this old, married-people business. I can't wait until he gets a sleep apnea machine.

"AAH! AAH! AAAAH!"

I ran into that sex-screaming girl during her first week here. She's not the sexiest thing. She returned my cheery "Hello, new neighbors!" by grunting at me and shuffling away like an overly medicated psych patient.

"She looks like Lurch from *The Addams Family* in a sundress," I told David. Because I'm a feminist I quickly added, "And good for her!"

At least she's getting laid.

The last time David and I had sex I got distracted by a dry patch of skin on his back. For a while, the only positions I wanted to do it in were ones where I could get a good look at it. After I asked him, "Is it itchy?" he ran to the mirror so I could show him where it was. That was months ago. Now we don't even talk to each other once we're in bed. Wait, that's not fair. A few nights ago, I asked him to turn toward the wall and stop blowing his whiskey breath in my face.

"AH! AH! YES! YES! AHHHHH!"

Oh, come on. She sounds like she's an amateur actor auditioning for community-theater porn. Though lots of sex stuff tends to sound fake to me. For years, I've complained to David, "Who says things like, 'Oh yeah, that feels so good?'" I once heard her laugh and that sounded fake, too. "HA, HA, HA, HA!" As if she'd been taught to laugh. "Here, let me write it out. It's HA. HA. HA. Yes! That's laughing!"

Finally, at two fifteen A.M. she fakes an orgasm.

"How are you so sure she faked it?" David asks me the next morning.

It's hard for me to believe that he wasn't pretending to sleep while he secretly recorded all her sex screams to listen to at a more appropriate time, like in the middle of the day at Home Depot.

"Of course it was fake! If it had been real we would have heard an 'Ow!' followed by 'Oh, just let me do it.'"

David doesn't laugh. I don't either. And I always laugh at my own jokes, but I'm distracted because David is sitting in his chair, his shirt is up over his belly, his unwashed hair is in crazy clumps, and three pairs of dirty reading glasses are perched all over his face.

"I wish you could see what I'm seeing right now."

I feel guilty as soon as I've said it and am about to add "because you look amazing," when he takes off his glasses and says with the slightest hint of anger, "Honestly, Lauren, from here on out, I don't give a *shit*."

There's a world where "not giving a shit" could be seen as liberated. Mature. But I wasn't ready to "not give a shit." You don't see me stumbling drunk around the apartment with my skirt caught in the folds of my back fat, granny panties stained with jelly, "I don't give a shitting" all over the place.

I'd promised myself and David not to give any power to what the psychic in Boise told me because, one: her office was in a strip mall above a Moneytree; two: because she'd made racist remarks about Mexicans ruining beach towns as I left her office; and three: because she was a psychic. But I can't help it.

Psychic Sheila told me completely unprovoked that my marriage was over. I'd gone to see her to get material for the play I was working on in Boise about the city of Boise. Psychic characters in plays are low-hanging fruit, but Boise is such a nice town full of nice people that I had to dig deep to hit the weird. Even the lesbians who live there don't complain, and lesbians complain about everything. My hope was that Sheila would be an interesting character, and she was.

With a cigarette dangling out of her mouth, she told me to "Pick a card, any card that speaks to you." I'd pick the card, she'd look at it, make a face—"Huh. I don't like this one. It's so . . . You know what, pick another one." It took me three tries before she liked my choice, or more likely, remembered what the card meant.

Sheila picked up the card, looked at it. The card was some newfangled version of a Tarot card and had a drawing of a goddess standing on a turtle drinking water at night.

"Oh yeah," she said. "Here we go. Your marriage is over."

She said it in this matter-of-fact tone that sounded like she was telling me it gets hot in September. I hadn't been taking any of what she said seriously up until that point, yet when she said this to me, I gasped and was immediately in tears. It was such a shocking thing. I tried to brush it off: "So is that always what a goddess on a turtle means? Or does it sometimes mean you're moving to a warmer climate?"

I'd stood up and told her I had to go. "And I don't think you should say things like that to people. You could have your license revoked."

She gave me a "geez, so sensitive" look and told me not to worry about it. "You get the house."

"We rent! We have a shitty little apartment! I don't want it!" Stumbling to gain my composure and not to let on that I was actually believing what a raspy-voiced, chain-smoking, middle-aged woman with Kate Plus Eight bi-level haircut and a pink running suit was telling me, I told her it was an upsetting thing to hear. "Only because, you know, I have a kid and the idea of—"

She shrugged off my concern about the collapse of my family with a "Your son will be fine." And asked me if I had any other questions I wanted answered.

Let's see, my marriage is over and oh, yes, am I going to get a new car? Any idea of the color? I'd run out to my rental car to call David and had started laughing somewhat nervously when I told him the story. He didn't laugh. In fact he didn't say anything. "David, can you hear me?"

"Yeah, I can hear you. I'm putting Leo to bed. Let me call you later." I didn't call him later because it felt like I was trying to stir up trouble. Plus, like I said, you can't really start any meaningful heart to heart with "But Psychic Sheila said—"

Her voice keeps popping up in my head at the oddest times. And I keep flashing to all the little angels she had all over her office. Angels holding her business cards; angels holding up her untouched *How to Be a Psychic* manuals on her bookshelf; angels holding her clock on her desk. I'm not going to give any weight to what that kooky lady who worked the hell out of her angels said to me.

I grab my robe and head to the garage to weigh myself.

Years ago, a therapist in Pasadena told me I needed to stop weighing myself every morning. "But how will I know how I'm *really* doing?" I asked her. Her theory was that a number cannot tell me and it would be best for my mental health if I got rid of my scale. It seemed a shame to throw it away completely, so I put it way up high in the bathroom cabinet behind the beach towels. I'll just have to start using my bank account numbers to tell me how I'm feeling, I told myself.

The scale stayed there for a few weeks, until a particularly brutal shopping spree at Costco destroyed our apartment's entire ecosystem. After that, the bathroom scale was moved to the garage to make room for twenty rolls of paper towels. I'd really hoped that it would prevent me from obsessively weighing myself, but instead it's meant that I have to come up with excuses to go the garage every day.

The next day I walk into the living room with my robe on and ask David, "Have you seen my bag of rocks? Hmmm. I'll be right back."

As I walk out the door, David gives me a "good luck out there" sad wave and turns back to his computer.

Right as I step out of the apartment, I hear Christina from apartment number five calling my name.

Christina's the only person at these apartments who has lived here longer than David and me. She's a fifty-year-old sexy brunette who, with her Chanel glasses, ivory Lexus SUV, and dewy skin, could easily be mistaken for a movie star or a Realtor.

Once when Christina was sick for two days, I texted her to see if she was okay and she texted back—"Jesus! I've been sick for two days and now you're checking? Thanks a lot. I hope I don't drown in my tub because you won't check until day three."

She's often referred to by the other tenants as "the combative lady in apartment five," but she's always been generous to me, giving me the hand-me-downs that her cleaning lady rejects. In ever-changing Santa Monica apartment land, where tenants come and go, she's my only friend, so I should stay on her good side. Over the years I even had some moments of what felt like love toward her.

There was a ninety-year-old lady who lived above Christina who died the first year we were here. A tiny woman, she wore bright purple or bright green polyester pantsuits every day. The hump on her back forced her neck down to her chest. Her right arm was higher than her left by at least five inches, in a permanent shrug. Slowly walking by our window, her white vinyl purse hanging off her lower arm, she did what no one ever did: She said hello. Unable to lift her head, she'd peek up like the sweetest shy little girl and wave to us. After she was moved into a facility for old folks, Christina visited her every day until she died. Christina told us how she was the only visitor the woman got and that she'd confessed to Christina that she'd never kissed a boy. "Can you believe that? I mean, I've been single for twenty years, but *that's* sad." They emptied out the lady's apartment after she died and Christina divided up the lady's dusty old phallic cactuses between the two of us. Watching Christina carry the cactuses that were too far gone to save to the garbage, I'd thought, please don't let me die here. I'm sure Christina was looking at those gigantic cactuses thinking, please god, let this not be the last phallus I see . . .

I was going to ask Christina if she'd heard the loud sex but she's too excited about her one-armed boxing instructor whose got the spirit of a two-armed boxing instructor to talk about anything else. "You don't even miss the other arm. It's *incredible*!" Last week she was raving about a powder you sprinkle on your food when you've eaten all you should that makes it taste like cow manure. "You just don't eat. It's *incredible*."

Christina asks me how David and I are doing. "I see him all the time but I never see you guys together. What's going on?"

Her *People* magazine must not have arrived yet. "We're good. I mean great. He's my sexy stay-at-home dad. I'm one lucky lady . . ."

We hear a door open and both turn around to see our neighbor Joel, pushing his bike out of his apartment. He's wearing a golf visor with fake spiked blond hair attached to the top. It would go great with a tuxedo T-shirt.

I tell him I like his hair.

"Oh. Right. Funny thing, lots of people don't even know it's fake. They think it's my hair. Pretty funny." Joel says this without a hint of "pretty funny" reflected in his voice.

Christina immediately starts yelling at him. "Listen, asshole, I'm sick of your shit!"

Joel calls her "crazy bitch" and tells her to fuck off.

Joel's lived in the apartment building for a few years, but his "witness protection program killer for the mob" vibe has made it difficult to get to know him. Rumor has it that Joel used to work on the stock market, but after he killed a bunch of people, he moved into a rent-controlled Santa Monica studio apartment to live out his days peacefully, riding his bike on the beach and soliciting prostitutes. He and Christina have been screaming at and threatening each other since the day he moved in.

According to Christina, it started when she asked him politely to take off his shoes when he was in his bathroom and he refused to do it even though she'd made it clear that his stomping around as he brushed his teeth at nine A.M. was waking her up and ruining her day. Christina had knocked on Joel's door to remind him to wear socks, and when he opened the door and saw her, he shoved her. She called the police and they haven't spoken since, except to yell at each other.

The idea of not getting along with my neighbors, even Lurch lady, is horrific to me. If I hated my neighbors I could't sleep at night. We are so close to one another—so intertwined. Did Nelson Mandela teach us nothing?

I tell Christina I hope she has a great day (so she'll like me), and then head to the garage.

I'm trying to find an even part of the cement floor to set my scale on when David comes in to get his bike.

"I'll be back around four."

"That's a five-hour bike ride, David."

"Oh, right, I'll be back at five."

His bike rides have been getting longer and longer.

"Are you avoiding me?"

He rolls his eyes and heads out. "Come on, Lauren! Don't. Don't start."

David and I took our first bike ride together in Santa Monica. I bought Jack a bike to ride to school and David went out and bought himself one the next day. That weekend we went on a two-hour bike ride along the LA River to our favorite sushi place. It was so fun. It was David's idea. He'd mapped the route, had it all figured out. We rode home, half-drunk in the dark. Thinking that David was far enough ahead of me, I'd stood up on the pedals and farted. David's head whipped around and he yelled, "Yeah, right?" He thought that I was commenting about the ocean air and the perfect night and had said, "Wow." We were so close he understood my farts. I've never told my "David talking to my fart" story without laughing so hard I can't breathe. Now it feels how it probably has felt to everyone I've ever told it to: gross and weird.

It's unusual for us to be this disconnected for so long. Usually after a period of blaming each other for our unhappiness, we see a good documentary about coma survivors or talk to a friend and come back to reality. That hasn't happened in a long time. It would be so lovely for him to fart to show me how he's feeling about our marriage or burp to me his fears about his life. Something. Oh, what am I saying? I've lost two pounds. Things have never been better.

Somebody needs to get this marriage relit. One of us needs to take control of the situation.

David returns from his marathon bike ride and I suggest that we go out next Saturday night. Together.

David says, "Okay." I ignore the fear in his voice and start to figure out which babysitter I should call first. My nephews in Indiana have a sitter with three teeth who shows up wearing her Minnie Mouse sleep shirt. We live near Hollywood. Our two main babysitters are beautiful young actresses. The younger and cheaper one, so to speak, is an acting student of David's who needed some work. Simone. Whenever she babysits I present her to Leo with "Hey! Look what Mama got you!" like a Vegas pimp.

Ava-Rose has been a professional nanny on the Upper West Side and is also very beautiful and sexual. I see that plainly myself but she always helpfully points it out as well: "I'm very sexual." She does a lot of spiritual work on herself. Her sexuality has always felt like the "treat yourself like the goddess that you are" school. I vacillate between Simone and Ava-Rose before deciding it doesn't matter. David won't notice either of them. His glasses are too dirty.

Saturday night arrives. I'm excited. It's been a long time since I've gotten dressed up. "Mama getting laid tonight!" I yell out from the bathroom. "Clip-clip here . . . clip-clip there. In the merry old land of Oz." Pubic hair is flying everywhere. David walks by the bathroom and sticks his head in. He doesn't seem to notice what I'm wearing or my age-inappropriate ringlet hairstyle.

He tells me to take my time in the bathroom because he's not showering. "I showered yesterday before my hike."

There's a knock on the front door. The babysitter has arrived. Finally, I'm going to be more dressed up than Ava-Rose!

I open the door. It's not Ava-Rose. It's the opposite of Ava-Rose. It's a short man with poufy hair from Long Island. It's Joel.

Joel has never knocked on our door before. Standing next to Joel is a disinterested-looking teenager with long straight hair down to her butt—Crystal Gayle or Mama Duggar hair, depending on your generation.

He's come over to introduce me to his prostitute. How progressive.

"Hey, Lauren. So listen. I got married. This is my wife, Svetlana." He puts his hand in front of my face so I can see his wedding ring. "There it is, so yeah, I'm married to her." He points to Svetlana, who nods at me gruffly.

"So if anyone comes around asking, we're married. She lives with me. Like husbands and wives do."

Is he hinting for presents?

"You seem very in love," I tell them.

I congratulate them, shut the door, and run to tell David about Joel's mail-order bride. He's in Leo's bedroom setting out his pajamas.

"David, it's the first time he's spoken to me in a nice tone! Last week he yelled at a grandma who was babysitting her grandkids to 'shut that kid up or I'll shut him up!'"

David wants to know why I'm so sure it's a fake marriage. "You never know, people get married for all sorts of reasons. Look at us!" He laughs heartily.

For the first time since we got married two years ago, I wonder if David really wanted to get married. How odd that I'd never doubted it until now.

A year into our dating we'd gotten engaged but called it off six months later and decided to wait until we felt more "stable." When I asked him again to get married, I explained that if he got hit by a car, his medical expenses would be more costly than a divorce, and so we should marry so I could add him to the great insurance policy I had through my union. "And of course I love you," we both quickly added after we talked about the money we'd save on taxes.

I acted like it was all insurance-based, but of course it wasn't.

Now I'm remembering how when I asked him, he shrugged his shoulders and said, "Sure." He'd suggested that it be cheap and quick. I said, "Like your mother?" Like I said, it was romantic.

There's another knock on the door. I half expect to open it and find Joel holding the girl's dead body—"Here! Hide this! Please. I owe you!" Thankfully, it is Ava-Rose this time.

David walks out of Leo's bedroom. He avoids eye contact with Ava-Rose and walks right out the front door. "See you outside."

I'm in the middle of reminding Ava-Rose about Leo's bedtime when she takes me in her arms for a hug and whispers in my ear, "You're beautiful. I know you don't believe it, but you are." No. I don't want her to get all heal-y on me. It disrupts the power dynamic.

I take back my control by saying, *"I'm pretty! I'm pretty!"* like Quasimodo, and then proceed to pour out every personal detail about my marriage to her. I tell her that I'm worried David isn't feeling manly enough. I tell her that he didn't say anything about me shaving myself down for date night.

Ava-Rose drops to the floor, crosses her legs, and pats the floor next to her.

"Lauren, come here. Right now."

Oh shit. Here she goes. She's pulled this kind of stuff on me before. After Leo was first born and I complained about not making enough money, she gave me a gratitude journal so I could attract more of what I was grateful for in my life. I ended up using it to keep track of my weight and make lists of people who had screwed me over.

"I want you to visualize the perfect date night—see it . . . *really* see it."

This is what I get for trying to trick someone into telling me I'm attractive.

"In my culture, if you visualize in front of another person it's considered rude. Okay, so you don't have to wash Leo's hair—"

"Stop it, Lauren. I know you're into this kind of stuff. I've seen your bookshelves. Just sit down." She pulls me down onto the floor next to her.

I pop right up—"Done!"

"I know you're being funny to deal with this moment, and that's okay."

Finally, she gives up and tells me that I can skip the visualization but she just wants me to remember that "if it hurts, it isn't love." I'm not taking any advice on love from an actress in her early twenties. At that age, I tell her, if it hurts it's an infection, and it is love because now you both have it, and you'll be together forever since your partner is the only one who will apply ointment.

How many more middle-aged bad-marriage jokes can I make? I sound like Erma Bombeck, or a bad sitcom without Asian jokes and canned laughter.

Ava-Rose comes at me for another hug-and-whisper session.

"The only reason I'm not laughing is because I'm not a big laugher, but I appreciate it. You're beautiful."

Date night is a disaster. Neither one of us has bothered to make a plan for where we are going. David wants to go to some happy hours he's been researching online. I want to have a night like we used to back in our dating days, where we'd hang out in the photography book section of Barnes & Noble trying to find the most "life-changing" photo we could. We'd show each other the photos of piles of dead bodies or funerals of stillborn babies from the Dust Bowl . . . something romantic.

In the end, we compromise and go to a Woody Allen movie about a middle-aged woman who loses her mind after her marriage falls apart, *Blue Jasmine*. At the moment where Cate Blanchett's character overshares with her young nephews, telling them, "Listen, boys, there's only so many traumas a person can withstand until they take to the streets and start screaming," I start applauding.

David suggests we skip going out after the movie to save money. We're walking up to our apartment arguing about the apartment and which one of us drinks more alcohol when we get to our front door to find Ava-Rose sitting on the couch drinking hot tea with the door to the apartment wide open.

"Don't you watch horror movies?" I tell her. "Murderers love babysitters!"

She responds in a very calm voice, "My safety and my happiness are under my control."

I grant her plenty of leeway, but keeping the door wide open in our hood at one A.M. is too far. Our apartment has a lot of foot traffic running beside it from the street to the back alley behind the building. We're the only building in the neighborhood without a front gate, making it the perfect shortcut to get from the park across the street to the back alley. There are some things that nobody feels comfortable doing in public that they will happily do in the privacy the alley provides, like changing socks after a long day or shooting up into their scrotum. We've had packages stolen off our front steps numerous times. Somewhere out there are some beach pirates, as a posse of homeless men who live on the beach like to be called, using Christmas coasters from a year-round holiday store in Indianapolis for their Mad Dog 20/20 and wearing Thomas the Tank Engine toddler underwear.

Ava-Rose is looking at me like I'm being insensitive to the plight of my fellow human beings. I'm not. There is a park across the street from us, and the folks who spend their days there are a part of our community. Some of the regulars I'd consider friends. The lady who spit on Jack on his way to school isn't just the spitting lady; she's *my* spitting lady. The bearded man with the giant beer belly who reads the newspaper saw me walking through the park with Leo once, irritated that there was no room for us to throw a football, counting, out loud, all the bodies that were spread out and sleeping in the park. Right as I got to twelve, he sat up and nudged his girl-friend, who was lying on a blanket next him. "I hope she's counting to figure out how many sandwiches to bring and not bullets." He called me out and he was right. I'd been walking around wishing I could rearrange the world for Leo like a Nazi propaganda film director.

"Listen, Ava-Rose. Just this week I had a guy, completely drunk, covered in blood splatters and dried pee, come up to me as I was walking out of the apartment and try to grab a cookie out of my hand. And when I told him, 'I don't think so, buddy,' he yelled at me to 'fuck off.'"

Ava-Rose asks me the same question that every one of my friends asked me after I told them the story: "Why didn't you just give him the cookie?" The truth was that I'd been saving the last three cookies to eat on my ride to work, but I didn't want to get distracted from the issue, so I tell her, "It wasn't about the cookie; he was threatening me."

Ava-Rose stands up from the couch and grabs her leg in one hand in some yoga circus move and looks me right in the eyes—like she likes to do—and gives me the report on Leo.

"So, I didn't put the nighttime diaper on because Leo told me he doesn't need them anymore because he just holds his penis shut all night, and I didn't do the dishes because there were some dishes from when I wasn't here and I was scared that if I did them it would be implying that I thought you should do your dishes. Does that make sense?"

David starts to insist on walking Ava-Rose to her car. "This neighborhood can get very 'land of the zombies' at nighttime," he tells her, but she peacefully refuses.

"Are you guys trying to act like you live in some tough neighborhood? You live in Santa Monica, come on."

She gives me *another hug*, whispers, "That must have been a really special cookie," winks, and walks out of the apartment with her shoes in her hand, barefoot. "And by the way—I love your apartment. I would kill to live here."

Date night ends with us listening to the sounds of the Florida newlyweds having sex for forty-five minutes.

At three A.M., I wake up to find David not in bed. When I realize that he isn't next to me, my heart starts racing, which seems a bit of an extreme reaction when he could have been having a pee or eating a bowl of cereal. I walk out to the living room, and there he is sitting in the dark watching *The Walking Dead*, wearing his sunglasses with a glass of whiskey on the table next to him.

I ask him why he's wearing sunglasses and he answers me like it was the most ridiculous question a person could ask another person.

"So I can see the TV, Lauren."

It gives me an awful feeling of dread that seems out of proportion to the situation. Maybe seeing a man sitting in the dark with sunglasses on in the middle of the night stirs up repressed memories of being date-raped by Stevie Wonder. But I doubt it. Stevie is an angel visiting us from another planet, here to spread love. All I know is that it bothers me far more than it should.

The Florida newlyweds are having sex all the time.

"Okay, she's giving him a blow job in their kitchen right now, so they'll be moving to the bedroom in about ten minutes," I say to Christina on the phone.

Christina thinks I should write an anonymous note.

"You'd be doing her a favor. They're the kind of people that will always be living in apartments, so you'd be teaching her a life lesson." She tells me she'd offer to do it but she's super-busy dealing with that "new wannabe singer idiot" who moved in above her. "The police wouldn't let me file a complaint about her singing in the shower but now her dumb-ass cat is knocking things off her bookshelf every morning, I totally have a case, but I have to act fast."

I write a note on typewriter paper in big block letters that looks like a first grader copied it off a chalkboard for handwriting class.

The note says, "I'm so glad you guys are having a healthy sex life, but I live in the apartment building next door and would appreciate it if you'd close your windows."

I watch their doorway for them to leave, and once I'm sure they're gone I run out and stick it in their mailbox. My hands are shaking like I'm planting a bomb. As soon as it's in the mailbox, I freak out. Why didn't I write it with my left hand? I forgot to melt wax on my fingers to hide fingerprints!

Today I don't even bother to make an excuse. "I'm going to the garage to weigh myself."

I pull the garage door open, a spring breaks and the door comes crashing down on my head. Before I know it, I'm in tears rolling on the ground in pain and hear the sound of Leo laughing. I look up and see him pretending to drink from a mud-encrusted liquor bottle he's pulled out of the bushes next to our building. David must have heard me scream when I hit my head because he comes running around the corner in his sunglasses—"Lauren, you can't leave the front door open like that! Leo went running out and I didn't even know he was gone!"

He walks over to Leo, takes the Mad Dog bottle away from him, and puts it back in the bushes. "David, throw it away—don't put it back."

"No, my heart goes out to these guys. I'd be mad if my stash was suddenly missing and I had to go to sleep sober," he says to me, and walks away with Leo.

Have I done something to David that I forgot about? Crashed his car? Had sex with his brother? I follow them inside and wait until Leo is down for a nap to ask him what is going on.

"You told me that you were going to give me credit for helping you when you produced *Bust*, but you never did. My name wasn't in the program."

"David, that was like seven years ago . . . Are you serious? I can't remember but I think the programs had already gone to the printer and . . ."

My god, he's obviously been looping this story in his head for years.

"Oh. You can't remember."

So I guess I did crash his car while having sex with his brother. He doesn't feel appreciated. Oh god, that's the worst. No, the worst is that it was seven years ago and I can't do a thing about it.

"Well, David, you look real pretty."

I'm not that funny anymore. Once that's gone I can't fall back on my looks. Oh boy. We need a new start. How on earth did he get so angry at me? What have I done? What can I do? Outside of anal, I'm open to suggestions, because I am completely confused as to why he is looking like . . . he hates me. It would be so awful, to be hated by the one person who knows me.

Eating breakfast while I'm checking for apartments for rent, I see Joel's child bride walk by our window and there's a woman with her. She's got short spiky blond hair on top of an older version of the young bride's face. Her mother. The two of them are chatting away and completely ignoring Joel, who runs behind them trying to get their attention. "Why don't I take you guys to a movie! Let me take you to a movie!"

His wife turns around and yells "*No!*" and keeps talking.

"But it will be a funny one. Tell your mom it's a funny one."

Christina texts me: "WHAT THE FUCK, LAUREN?! HE'S CRAZY!"

> "She married him for a green card and he's been putting together some wedding-bliss bed from Ikea and potting plants for his front steps like he's a fucking newlywed! Oh my god. If the girl wasn't Russian, I'd turn him in so fast, but the Russian mafia makes the Sopranos look like the fucking Girl Scouts."

At the end of the week, I hear a screaming fight. I'd miss one of the words and Christina would fill me in. "She didn't do what on Tuesday?" I'd text Christina. "She didn't call him after she got off work." It's an epic fight. If we weren't scared of Joel being another Whitey Bulger, I'm sure someone would have gone over and tried to break it up.

"Her voice is so calm because you can tell she doesn't give a shit," Christina texts me. It's twenty minutes of yelling: "You whore!

What the hell do you think you're doing? I did all this for you and you don't call me when you're late?" Followed by silence. Followed by the sound of a suitcase being wheeled down the sidewalk.

Christina texts me: "Jesus, that was quick."

David, who is the non-snoopiest, most mind-your-business, most anti-gossip man I know, opens the curtains and watches her go. She's long gone and he's still staring out the window.

I feel completely alone. Like Joel must feel.

Last night I brought up the issue of me not giving David credit for helping me with *Bust* again. He told me that I'd never believed in him, and I didn't know to convince him how untrue that was. Saying it really loudly and pounding myself on the chest as I said it didn't seem to help. He told me that I took all the glory for myself. "But what good is glory if you don't have people you love to share it with?" I'd said. It sounded clichéd, but I meant it.

He's started to say things like, "Lauren, you're the kind of person who . . ." I jump in as quickly as I can with "Is good with ducks?" When he said, "Who doesn't care about people," it was actually a relief, because while I didn't love that, it wasn't going to haunt me for days wondering if it was true. I can be easily convinced that I have a lot of displeasing personality traits, but not caring about people isn't one of them. The other day a homeless guy asked me if I had any change I could spare and I told him no but I had a smooshed granola bar in my purse if he wanted it, and he said not only did he want it, but it was perfect because he couldn't chew that well anyway and pointed to his toothless mouth. So don't tell me I don't care about people.

David has been wearing his sunglasses constantly. He never takes them off. He brushes his teeth with them on.

He's leaving me—one body part at a time. My life has turned into a Raymond Carver story.

One A.M. It's completely quiet. No fake sex.

The next day it's quiet too. No fake laughter either. Oh god, I worry. Maybe it wasn't fake and my note killed her spirit, made her feel ashamed. What if after this, she's never able to relax or have an orgasm again? The first night after the note, I bet he wanted to have sex and she'd started crying, "No! No! Don't you get it? I'm a freak!"

I didn't hear any crying. I heard nothing.

I lay awake in bed, picturing her husband holding her as she sobs as quietly as she can. Her vagina has dried up forever like a bad apricot.

The next morning, Florida girl is pulling a suitcase down the sidewalk. Oh my god, I've broken up the marriage. I text Christina. That's two suitcases pulled by women whose marriages have fallen apart. One of the wheels on my roller bag is stuck. Not that it matters.

"You're insane. And if you did, who cares?" Christina says. "She probably takes her roller bag to the library with her. Listen, she and her husband are going to break up and the next guy she's with will thank you for stopping those fake sex sounds. And so will every neighbor she ever has."

Later that day, on WestsideRentals.com I find an adorable Craftsman three-bedroom house in Santa Monica for twenty-five hundred dollars. Most houses go for at least five thousand. At least. I email the owner immediately and look out my window and see Lurch.

Outside getting her mail. I walk out to the mailbox to see if she suspects me. The guilt is killing me. Marriage is hard. They didn't deserve this. I go up to her and she grunts at me. It's a friendly grunt.

"Hey!" I say, full of guilt. "Man, I got a note in my mailbox from the neighbors complaining that our kid was too loud. It came from the building next to ours. Not our building. I think the building over *there* has some very unhappy people in it that won't let people be happy. Geez. Anyway—I'm just going to ignore the note."

She looks directly at me. Her hair, beaten to death by curling irons, is held back on each side by barrettes intended for a little kid. She doesn't look guilty. Or relieved. She just looks blank.

"We're moving," she blurts out. "We were only living here until our house was ready. So I don't really care."

Her head slumps to her chest and she shuffles away. Happy. She's got her man. She doesn't care what anyone in this building thinks of her because this was never her home anyway. Now that really is one Lucky Lady.

A door opens. It's Joel.

"Listen, Lauren, let me ask you something."

Joel points to a large floodlight on the side of the building. "Okay, now, you ever see that light working?"

I tell him that I hadn't because it was true. I hadn't.

"It's always been dark out here at night—right? 'Cuz that light—it's never worked—right?"

"Um, right . . . I didn't even know it was there, actually."

"Yeah, that's what I thought. Okay, well, I changed that light bulb and so now it's working and I've been asking around and the other tenants are all saying how nice it is. How safe they feel now. Right? You feel safe?"

I didn't feel any safer.

Joel touches his novelty hair and nods at me. "That's right . . . you feel safe."

My phone rings. It's Christina—

"If Joel asks you if the light has ever worked before, say yes! He's trying to extort money from the owners. So just say yes, it's always worked! And, hey, what's up with Ray Charles? I saw him coming last night and I was like, hey, freak, it's nighttime. Take your sunglasses off. How do you stand it, Lauren? I don't get it. Hey, do you ever wonder if something is going on with David and that babysitter? Not the New Agey one but the one with the big boobs?"

She reads too many *People* magazines.

Joel very patiently waits for me to get off the phone with Christina. "You done?"

Yes, I'm done.

"How long have you lived here?" Right as Joel asks me this, the light makes a popping noise and goes out.

"Cocksucker!" Joel takes off his hat and stomps off to his apartment.

By the time I get back inside, the owner of the house has responded—

"The place is yours! Enjoy! I'm currently tending to business affairs in Nigeria. Would you be so kind good friend to deposit a check for $9,000 as quickly as possible?"

It's a scam. A fake listing. That's okay. Wherever you go, there you are. Right? We live eight blocks from the beach. #grateful #blessed

I go into the living room determined to find a way to remind David who I am, who we are, and there he is, sitting in the dark watching *The Walking Dead* wearing his sunglasses again. I ask him if I can talk to him for a moment. He pauses the TV and turns his head toward me. I ask him if he could take his sunglasses off and he tells me, "No, Lauren, I can't," and un-pauses the show.

Impending doom starts to make life feel surreal.

At a dinner party I hear him telling a little clan of attractive women that he's the sole caretaker of Leo. One of the women sits next to me at dinner and asks me if I've had a chance to meet that man over there, and points to David. "He's amazing. He's a widower and stay-home-dad taking care of his kid full-time . . ." She doesn't even know I'm with him.

In the car afterward I ask him why he said that. "You keep telling me how you're 'happier than you've ever been in your life' being a stay-at-home dad, but you seem so unhappy. At least with me. I can't take it anymore. Listen, David, if you're not happy, if you don't want to be married, then let's split. We'll be good co-parents. We'll—"

"Yes. I think we should."

Everything I say is a lie or a test. Remember?

I didn't mean it. I was only saying all that to try to scare him into showing a little love. But he jumped right on it. By the time we got home it was decided that we'd have a trial separation. In the apartment I tried to stifle my sobs so Christina wouldn't call the cops on me.

Maybe the entire apartment building saw this coming, but I didn't. Not really.

The obvious choice was for me to move out with Leo. After all the years of me complaining, here was my chance to find sunlight and non-felon neighbors. Finally, I will get out of this dark, awful place. Filmmaker friends of mine from Seattle had a place they rented out in Venice. Venice has always been my dream place to live. At least on the Westside. They welcomed us the first night with vodka and pie. My two favorite things in the world. Tonight before I walked out of the apartment, David and I hugged each other so tight. Heartbroken. Both of us. I walked away thinking "no no no" and waited for him to come running to me or call or text. Nothing.

I've had many nights alone in the past four years, but tonight is my first night "alone" even with Leo asleep on the floor next to me. I made a bed with every blanket and pillow that I could find.

I wanted a better place for him. This place is smaller and too "rental"-like. I'd wanted some immediate perk that Leo would be excited about. I had some dumb idea that if I could leave on a fancy swan boat it would immediately make our future look brighter. I wanted to take him away to a castle.

I'm on the couch because the bedroom didn't have a bed big enough for Leo and me to share and we wanted to be near each other.

It's true what they say. It is easier to be suffering in a bad relationship than to leave.

I can't tell what's happening.

I mean . . . this is happening. *My When Things Fall Apart* book is back at my apartment. Our apartment. The apartment. What happens again? What happens when things fall apart?

I bet during the day it will be better.

It's so quiet. No texts from Christina dinging my phone every five minutes. No fake sex. No sounds of Joel yelling at whoever is in front of him. Leo and I ate our breakfast on vacation rental plates and drank out of vacation rental cups on a bright cheery patio with a perfect view. Nothing but sky overhead.

I can remember being curled up on the floor of my closet when I was nineteen years old because my boyfriend had canceled a date with me five minutes before I was about to leave the house. I sat on the floor sobbing. Waiting for him to change his mind. Waiting for him not to be doing this. For someone to save me. If I wished he was sensitive, I should have been sensitive to him. Be kind if that's the world I want.

I have been on the floor waiting for David to be kind to me and care that he hurt me, and I cannot tell if it's me making this happen. I'm forty-five and I'm sounding like I'm twelve. I'm back to it. I knew we would never connect unless I was suffering. I also knew that I was a hard person to collaborate with and thought of myself first too often. It's possible for both things to be true—I have something to learn *and* he's been horrible. But I don't have to lie on the floor of my closet waiting for him to not be who he is.

I want my apartment back. That's my home I made.

After spending two nights there, I called David. "Leo and I are taking the apartment. You find someplace else to live."

Welcome back home. The apartment looks so good. It's nighttime and I clearly see a hummingbird—the moon is so bright. The plants and trees are lit up and sultry. A little surreal, like a Disney ride through the jungle.

Right before I'm about to walk inside I turn around, and like Salieri in the final scene of *Amadeus*, I greet my people. I'm the patron saint of rent-controlled Santa Monica apartment living. Hello, Joel. I absolve you. Hello, Christina. I absolve you. Hello, Lurch. I absolve you; never mind, you already moved. Hello, my spitting lady. I absolve you. I think about absolving David but it seems a little premature, so I walk inside and leave the front door wide open so I can smell the jasmine.

To All the Gays I've Loved Before

The sound of Eddie the mailman's wad of keys jingling up the sidewalk signals my favorite moment of the day. The mail is here! Not wanting to seem desperate for good news that the mail never brings, I hide behind my curtains, ready to run right out the moment Eddie slams our apartment building's mailbox shut—*slam!* That's it. He's done. I bolt out of my apartment, and as I round the side of the building, Eddie isn't walking away from our mailbox; he's walking toward it. The noise I heard had been the mailbox next door slamming shut, and he was just now coming to ours.

With a put-on "Oh, are you here? I thought it was Sunday" look, I take my pathetic little stack of mail from Eddie. No twelve-dollar residual checks today or cards from my mother with one-dollar bills taped on the inside to buy myself a Diet Coke. There's a notice warning Santa Monica residents that if they choose to go swimming at any of the Santa Monica beaches this summer to be careful not to get any water in their mouth unless they want anal leakage.

Sadly sorting through my tiny pile, I find a letter from my old high school, North Central. There's something that sounds like sand swishing around inside the envelope—an invitation to a beach-themed high school reunion? Knowing my old school, it's more likely that the reunion would be an American pride "Love It or Leave It!" theme and the envelope is filled with anthrax. I don't care what the theme is; I'm not going to fly across the country to drunk-sob *Am I pretty now?*" in the face of a pudgy middle-aged white man wearing that "don't tell me you're not asking for it" combo of khaki pants and a tucked-in blue dress shirt.

The suspense is not killing me as much as my imagination is. I rip it open. It's an invitation to a party celebrating fifty years of my old show choir, the Counterpoints. Red glitter pours out of the envelope all over the sidewalk.

> *COUNTERPOINTS ALUMNI!*
> INDIANA'S MOST PRESTIGIOUS SHOW CHOIR IS 50 YEARS OLD!
> JOIN US FOR A BLACK-TIE GALA AFFAIR AS WE CELEBRATE OUR GLORIOUS PAST WITH PERFORMANCES BY THE CURRENT COUNTERPOINTS CHOIR!

High school existed in two places for me: theater class and Counterpoints. "Once a Counterpoint! Always a Counterpoint!" A large banner with our motto hung in the rehearsal room. It was written in pizzazz-y exuberant letters and followed by four exclamation points. It was screaming at us to "Put on that Ritz!" "Stomp at that Savoy!" "Be My Funny Valentine!" The rest was of high school was a blur of acid-washed jeans and Hostess fruit pie lunches. Little clumps of musical theater geeks would run full speed, like a nervous herd of chubby gay zebras surrounded by lions, to get to the safety of swing choir rehearsal. The grand pooh-bah of swing choir was the director, Robert Critzer. Mr. Critzer was grandiose, mocking, and snooty and far too talented to be teaching high school show choir in a window-less room in Indiana.

As members of the elite Counterpoints, we left school, sometimes several times a week, to entertain at children's hospitals, shopping malls, Jewish community centers, and old-age homes. Lots and lots of old-age homes. Critzer preferred a senior citizen audience. They had respect for the music he loved—Fats Waller, Cole Porter, any-thing from the big band era. Thanks to the pillows that propped them up and the nurses who clapped their hands together, they were an attentive and enthusiastic audience.

I didn't walk around talking about how much I loved being in Counterpoints, but love it I did. We all did. Nobody had to be there. It was not a graduation requirement to know how to wear a bowler, carry a cane, and sing "Puttin' on the Ritz" to the sound of oxygen tanks. It was an elective.

My Counterpoints pride was fierce and I did love all the bells and literal whistles of the choir, but most of all I loved Mr. Critzer.

Mr. Critzer wore dark green polyester suits that helped con-firm the rumors that teachers made only slightly more than wel-fare recipients. When conducting, he took off his jacket, revealing neatly pressed dress shirts that always had yellow armpit stains. That grand diva of the music department wore Goodwill clothing when he obviously belonged in white fur capes.

Critzer refused to let us do what all the other (lesser) choirs were doing, like break-dancing to an a cappella version of the little-known and often mistaken for Kenny Hollywood's "Eat Me I'm a Danish" (a parody of "Rock Me Amadeus") in full-length pink taffeta. "Listen, I'm sure it does bring their audiences to their feet," Mr. Critzer would say whenever a Counterpoint would report on the life-changing show they had witnessed over the weekend in hopes of convincing Mr. Critzer to let us do more popular songs, "but when you're performing in the mall, everyone's usually already standing."

The gala planning committee must have blown their budget on glitter and stamps because the invite is on a flimsy piece of eight-by-ten copy paper and looks like it was formatted with an old Word template usually used for nursing home announcements promoting free movie nights and callus shavings.

Included with the invitation is a single-page "History of Counterpoints." I do a quick scan for my name. It's not there. There's no reason it should be; I've just developed a bad habit that I can't break of scanning for my name on any written document. About two-thirds of the way down the page, I see Mr. Critzer's name.

> *Bob Critzer, the choir's former director, earned a master's degree from Butler after completing a BA in music from UCLA in 1964. Like all members of the choral factory, he had excellent keyboard skills and was an exceptional teacher of music appreciation and history. His lectures were of college caliber. He was also a perfectionist in his expectations re performance. Bob served as director until his untimely death in late December 1986 at the age of 44. Bea Arthur took over leadership until the end of the 1986–1987 school year.*

That's it? Untimely? Is it "untimely" to die of complications related to AIDS? I don't expect them to do some big dramatic "Ode to AIDS" musical number like *Glee* would do. But come on. Why not at least give Mr. Critzer something special? Some post-life honor. I bet they wouldn't even admit it was AIDS today; that's how backward it is there. Even the gayest thing in the city, swing choir, won't admit to it in a red state.

Untimely, come on.

The words "you homophobic faggots" slip out of my mouth.

Eddie's head jerks up from his mailbag, "No check again, huh, Lauren?"

That's right. Eddie can hear me. I forgot how his headphones are just a glorified headband to keep his long hair out of his face. I found that out the day David and I were walking behind him and I commented that Eddie had the calves of a six-hundred-pound man. Without turning around, Eddie yelled back at me, "I walk a lot!"

Eddie and I keep it real with each other. When I was teetering on the edge of bankruptcy and he handed me a stack of fifteen residual checks that added up to forty-six dollars, I openly wept in front of him. The day Anna Nicole Smith died he was so distraught I had to sit on the steps with him until he had the strength to go on.

Not wanting Eddie to think I walk around screaming "homophobic faggots" willy-nilly, I fill him in.

Eddie stops sorting through a pile of Bed Bath & Beyond coupons and shakes his head solemnly. "That's rough. Rough. I can't believe it. Anyway, you know they got a karaoke night on those Carnival cruises and you know my song, Lauren? 'Summer of '69.' I been singing that song for going on twelve years. That's how long I've been going on those cruises. Matter of fact, they just upgraded me to VIFP status. Very Important Fun Person."

Eddie points to his headphones and gives me a "Sorry, gotta take this call" guilty shrug, slams the mailboxes shut, and takes off down the sidewalk. I guess his headband is plugged in today after all and he's got an important incoming call. He's already zipped down to the end of the block, pushing his little mail cart in front of him: "Hey, man, what did I tell you, Peyton chokes in the postseason . . ."

There's a VIFP who knows how to relax and enjoy life. The

apartment buildings around me are filled with young easygoing dudes like Eddie. VIFPs in the making. They work hard. Play hard. Jog on the beach. Drink tequila. Keep it simple.

I need to do more of that in my life, and I will, right after I avenge the death of my high school show choir director.

The longer I wade around in this puddle of red glitter, the more outraged I become. How many wrongs can there be around one man's death? It's time to make it right. If I know that somewhere in the world gay men are being hurt, even if they're already dead, I cannot bear it.

"I love gay people" flies out of my mouth all the time. As if "gay" is all anyone needs to know about a person. As if once I say "gay" you know exactly what to expect. It's a simple description, like saying something tastes like popcorn. "Oh, stop there, I get it." It's such an overgeneralization. The problem is that in a huge, big, generalized "gay pride parade" way, I do love gay people. I love them at my job, in my home, at parties, and at the movies with extra butter.

Gay issues have always been my issues. They affect my job, my community, my quality of life. Gay boys are my canary in the coal mine whenever I've been deciding if I could live in a city. If a delicate creature covered with bright yellow feathers can't thrive in a city, I won't be able to either. If I can't drive my car straight, but not narrow, into the gayborhood or "follow the rainbow flags" to gay karaoke or turn right on Harvey Milk Way to get to my gym, I can't possibly imagine living there.

Holding the invitation in my hand, I mull over how it all started with Bob Critzer.

In the three years he was my choir director, the nicest thing I remember him saying to me was, "You look much thinner. You should have throat and sinus surgery more often." Three years of bitchy banter sounds exhausting, but I was younger then and it flew by like a three-day weekend in Provincetown. I heard the term "fag hag" plenty of times in high school. I hated it. Neither the fag nor the hag comes out sounding dewy, sweet, and kind. I wasn't a fag hag. I was just a teen with a weight problem who loved a man with chiseled cheekbones and a caustic wit. A simple midwestern gal who loved her gay choir teacher. Nothing more.

The first time I saw Mr. Critzer was at show choir placement auditions. He breezed into the choir room, his nose tilted up in the air, one hand cradling a giant stack of sheet music and the other swinging out to the side and randomly gesturing, like he was composing music as he walked.

He gave a quick "I hate you all" glance around the room and then sat down at the piano and started trilling up and down the keyboard like Liberace.

In order to get into Counterpoints you had to be able to sing "On a Clear Day." It was a tough and humiliating song with painfully high notes and throat-ripping low notes that only a four-pack-a-day smoker could hit. It was so difficult that people would either whisper the entire thing or belt it out off-key. It was like a talent show at an insane asylum for deaf people. I stood in front of Mr. Critzer for my audition, shaking with nerves. He gave me a squinty glare that probably meant "You're a dime-a-dozen low-voiced alto who will look fat in our dresses," but I saw it as "You and I are bigger than high school; we are divas. Let's show these rubes how it's done."

I opened my mouth and started singing. Critzer stopped playing the piano and looked out the window. "Sorry. I thought for sure that a semitruck just went rumbling past. My *god,* that's a low voice." It was humiliating to be compared to a passing big rig, but it was also an honor. He hadn't said a thing to any of the other students auditioning. Not even the few rare perfect-pitch sopranos.

Singing had always been something I loved to do, but I'd never considered myself to be especially gifted until I was standing in front of Mr. Critzer. High school was full of opportunities for trauma. There was a large jock kid who would moo like a cow whenever he passed my locker. There were fistfights in the hallways and moments of silence during the vice principal's morning announcements for the young boy or girl who had been killed in a car wreck over the weekend coming home from the prom. Even with an old-timey song like "On a Clear Day," it was so enjoyable to have a way to release all the tension and emotions just by opening up your mouth wide and letting sound come out—"singing," I believe they call it. Critzer always pushed me to open up even wider, go even deeper. I was so hungry for it, you would have thought I was singing in secret under Taliban rule.

Thanks to the low turnout of five-hundred-pound gospel-singing black men, I got in.

He kicked me out the first week.

Before the class bell rang, I'd been regaling my fellow altos with my classic "The time a guy sneezed into my mouth when I was going downhill on a roller coaster" story. Mr. Critzer came rushing into the choir room, threw down the ridiculously tall stack of sheet music he was always carrying around, and with wildly dramatic facial expressions and sweeping arm movements (he looked like Norma Desmond directing traffic), he silently mimed his commands to us to "All rise . . . eyes on me . . . deep breaths . . . wide face . . . one and a two and a—"

Normally, I couldn't take my eyes off of him, but I was almost at the point in the story where I sit in the church van for the rest of the day, petrified that nobody will ever want to kiss a girl that has had another man's snot in her mouth. Mr. Critzer slammed his hand on the piano. "LAUREN WEEDMAN! If Jesus Christ himself were standing up here, you would not stop talking."

His face, which was already pretty ruddy, turned bright red.

In Indiana, to hear Jesus Christ's name said out loud in a public school without being followed by "is my lord and savior" was shocking. It had a bit of a "motherfucker" spice to it.

That's probably how he talks to his friends, I thought. He's speaking to me as an equal. A peer.

"Listen, if Jesus Christ were up there, I believe I would stop talking. Though it depends if it was the foxy Richard Gere–looking one or the Willem Dafoe, am I right?"

He kicked me out of the class but let me come back the next day. A week later he gave me the scat solo in a Cole Porter medley we were doing, so he believed in my talent. Either that or he really did hate me. "Zat do zat do zay bud du du duah day zu" was tough to memorize.

That first year in Counterpoints was also the first year I started waking up in the middle of the night with full-blown death anxiety. All those moments of silence during the morning announcements for our departed classmates got to me. The fact that I didn't know them personally didn't matter. It felt like I'd reached the age where I was finally eligible for death. They got my application and I qualified.

The anxiety attacks could be avoided as long as Spook, my cat, let me sleep through the night. Spook was a long-haired white killer who would swallow baby birds with no chewing; she'd just gulp them down whole like she was taking her One A Day vitamin. Her favorite way to pull me out of a deep sleep was to knead on my chest with her paws. Her kitty breast exam would be followed by her trying to stick her paws into my mouth. Even if she started to lick my teeth I tried to keep myself from fully waking up because I knew that once I was awake I'd start thinking about eternity and my place in it. I'd throw Spook out the window so she could go give some baby squirrels death anxiety and lie on my bed, staring into the darkness. "There will come a day when there will be no more Lauren. At first it will be 'Lauren's been dead one year,' and then, 'Oh, she's been dead around ten years now,' and eventually, it will be, 'Wait. Who's Lauren?'"

I'd sit up in bed, my dried-out mouth wide open, and let out a silent arid scream. The only way to pull myself out of the blackness was mind control. I'd actually say to myself, "I am going to have a sexy fantasy . . . here it goes."

My go-to fantasy was to imagine a life-size naked Ken doll standing by my bed. Nobody was around to see, and I was allowed to do whatever I wanted to do to him. He'd let me knock on his plastic bump and kiss him. After that, we'd lie on the bed and hold hands. This was eerily similar to my sex life with many of my future closeted gay boyfriends. Sometimes if Ken wasn't up to the task of trumping my disappearance off the planet, I'd bring in the big guns. David Bowie. The "personal assistant of David Bowie" fantasy was always the same, and it always worked to get my mind off my place in the universe. We never had sex, but he loved me deeper than he could ever love any of the supermodels he had sex with. He'd tell me how he loved my personality and wanted me around him for the rest of his life. He could be himself with me. Even in my sexual fantasies I was a fag hag.

The best time to catch up on any sleep I lost to the abyss was during my teacher assistant hour. Second semester, I'd offered to be Critzer's assistant and sit in his office for one period a day to help him with whatever he needed help with. Nobody understood why I'd want to do this. "Do you need an extra hour of him yelling at you?"

I knew he wouldn't yell at me one on one, and I never saw it as yelling anyway. When I asked him about assisting him, he'd said, "Oh please, no." But I begged him, and he let me. He was never in his office. So where was he? The idea that he'd be sitting in the teachers' lounge, drinking a Capri Sun and chatting about gardening and the symphony with the other teachers seemed impossible. In fact, I never saw him talking with the other teachers. Maybe he felt a little above them. It was rumored that he'd left Counterpoints to pursue his career as a classical pianist, only to be back one year later. Mr. Critzer was a very private man. You could rely on most teachers to snap under the pressure of teaching high school kids and overshare about their divorce and their mentally challenged daughter they were forced to institutionalize, but Mr. Critzer kept his personal life a complete mystery. When he was playing music and directing he was a force, but out in the hallway I'd notice him struggling to carry enormous stacks of music theory books, weaving in and out pods of loud high-fiving jocks, rolling his eyes and shaking his head at them. Which was exactly how I felt. My world was entirely set in my music and theater classes, where a funny chubby girl who dressed like a forty-two-year-old Jersey housewife—Sun-In blond hair, blue eye shadow, and orange tan set off by my full-length baby blue sundress—could thrive.

The one time he came into his office to pick up some folders he looked surprised to see me. I took that opportunity to create an awkward moment where I asked him how his dating life was going and gave him an "I know you know that I know" kind of nod so he knew that he could speak freely. He grabbed his brown paper bag lunch and walked out.

It always blew my mind when people refused to see that Mr. Critzer was gay. Nowadays my so-called gaydar gets me in trouble all the time as I walk down the street declaring, "Gay, gay, not gay, kind of gay, gay for Alec Baldwin," but at the time I was one of the few kids who knew that Mr. Critzer was gay and one of the very few who had no problem with it. This was in no small part thanks to Sid and Sharon Weedman.

Long ago, the conservative, cat-sweater-wearing, easy-listening-music Republicans I called parents had been show folk. My father was a theater production major in college. He stage managed musicals and my mother danced in the chorus. All of my mother's dance partners had been gay. My father fell in love with my mother watching her being tossed from one gay man to another in the production of *The King and I* at Butler University. Most of our Indiana neighbors held on to the popular "homos are fudge packers on a butt bus to hell to have sex with a donkey" attitude, but I grew up with family friends like "the two Jims." I'd asked my dad if they were brothers with the same name who fell on hard times and were forced to live together, and he'd told me simply, "Nope. They're gay." This "Tall Jim loves Big Jim" matter-of-fact attitude had been introduced to me at a very young age. Of course, it was also presented to me at a Klan rally while my father's lover molested me, but no childhood is perfect. (Oh, gurl, no you didn't. Snap. Head roll, etc.)

There I was, marching in the hallways, screaming for everyone to *"wake up and smell the gay coffee!"* whenever Critzer came up, while each of my high school relationships featured a moment when I was pulled aside by a well-meaning friend and told that my talented makeup artist / choreographer beau was gay. If I had a dime for every time someone tried to convince me that one of my high school boyfriends was gay, I'd have eighty cents. That's not one boyfriend and eight confrontations. That's eight boyfriends, one confrontation each.

My first year of Counterpoints I fell in love with a delicate-boned tenor named Brett. Kerry, a shrill soprano with long red hair, pulled me aside before our big band medley rehearsal and said, "You know how people are always screaming '*fag!*' at Brett wherever he goes? Like at the mall and church and while he's sleeping? Do you ever wonder why?"

Jealousy, I thought. People were jealous. He was confident and talented. He was so much more passionate about music and movies than other boys.

If someone were really gay, would they swish down the hallway and slap football players' asses? Would they sketch naked boys with gigantic hard-ons in their journals? *No.* That would be far too obvious.

Brett had a toilet seat hung on his bedroom wall and if you lifted the lid up, Woody Allen's face looked out at you. On our dates he'd invite me to his parents' modest ranch-style home and make me hummus from scratch while wearing one of his mother's dresses. The night would end with us talking in English accents as we wished each other "Good night, dahling!" and air-kissed each other, "Mwah! Mwah!"

On the drive back to my house I'd be giddy with love, thinking this is what it must have been like to have been a part of Andy Warhol's Factory!

Except with less sexy time. Our romantic troubles were entirely my fault, I told myself.

Waiting for me to roll my control-top underwear off and stash it under the front seat wasn't a teenage-boy aphrodisiac, so I stopped wearing them to show my openness to adventure.

After three months it didn't make any difference, and I started to get frustrated with Brett's lack of physical affection toward me. One night, parked in my Chevy Malibu Classic after his five hundredth blow job, I brought it up.

"Hey, do you think that you'd ever want to . . ." I nodded toward my lap.

"Tie your shoes for you? Never."

If I had to get too detailed about it, I knew that I'd end up talking myself out of it. Better to keep it light and jokey.

"You knowa whata I mean. Ia scratcha your back, you scratcha mine?"

Brett took a deep breath and turned to face me, "Listen, Chef Boyardee, I wouldn't hold your breath on that one because you'd die. Weren't you there when I made my announcement in the lunchroom about how even the word 'vagina' makes me sick? It sounds like something that if it got on you, you'd be like, 'GET IT OFF! GET IT OFF!' I know that I spoke for every person in that cafeteria when I said that it's a myth that anyone wants to spend anytime down there at all. You can send me a postcard because I won't be visiting." He looked down at his watch and screamed, "I'm late! I'm doing makeup for *The King and I*. I have to turn twenty doughy-white Hoosiers into Asians. Wish me luck."

I had lots of gay-boy crushes before high school. It started in eighth grade with Marc Borders. After puberty, I was drawn to the sweet, playful boys. The ones who were quick to laugh and just as quick to grab my arm as we marched down the mall singing "We're Off to See the Wizard" at full volume and doing the little dance step that went with it, too. Even back in eighth grade I had well-meaning friends who were trying to clue me in that my boyfriends were in love with boys. "I saw him making out with this guy and then he gave him a rose and yelled 'I love you!' as the guy drove off." It all sounded to me like crazy made-up urban myth stuff. Their stories were as real to me as "my friend of a friend put her gerbil in the microwave one time . . ."

It was Brett who, at the beginning of junior year, stopped my friend Wendy and me on our way into Counterpoints rehearsal to tell us that Critzer was out sick with a chest cold.

Wendy suggested we skip class and go get some biscuits and gravy at Shoney's all-you-can-eat breakfast buffet. "If Mr. Critzer isn't there, it's a waste of our time." Wendy was a buxom redhead who dated straight boys and had a crude sense of humor that would have put Don Rickles to shame. I agreed with Wendy. I always did or else she'd titty punch me and tell me I smelled like a maxi pad.

After a few weeks of Critzer's on-and-off absence, we had it down to where if we walked up to the rehearsal room and heard any voice that was not Mr. Critzer taking attendance, we'd just keep on walking out the front door of the school. It was easy to slip out of the school when you were in show choir; you just threw some red taffeta over your shoulder with the "Don't you dare. *I'm a Counterpoint!*" snooty attitude that Critzer instilled in us and everybody assumed you were off to sing for some old folks somewhere. Whenever we got scared about being caught by the school cop we'd start singing the *Ain't Misbehavin'* medley for which we'd won first prize at state competition the year before. Thanks to Mr. Critzer's insanely complicated arrangement, the focus it took to sing it helped keep our nerve up to make it out of the school and into Wendy's car. We'd hold our final note—"saving my love for youuuuuuuuuuuuuu"—until we had safely made it off school property.

One day we were rushing past the Counterpoints door singing the alto part of "I'm Gonna Sit Right Down and Write Myself a Letter." It was so low we sounded like those throat-singing monks or a didgeridoo, and our low, rumbling vibrations caught the attention of Mr. Tucker, the vice principal. He was on his way into the Counterpoints room to make a special announcement. "You missed the door, ladies," he yelled at us. Oops! We stopped singing and sulked back into the room. Starving.

Mr. Tucker was a serious man who frowned a lot and stormed through the hallways with a giant wad of keys dangling off his belt like some sort of gladiator weapon. Tucker had been a football player and had a smooshed face that looked like someone had sat on top of his head. Or his helmet had been on too tight. The expression on his face was always very gloomy. He could be letting you know that he just saw a puppy licking a lollipop and it would still feel like Vincent Price trying to scare the shit out of you. That day his news actually matched his face.

"You all know that Mr. Critzer has been ill. Well, I wanted to let you all know that he's gotten very sick and he's been moved to intensive care."

The choir got very quiet except for Jill, a high soprano who also happened to be Mr. Tucker's daughter. She broke out in sobs. Wendy leaned over and whispered, "Man, she'll take any opportunity to break down so her daddy will hold her." Jill and her father were infamous for calling, "Love you, baby!" "Love you, Daddy!" if they crossed paths during the school day. Their love was so open that we just assumed that they were a couple, which would also explain why Jill always brought stuffed animals to school to comfort her. In reality they were simply a father and daughter who loved each other, and that made us jealous so we turned it into something disturbing so we could handle it.

Jill was so distraught that her father had to French braid her hair to help calm her down. Something felt fishy. A week ago Critzer had a bad head cold and now he's in intensive care? "Come on!" Wendy had said to me after class. "He's a gay man in this conservative, boring midwestern town. Some boy probably complained that he winked at him and they fired him and now they have to create this totally unbelievable 'in the hospital for a runny nose' thing so they can cover their gay-fearing asses."

I agreed with Wendy, and this time it was because I thought it was maybe true and not just because I was trying to avoid the titty punch.

Holiday break (or, as it was called back in my day, "The Superior Race's Break for Christmas and Skiing") had just started. I was coming home from Christmas shopping at the mall, acting like the bags hanging off my arms were full of presents for my family—"Don't look in here! It's your present!"—when in reality they were full of Little Debbie snack cakes for me to binge on, when Wendy called to tell me that Mr. Critzer had died. Her mother had seen his obituary in the newspaper.

It had gone from "Mr. Critzer has a cold" to "Mr. Critzer is in the hospital" to "Mr. Critzer is dead" in six weeks.

Wendy was the first person I knew who suggested that maybe his death was AIDS related. But how could that be? He didn't look all frail and awful like the people I'd seen on the nightly news. It was all so sudden and bizarre. The obituary said he'd died from pneumonia. It made no sense to me whatsoever. He might as well have died from stubbing his toe.

The last time I had seen Mr. Critzer, we'd been getting ready to perform at an upscale (it had carpet) old-age home. Wendy and I were unloading top hats and canes off the bus, laughing about an incident that had happened the last time we'd performed at a nursing home. During that show, an elderly man in the front row had keeled over in the middle of our rousing version of "Up, Up and Away." He'd done it right on the lyric "Up, up and awayyyyy." It was like he heard it and thought, that sounds good, and down he went. The tiny lady he fell on had been really enjoying the show and was annoyed at the interruption. She pushed him off of her, let him fall to the floor, called, "*Nurse,*" and scooted her chair over so she could enjoy the rest of the show. There wasn't much to hear at that point. Most of the choir was unable to sing due to their complete horror at witnessing what they'd thought was a man dying during the show. Thanks to the healing power of music or the end of his seizure, the man popped back up before the nurse got to him and started clapping as if nothing had happened. Wendy and I were in hysterics remembering this when we spotted Mr. Critzer sitting by himself in the very dimly lit hallway. "Shit," Wendy said when she saw him. "He's back. Hopefully he won't smell the biscuits and gravy on us. Here, take a mint."

"You two just never shut up, do you?" Critzer said when he saw us heading his way. His normal "Get these ignorant hayseeds away from me" tone and disgusted eye rolls were gone. His zing was gone. He looked small and tired. My immediate instinct was to cheer him up. "You'll be sorry you're always telling us to shut up when we're up there accepting our Oscars," Wendy said to him.

For years after his death we replayed what he said back and it never stopped breaking our hearts, and to be honest, freaking our shit out.

"Oh, I'll be long gone before that happens."

At the time, I'd been angry that he was implying it was going to take so long.

After we got back from our holiday break, everyone was in shock. Counterpoints not only lost our captain; we lost our minds. A sweet old white lady, Bea Arthur, was standing behind Mr. Critzer's piano our first day back. Mrs. Arthur had been the one who had taken over as the director of Counterpoints the year Mr. Critzer was gone pursing his career as a pianist. She'd come out of retirement to help out until the school could find a replacement.

Mrs. Arthur had the unfortunate job of leading the choir through a "grief session." The sopranos wanted to sob and hold one another. The only thing I wanted to do was visit the hospital where he died. Talk to the nurses. Get some information.

Mrs. Arthur asked us to circle up our chairs.

"I know this has been an emotional time for many of you. Losing a teacher is hard. Losing a friend is even harder. So I thought we could just take some time to just remember."

Things were going to get ugly, swing choir—style. Shrill and dramatic. Alison, a contralto who had given Valentine's Day cards the year before to everyone in the choir that were signed "Love in Him" (which, it had to be explained to me, meant Jesus; I thought it was some R & B way of saying "Put some loving in your man"), came after Wendy and me with such venom you'd have thought that we were the ones who killed him. Based on the looks on their faces, it was clear most of the choir felt like Alison did.

She started off calmly asking Mrs. Arthur why the funeral, which took place a week after he died, had been held in a strip mall. We had all gone.

Mrs. Arthur explained that the family chose the location.

My dad had told me that no regular home would handle his body. So they had to rent out an empty store space in a strip mall. It had been some sort of Mail Boxes Etc. store. The leftover shelving on the walls and packing tape in the corner of the room supersized the dreariness of it all. Thanks to the bizarre choice somebody made to have an open casket, we all had a chance to look at his body. For a dead person he looked incredibly healthy. Certainly not gaunt or ill in the way that I'd come to envision AIDS deaths. As always, the sopranos were in their own operatic world of emotion. Alison took her moment in front of the body, wailing and sobbing. All the sopranos were collapsing into each other's arms. "My god, I touched his hand! He feels like chicken. No. This can't be. *No00!*"

The thing I was most struck by was the pair of oversize Charles Nelson Reilly glasses Critzer had on. We'd never seen him wear them. Wendy's theory was that someone's glasses had fallen off their face as they filed by for the viewing and the person had been too skeeved out to retrieve them, thinking, "Forget it. I'll get another pair." Was nobody around after he died who knew what he looked like in life to advise the funeral home? Or were those glasses symbol number 344 that I knew nothing about him?

Through her tears, Alison continued to dominate the grief circle. Now she wanted to know if the older lady standing in the back of the room at the funeral had been his wife.

"No," Mrs. Arthur said, her voice full of patience and kindness and just the tiniest hint of "you dumb ass," "that was his mother."

Alison addressed the entire choir, speaking through a crazy frozen grin and staring straight at me and Wendy. "I just want to say that I loved Mr. Critzer a lot. And I am tired of some of the rumors that are being spread."

Wendy and I were losing our minds.

I can't remember who said it, Wendy or I, but one of us stood up and yelled, "He wasn't married because he was gay and he probably had AIDS!" I'm thinking it was Wendy since she was more of a yeller. When it came to dealing with large groups of my fellow teenagers, I was more of a nodder and a "yeah, that's right" type.

Alison whipped around to face us, her smile gone. "I would think that you two would feel bad enough as it is. You wasted his time, and he didn't have that much time to waste. You disrespected him when he was alive and you are disrespecting him now that he is dead. He worked all of his life to arrange music, and it is not easy to arrange music. Especially some of the complicated medleys that we've done this year. And then he died without ever having a wife or having kids."

Mrs. Arthur glanced over at Wendy and me. "Let me just say this. When he died, he was in the AIDS ward."

The truth, or the indirect implication of truth, felt so good, but not to Alison, who let out a frustrated scream.

"Ahhhh! The principal told us that he died from pneumonia! Why would the principal lie to us? What does he have to gain? He's already the principal!"

Desperate for some sanity and for the bell that signaled the end of class to ring, Mrs. Arthur turned to the boys to save her. "Any of our boys have any experiences they'd like to share? Maybe a happy memory?" A pale, underfed senior who had been ordered by Mr. Critzer, "Never sing. Lip-synch," raised his hand. He had sweat dripping down his forehead and his voice had a pervy quiver to it. "Once . . . I was watching TV and . . . umm . . . I saw a gay channel. Gay stuff." His touching remembrance opened the door for Eric, a skinny black tenor, to share his equally unrelated homophobic thoughts about his cousin who was a lesbian "and her big thing was that being a lesbian is a lot more than just not caring what you look like." Alison started wailing about how unfair it was that she couldn't bring her Bible to school but she had to "sit here and listen to this!" Brett and the other closeted gay boys in the choir sat in complete silence.

I was surprised by how truly stricken with grief some of the students were during the grief session. They didn't know him. Not like I did. Now that I think of it, I might have seen Mr. Critzer in those glasses at some point. In fact, I'm sure I did. It was in his office. He put them on in order to read lyrics printed on the back of a record album. I think. Or maybe he wore them to drive and he came to one of our shows at the JCC with them on? I'm not sure. The image of him in the casket with them on has scared all my other glasses-wearing memories away.

The bell rang, and how Mr. Critzer died was never mentioned in choir again.

I'm buying a plane ticket, and I'm going to the gala. Bob Critzer was never properly mourned, but he's going to be. I'm going to wear an oversize white T-shirt with a spray-painted picture of Mr. Critzer's face on the front, like they do with murdered rappers. I'm going to write LOSE WEIGHT—ASK ME HOW on the back to lure people in. People will tap me on the shoulder: "Excuse me, can you tell me a little about your weight loss plan?" "Sure!" I'll say. "What you want to do is focus on expending more calories than you're taking in. You could also GET AIDS AND DIE ALONE LIKE ROBERT CRITZER DID!"

Wait a minute, I should be calling the planners of the gala directly and giving them the good news. I'm a regular on a "It's not TV, it's HBO" show, *Looking*, for god's sake! The show is about a group of gay boys in their thirties living in San Francisco looking for love. I'm the straight one. The "approachable" one. My character, Doris, is the "fruit fly" or "fag hag" fun one! Paid to be a fag hag. Sometimes the good Lord does have a plan.

Just because two gay pride parades turned me down after I e-mailed them and offered to sit in a convertible and throw butterscotch hard candies and condoms at the leather-bound gay men pushing their babies in strollers (actual babies, not men dressed as babies) along the parade route doesn't mean that I still don't have some "I'm on TV" sway. I'll offer to give a speech about how the choir changed my life and give Mr. Critzer the memorial he deserves. Why didn't I think of this before? And why don't I have more followers on Instagram? The other actors have hundreds of thousands and have to use fake names to avoid being stalked. I'll do a little shout-out about my social media presence during my gala speech.

I may have to lie and say that the sexy boys I'm on the show with are coming with me. I'd love to have those boys with me. What if I showed up with the main actor, Jonathan Groff? Jonathan was on *Glee*, a show about swing choirs! They would lose their minds after I lost mine. I'd forget about correcting the wrongs of show choir history and would spend my whole time making Jonathan leave voice mail messages for my friend's kids as the moose from *Frozen*.

Before I get too crazy with it, I should make sure that Critzer

really has been forgotten all these years. If there's a half marathon in his honor or a musical about his life, I could look like a
real ass. *Glee* could have done an entire episode about him; my
TV's being used exclusively to play Wii *Just Dance 2014*, so I
wouldn't know.

If you died before the Internet came around, you're really dead.
I've been scouring the Internet for more than an hour and I can't
find anything about Critzer anywhere.

Finally, I type "find a grave site" into my search engine and I
find a website called Find a Grave and there he is. His gravestone
is small, gray, and rectangular, with his name and birth and death
dates on it. That's it. "Robert E. Critzer 1942–1986." There's a section below the photo of his grave for "family information." Mother,
father, sisters and brothers, and so on. It's blank. For fun—because
forget Tinder; nothing is more fun than trolling through graves—
I type in the last name Critzer and find three other Critzers buried in the same small graveyard in this little Indiana town.

My *Murder, She Wrote* mode kicks in, and I sign up for a temporary membership at Ancestry.com to see if it will list his parents' names. It does, and it was their graves I'd found. The section
for family members is filled in on their pages. Nobody lists Bob. I
have a very strong urge to drive to his grave and stick a plastic
sunflower by his gravestone. Next I'll be buying Beanie Babies at
the gas station to stack on top of his grave, so I better stay home.

I'm back on Ancestry.com to cancel my temporary membership
since I'm always forgetting to cancel subscriptions. I'm probably
still paying for *Tiger Beat*. They have a copy of his birth certificate.
Santa Monica, California, is listed as his place of birth. I'm in Santa
Monica. That's where I am at this very moment. I live here. He was
born here. The city where I'm sitting right now was his place of
birth. This is a sign. I give his spirit a little jazz hand high-five.
"Don't worry, Bob. I've got this."

You know who may be able to help me? Those gay-loving hea-
thens back in Indianapolis, my parents. Mr. Critzer was close with
one of my dad's good friends, Charles, an arts writer for *The Indianapolis Star.* My dad had called Mr. Staff after hearing the news
of Critzer's death, and he had been the one who confirmed that
he'd died from complications from HIV.

Charles and Bob would go see the Indianapolis Symphony
together. Maybe they were a couple. I've never asked.

My dad answers the phone.

"Jake's pool hall. Jake speaking."

He asks me if I'm doing anything exciting.

I tell him how I'm trying to find out more about my old choir
director Mr. Critzer.

He tells me that's not very exciting.

"Anything else? Any movies with celebrities we'd know? Or is
it all the gay show still?"

"The gay show was canceled, and no big movie plans. So do
you think I could call Charles and ask him about Mr. Critzer?"

"He's dead."

"Is everybody dead?"

"Yep."

My dad was a big speech giver back in the day. He'll like the
idea of me crashing the gala and giving a speech about Critzer.

"Save your money. They're never going to let you do it."

"Actually, Dad, I think they might. I *was* on *Looking* and
that's—"

"The gay show? Nobody watched that. Isn't that why it got
canceled?"

The next morning, my dad sends me an email with a link to an
article in the *Bedford Gazette.* The first thing I do is scan the article for
my name—old habits die hard—but Bob's name is there. The article

is profiling one of its locals, Judy Harris. She's starting a musical theater company at the Bedford community center. Judy talks about
being in Counterpoints. According to her dates, she was in Counterpoints the same years I was. Her name sounds vaguely familiar.

In the article, she's talking about how Bob Critzer was her
greatest mentor.

Maybe she was a year ahead of me. Why don't I remember her?

"If it wasn't for the belief that Mr. Critzer had in me I would
have never made it into Carnegie Mellon music school. We all
need teachers who are willing to not only write the recommendation letter but make that extra call."

He made a call for her? I'd asked him to write a letter to help
me get an audition with a local vocal coach for after-school lessons, and he'd told me that he never did that sort of thing. Ever.
She goes on to say how important it had been to hear from her
greatest mentor that she had talent. That in addition, the honor
of having "private vocal lessons" with him the last few years of his
life changed her life. She hopes to pass some of what he taught her
on to her students. He gave her private lessons, and even more
shocking that that, he told her—to her face—that she had talent.

I'm not going to the gala. Not because he never did any of those
things for me but because they've probably already asked Judy to
give the speech, which she'll be thrilled to do after she gets done
running in the twentieth annual Bob Critzer 5K.

That night I've calmed down considerably. I'm going to the
gala not for social activism or to increase my Twitter followers but
because I bet it's going to be a fantastic evening of song and dance.
That's the way Critzer would want to be remembered. Big hands,
big faces, deep breaths, red glitter, and five-part harmonies. Not a
forty-six-year-old straight woman screaming "IT WAS AIDS!" in
people's faces as they peel their shrimp.

Thinking about how I was just looking for an excuse to publicly emote all this time, making me no better than a soprano, is a bummer. Since my David Bowie fantasy stopped working when he tried to form the band Tin Machine, I've had to find other ways to survive dark nights of the soul. In Portland I made the slightly pathetic discovery that if I'm having a awful evening, instead of hopping right back on Tinder to meet the next sex addict who will capture my heart and leaving me sobbing in the rain, I can instead walk very slowly, back and forth, in front of a packed gay bar until someone recognizes me, and my Friday night, and my soul, is saved.

I had to walk back and forth four times in front of the Abbey in West Hollywood tonight before I heard a boy scream and yell, "DORIS!" He probably saw me and immediately knew what I was doing. Who cares? I feigned surprise at finding myself in the heart of the gayest of gay bars.

"Oh, is this a gay bar? Is that what all those rainbow flags mean?"

It's gay karaoke night. Things are looking up. An ornery little Gay-Asian named Tag is by my side all night. After we share our stories of heartbreak and broken dreams with each other Tag insists my troubles would be solved if I accept I'm a lesbian and or have gender-reassignment surgery. His bold sassiness makes me giddy. The more outrageous he is the more delighted I am. When I ask Tag to check to see if "On a Clear Day You Can See Forever" is in the karaoke songbook, he suggests I stick to songs about crazy woman wandering the streets with dead flowers in her hair. "Honey, get to know yourself. You're an alto and that's your genre."

I'm at the bar until closing, hugging beautiful boys, laughing myself into coughing fits and singing Helen Reddy songs. I mean, come on, you gotta love those gays.

Gang Toast

Round white spots have appeared all over my shoulders and chest. It looks like I fell asleep in the sun after somebody's coin purse spilled all over me.

My dermatologist, Dr. Adair, insists it's not a big deal. "It's just a fungus."

Oh good. I was worried I'd caught ringworm from the manure-covered donkey at the farmers' market petting zoo. Whew, it's only a fungus.

"It's like athlete's foot, but all over your body."

No more details are needed. Fungus really ends the meeting.

Dr. Adair's skin is so perfectly white and smooth, you could use it as a dry-erase board. A fungus would slip right off her. Fungus grabs right on to me and won't let go. It announces to the world my secret that I don't always shower after I work out. I really can't keep a secret.

The final diagnosis—tinea versicolor—is also known as "You're Disgusting."

My body doesn't want me to date. It's not letting me. I'm the one who wasn't showering after spin class, so maybe I was getting in my own way, but it is odd that the night after I put myself on Tinder I'm covered in fungi. Honestly, I'm not completely ready to start dating, but I thought if I went on Tinder and saw someone I knew whom I'd always wished I could date, maybe that would be a good way to start. I got as far as writing a jokey profile blurb—"Looking for a man to pay for my other fake boob and raise my child while I have sex with your brother"—and lost my nerve. There're a lot of stand-ups and men giving speeches at weddings ("not my own!") on Tinder. Lots of men holding microphones in front of brick walls.

Apparently the fungus is very heavy on my back. There could be a KICK ME sign from middle school back there. It's been forever since I or anyone else has seen my back.

Dr. Adair mentions an ointment I could use but suggests it would be a lot faster if she prescribed some pills for me. "It's super-easy. Just take the pills for four days, avoid alcohol, and—"

"Is there an easier option than the easier option?" I ask. "Like maybe a skin graft or heavy makeup?"

It's not that I can't go four days without drinking, but I don't want to go four days without drinking. If it means I'll be limited to dating within the fungus community or even have to start shower-ing, so be it. I'm not ready to give up my three glasses of wine a night. Not yet. It would be a shock to my divorced system and could even be dangerous. What if I had seizures—or worse . . . feelings?

Dr. Adair tries to frown at me, but thanks to her perfectly dis-tributed Botox injections, it's more of a blank open stare. But her tilted head and hand on her hip communicate what her face no longer can: "If you can't go four days without drinking, I think we need to have a different conversation."

"Hey, unless that conversation is about good wines under ten bucks and the latest episode of *Orange Is the New Black*, I'm not sure I could stay interested!" I say. Then I ask her if she could tell me about the ointment and if she could not say the word "oint-ment" and use "lotion" instead.

The lotion was a perfectly viable option, except that it was to be applied twice a day and I should be sure to have my husband or my partner help me with the hard-to-reach spots in the middle of my back.

"I don't have a husband or a partner. I'm divorced."

Dr. Adair is a dermatologist married to a plastic surgeon; the words "I am divorced" are not ones she's unfamiliar with. I've been divorced twice now, so you'd think it wouldn't feel so awful to say those words, but it does. I'm still so confused as to how I got here. No, I'm not. I know how I got divorced. I'm just completely unsure of how to move forward. My friends keep telling me, "You need to be single for one year, at least." I had a nice sex fling right after I split with David, and that was even hard to negotiate. After sleeping with the guy, whom I'd known for years, I wasn't sure how it was supposed to move forward. When do you say "boyfriend," and how do you know when it's over when everyone is so busy with jobs and kids? How on earth would I ever fall in love again? All is not lost. I have my fungus to keep me company.

Dr. Adair wants to help me get rid of my fungus. She's gone through this before with some of her elderly patients who live alone. "What I have them do, and it works really well, is to take the oint-ment and spread it on a doorjamb, and then they can lean up against it, rub up and down to distribute the ointment over the infected areas. Do you understand what I mean?"

If I apply fungus ointment with a doorjamb, if I take off my shirt and rub up and down against a door frame, like a bear scratching its back against a tree, I will have hit a new divorce low. I cannot think of a more depressing divorced moment besides signing the actual divorce papers.

I'd rather take the pills. I don't care if the white wine I won't be able to give up causes partial paralysis.

I can't start dating right away anyway; I'm leaving for Boise for a week. Dating in Boise would be impossible. Even if I'm just looking to have some crazy divorced sex. It's such a small town, it reminds me of the joke I heard a comedian tell about being in a small-town airport and hearing an announcement over the PA: "Hey, Paul. Come here." The guy was so funny, but I can't remember his name. I'll find him on Tinder when I get back in town.

I'm going to Boise to host a fund-raiser for the Boise Contemporary Theater. I'm looking forward to seeing my friends and breathing clean air, but I'm dreading the live auction part of the fund-raiser because I'm going to be auctioned off like a heifer. It's "Dinner with Lauren Weedman and six of your friends catered in your home by a local fancy chef." There's something about being single now and wanting to date, wanting to be wanted, and standing onstage as somebody begs for money for you. "Do I hear three hundred? Three hundred over here? Three hundred over there . . . You're not going to find an overbite like that anymore, people. Orthodontics have come too far; she's rare. Honey, dance around and show them how you can entertain yourself. How about two-fifty; let's start at two-fifty." I'm going to get so marked down that the part-time lighting guy who works at the theater could afford me.

Once I'm actually in Boise, I meet up for some pizza with my friend Keily, a feisty little lesbian poet with a Mohawk who is sick of hearing me make fun of myself.

"Shut up. You could get a hot young guy so easy. Stop saying you're a fungus-covered heifer!" She laughs and gives me a high kick to the hip. "Oh man, you're killing me, Weedman!"

She's punched me so many times with her bony little fists since we've been walking to lunch, I had to ask her to walk on the other side of me because my right arm was getting sore.

When I do meet someone good-looking, I get so blinded by the thrill of a handsome man's attention I overlook the little voice in my stomach that yells at me, "Bitch, please, stay away from that man! You don't mess with a self-identified sex addict! No more 'Oh, I've done some bad things that I deeply regret but I've changed' or 'Oh man, I forgot my wallet in the car again.'" Apparently, my inner voice is a scene from *How Stella Got Her Groove Back*.

The fund-raiser could turn into a form of speed dating for me, according to Keily, if I grabbed a chair as I'm being auctioned off and started humping it. "And even if you didn't get a date out of it, you'd freak the shit out of all the wives."

Keily is more punchy and roundhouse kicky than normal because she's getting her first tattoo tomorrow. A local tattoo artist who won a Baked Potato Best of Boise award last year designed a Celtic symbol for strength that he's going to draw on Keily's arm. Keily knows exactly what she wants, where she wants it, and what it means to her. I may find that inspiring; I may not. I'll check with a few other people who know about that sort of thing better than I do before I decide.

"Weedman! You should get one with me!"

Funny she'd mention that. I've been throwing around the idea of a second tattoo. A little design to symbolize this recent life change. As if I'd ever forget.

Getting a tattoo at my age feels a little weird. Ten years ago, when I got my first tattoo, I was already worried about what would happen to the integrity of the design as I aged. I imagined being seventy, with my grandkids trying to clean up their old bearded grandma. As they were retying my nightgown, they'd notice something they'd think was dried food in the wrinkly folds of my chest skin. "Oh, let me get a wet rag and get that, Grandma."

"That's not dried spaghetti, kids," I'd say, pulling my skin out to straighten it. "It's a lone wolf howling in the silhouette of the full moon. It's not bad hygiene. It's a symbol of Grandma's core loneliness!"

But then I realized that old skin will just be a big mash of moles, scars, bumps, holes, and waffle-iron burns, so who cares.

How can I say no to Keily, the only gay in the village? I'm always trying to get her to admit how hard it must have been growing up gay in a small town in a red state. She denies it, but I don't believe her. There must have been a few stares at the rodeo. Whispers behind her back at the annual potato festival, if there is an annual potato festival. Her mother was diagnosed with cancer recently. I love her mom. I don't want her to tell her mom that I wouldn't get a tattoo with her. Her mom will think it's just like when nobody would sit next to them at the potato rodeos.

Getting some "ink" would be the perfect subculture/hipster/ midlife crisis "I'm with you, sister" thing to do. I have no idea what I'd get or where.

Like a Native American chief receiving a vision, I proclaim, "The lesbian with the Mohawk knows her heart, and the black hawk has flown the skies at dusk. It is time for me to get another tattoo."

The phone in my hotel rings at eight A.M.; it's Keily.

"Weedman! Get up! You're getting a tattoo today! My guy's booked months ahead of time, but I found a place that can take you today. Get in your car and start driving!"

That isn't going to happen, I tell her.

I'd planned on looking up some design ideas last night, but instead I ended up going barhopping with a very handsome pilot from Georgia. He sat next to me at the hotel bar, and after we talked about flying for Delta and the differences between Atlanta and Boise, he offered to get me out of the stuffy hotel bar and show me some local bars. His name was Dale. He wasn't really my type, and thank god. This guy had a job and owned houses in two different cities. Not a lot of "funky independence" art lover coming off him, but I'd thought that was much better. I felt safer. He's a "do the right thing" guy, I thought.

Fast-forward three hours later. Mr. Do the Right Thing was drunk whispering in my ear in front of a table of his friends: "I'M GOING TO LICK YOUR PUSSY." His friends were mortified. "I've never seen him like this. I'm so sorry. Hey, Dale, cut it out, man." Dale put his arms up over his head and stumbled backward, slurring, "It's all good . . . I'm all good," only to do it again two seconds later. "DON'T YOU WANT ME TO LICK YOUR—" "Dale! You have got to stop. You're not getting anywhere with her like that, man." Stumbled backward, arms up. "We're good. It's all good!" I'd gotten nervous after the first few drinks when Dale started telling me how "we are the smartest people in Boise" and how nice it was to have "intellectual discussion after being around all these dumb porkers." This was after I'd asked him to pass me a napkin to spit my gum into. The local bar he took me to was a sports bar full of hard-core-looking white people. I'd stupidly bragged to Dale about being on *The Daily Show*, a problem I had the last time I was single twelve years ago. I couldn't get through any first date without mentioning it. It felt like bragging about owning a boat, except that I was fired so I don't know what I was bragging about. Dale didn't act impressed but apparently he was because he must have mentioned it to some of his buddies at the bar. Before he started shouting his lurid whispers in my ear, he was telling me about a compulsive-hair-pulling support group his ex-wife goes to.

That was six hours ago. I'm a little shaky. Keily cannot believe I had a night like I've just described. "That was here? In Boise? Are you sure you weren't in Eagle?"

Today is not the day to get a tattoo.

"Shut up! Your artist's name is Virginia. Weedman! That's my mom's name! It's a sign! My mom says you're like a daughter to her, like family, even though we never see you, by the way. Because you're a total dick, Weedman."

That's a low blow. Bringing up her mom. She knows I love her mom.

Last night was awful, but at least I walked away with my dignity. I didn't do anything ridiculous. Dale started out very normal. I'm not sure what he was doing hanging out at the hotel bar, but it was nice until it wasn't and then I left. That's dating. One down, 8,999 to go. You know what? Maybe it is a sign. My therapist had told me that yes, my family had broken apart, but I was going to get another family that was going to be so much bigger than I'd imagined it. This is what he meant. Keily is my sister. She is a part of my family and she's driving me nuts. To shut her up I'll get a tiny little star in invisible ink on the bottom of my foot.

Anywhere you want to go in Boise, Idaho, is never more than a five-minute drive. I've been on the road to the tattoo parlor for about seven minutes. In those extra two minutes the entire city changed. It's dustier. More "Hmmm, so what happens out *here?*"

The moment I park my car in Ink You's parking lot I have a very bad feeling. A *Breaking Bad* meth house, Satan screaming "GET OUT!," blood pouring down walls, pig head in the window bad vibe. At first, when I caught myself judging the gravel in the parking lot as "dirty," I thought I was nervous and looking for any reason to back out of getting the tattoo.

The front door of Ink You is locked even though a giant sign says OPEN. There's a dreadlocked white guy standing inside watching me struggle and struggle to open the door. He screams "PULL! PULL!" angrily at me, refusing to walk over to the door. Based on his skin tone and body weight, he looks like a guy who's had his fair share of struggling to open things in his life. Doors, drawers, veins. You'd think he'd have a little empathy. Suddenly a guy who looks like he's in ZZ Top runs from across the street, bangs his motorcycle helmet on the glass door, screams, "IT'S FUCKING LOCKED!" and walks away. My hero.

Dreadlocked guy unlocks the door. I make sure to tell him that I'm not with that guy who banged on the door but I do have a ten A.M. appointment. He asks me what sort of design I'm thinking of, and I ramble on like a drunk slam poet describing how "truth is truth," and "letting go so that what is shall be." I keep waiting for him to stop me, but he never does, so after ten minutes of talking in circles I wear myself out.

I tell him that I have a general idea of what sort of tattoo I want to get but was hoping to do some brainstorming with the artist who had been recommended to me, Virginia.

"She's not here yet," he says and tells me I can browse through some tattoo albums and see if I find anything in there I like.

Dreadlocked guy, who could also be called "chapped-lipped guy," grabs a beat-up photo album and tells me to have a seat in the waiting area. "Are you sure this isn't the Cheetos-eating area?" I joke, referring to the large amount of Cheetos crumbs on all the chairs. He answers, "No, it's not."

The photos in the albums are close-ups of people's red, swollen, and heavily ointmented finished tattoos. It has more of a "medical record of painful skin infections experienced by biker gangs in the seventies" feel than a sales tool for a tattoo parlor.

A young girl in an ill-fitting T-shirt with a baby in her arms appears from the back. The first thing I thought when I saw the baby was "Wow, that's a bigheaded baby," but now that a debate has started between the mother and dreadlocked baby daddy over whether the baby looks inbred, I'm offended on behalf of the big-headed baby. I can think his head gigantic, but those are his *parents*. They should think he looks like them.

Dreadlocked guy screams "FUCK!" and jumps back like he's seen a spider on the baby's face. "Okay, one of his eyes is way fuck-ing bigger than the other one and it's freaking me out," he says and pounds on the counter with his fist.

The mother tells a story about a dishwasher she worked with who had been a twin "and he was inbred, too," and neither of the brothers looked anything like what this baby looked like. "Wouldn't you know if your baby was inbred?" she asked.

I smile politely at the little impromptu family meeting that's happening behind the counter and flip through the pages of the photo album like I'm reading a Crate & Barrel to help cover up the "I HAVE GOT TO GET OUT OF HERE" panic that has now fully set in.

I can't get myself to just stand up and leave. I don't want them to think their talking shit about their baby has turned me off. If I walk out now, it looks like I'm judging their lifestyle. Like I think eating Flamin' Hot Cheetos for breakfast is so beneath me.

My first tattoo was so much better. It happened on the beach in Tahiti and was a blissful experience from start to finish.

It was designed by a French Polynesian man in Mooréa, Tahiti, whose real name I am sure is something like Ra'iarrii' and means something mystical like "those who live in the sorrow of a whale's dream and smell like mangos," but he took one look at my sun-burned face, Ellen DeGeneres haircut, and wristbands from my all-inclusive resort, and said, "Call me Fred."

My mother and father had decided that instead of leaving us money after they died, like nice parents do, they wanted to spend their money while they were still with us. Our inheritance would be the memories we created together of touring vanilla bean factories and learning how to make a coin purse out of a coconut. The day I got my tattoo we were scheduled to have our picture taken kissing a dolphin. I'd bristled at the idea of paying anyone to kiss me, especially a dolphin. While my sisters were scraping their tongues in anticipation, I was doing research to find out where dolphins' ears were so I knew where to whisper, "You don't have to do this." Thank god I got over my "fat American on vacation exploiting animals" hang-up and ended up going. Otherwise I'd never be able to say how an hour before I got my first tattoo I was kissing a dolphin. Plus, I would have missed out on my sister Joyce's first kiss.

It was that sweet spot in my life where someone whispering "I will love you forever" in my ear didn't make me punch the wall and scream, "LIAR!" I was thirty years old and about to be married. For the first time. I believed in love, and for a brief few years I believed someone could love me. As I walked out of the resort to find a place to get a tattoo, my dad came running after me and handed me fifty bucks. "I said I'd pay for everything on this trip, so let me pay for this." I swear he had tears in his eyes. Maybe he wished he could go too. Perhaps he was proud of me. Or maybe they'd all discussed switching resorts and not telling me.

The Canadians who ran the moped rental hut told me, "Find Fred." I did. I found him sauntering down the beach carrying a guitar in one hand and twirling a tiny white flower in the other hand. Finally my life felt like a commercial for tropical body splash. He was naked except for a loincloth that was up his ass. I don't mean he had the entire thing shoved up there, but it was very minimal coverage.

I'd seen a lot of people on the island wearing them but had assumed that they were just Hooter-ing it up for the tourists. Fred made it look natural. Like it was god's intended uniform. When I first spotted him, I ran up and stuck out my hand like I was running for mayor, but instead of shaking my hand and promising his vote he reached out and stroked my hair. He stroked my arm. He stroked my face. After he got done tenderizing me, he asked me in very halting English, "What do you love?"

Fred's spiritual vibe unlocked the hula-dancing mute in my soul, and I started acting out little scenarios about nature and love. I was trying to tell him that I was getting married soon and that I was a Pisces so I did a lot of grabbing my heart, pointing at the ocean, and drawing smiley faces in the sand. At one point I mimed taking handfuls of sunshine and shoving them in my heart. It looked like I was doing an experimental dance piece about a woman who dies from open heart surgery. But he got it. He nodded, grabbed my hand, and led me to his hut.

After an hour of lying on a pile of pillows looking out over the Pacific Ocean, I had a Tahitian tattoo that looked like the ocean flowing into the sun on the side of my left calf. It flowed so organically with the lines of my lower leg that it looked like the waves and swirls of the tattoo had been there first and my body organically developed around it.

It was the highlight of the trip for me. It was magical and amazing and I've never regretted that tattoo for a moment.

Of course I hadn't been through 9/11, *The Daily Show*, herpes scares, hot babysitters, and two divorces.

So maybe, just maybe, my expectations for my second tattoo were too high.

"Do you have any books of tribal designs?" I ask. Dreadlocked pulls down what looks like a coffee table book, dusts it off, and tells me that Virginia is parking her car and will be here in a minute. The tribal book is more what I'm looking for. On the "Designs of the Hopi Indians" page I see something that speaks to me. I show Dreadlocked. "How about something like this—just this circle and the three dots and the lines?" I like it. It's got a Zen/Basquiat/ tribal feel.

He glances at it, turns his head, and yells toward the back, "Virginia!" We stand in silence for what feels like a solid five minutes waiting for Virginia. He doesn't call her name again. I guess he knows she needs to be screamed for only once. I take the time to imagine cleaning under his fingernails.

Virginia appears from the back. She doesn't look well. She's about thirty, very pale and very thin, with greasy hair kept in place with plastic barrettes shaped like bows. The kind you see on little kids, nineties hipsters, or the wigs of the mentally ill. Her neck and arms are covered in elaborate tattoos. She shuffles her feet when she walks and has her hands stuck in her pockets, which I soon discover is to help keep them from shaking. In a teeny tiny voice she asks me, "So what are we doing today?" I show her the Hopi design. "Okay, circles are really hard. They're the hardest things you could ever get."

The last thing I wanted to do was to cause her more stress, but it did strike me as fairly shocking that something as common as a circle would be such a big deal. "You've got an Escher painting on your neck. Wouldn't that be way harder?"

"It's actually way easier."

I offer to wait while she practices on an eggplant. I'm trying to help her out. She keeps glancing toward the back where Dread-locked has disappeared.

"If you'd rather have that guy do it, I'd be okay with that. Please don't feel you like you have to—" I offer, thinking maybe she wants a way out, but this clearly is not the right thing to say because she starts to panic immediately.

"No! Nonie can do this. Please! I want to try. Can I at least try?" Oh god.

Virginia asks me if I'd like a drink of water. I tell her no but she should go ahead. She turns toward what I assume is the direction of the water, lets out a loud exhale, and turns back around.

"You know why I want to do this? Because it scares the shit out of me. And I'm sick and tired of being scared of everything. I woke up this morning and I was scared of my cereal, so I'm like, what's next? You know?" Before I can answer, "Me leaving!" she gives me a weepy smile and invites me to "come on back!"

As she outlines the design on my wrist, I stare at the top of her head. Study her pale skin and sprinkles of dandruff caught in her hairline.

She tells me how she's a dancer. I ask her how she likes living in Boise. "Well, I love snow but I hate snow." I try not to look at her dandruff again. You know what? I like her. The fact that I'm not at some slick LA "I'm Johnny Depp's artist" tattoo shop is perfect. A little shaky artist girl in Boise. This is perfect. She looks exactly how I felt so many days these past six months. I'm not walking out on her. She's going to give me the best tattoo of her life. You and me, Virginia. We are making this happen. This tattoo is going to be the beginning of our new lives.

I ask her how she's doing. "I did not sleep well last night."

Oh, that's it. She's just tired!

"I had this dream where I was in an empty apartment and I looked out the window and I see a bridge and it's covered with people. Like four thousand people walking across it. It was like a big Brooklyn Bridge. Then I look over on the wall in the apartment and there's a button and I just walk over and before I even think I reach out and I hit the button. And when I do the bridge collapses and I watch all these people falling."

She takes a moment to finish what must be the circle—I can't get myself to watch—and looks up at me. "And I think—oh my god, I just killed four thousand people."

She stares off like she's seeing the mass murder happen in front of her, makes one last mark on my wrist, and sits up.

"Okay—there's your tattoo."

Circles really are hard. The circle is ever so slightly lopsided. That's not the worst part—the worst part is that it's just a horrible tattoo. I've seen jail tats that had more style. It's awful. Really awful. Three blue dots in a triangle shape. Three small stubby lines underneath the lopsided circle. The ink looks like it's already faded. Like I've had the tattoo for years.

I mumble "Thank you" and stumble out of my chair. I need to get out of here as soon as possible so I can get back to my car where no one can hear me scream.

Later that day, Keily comes to my hotel to show me her tattoo, which is perfect and she loves it. I show her mine. "Is that really what you asked for?" she asks.

On the plane ride back home I sign up for OkCupid and by the time I land I've set up a date with a reality show ("we prefer the term unscripted content") producer, a journalist from the BBC, and a pool-care guy.

My friends are all throwing rules at me. "Don't sleep with anyone until after three dates." "No guys who don't have jobs." "No guys without kids." "No guys with kids." "You need a guy who . . ." And then all my bossy girlfriends, my birth mother, or Eddie the mailman tells me what I need.

At first, I like all of them. For the first five minutes they all seem way better choices than I've ever had before. I'm not sure why.

After three dates, it's the most depressing parade of sad broken robots in the galaxy.

Four months of dating. I'm in the doctor's office with a fever and a kidney infection. The most promiscuous friend I know—I'll call her Stan—tells me that a kidney infection is "the whore's disease." "My doctor said it was stress related," I text her from the pharmacy waiting for my prescriptions. "He's being nice. He feels sorry for you because of your age."

It's like I'm trying to get love through all the wrong holes. I'm not sure what the right hole would be. The hole in my heart?

The odd thing is that none of the dates mention my tattoo. They don't notice it. Maybe if it had been right above my mouth it would have warranted more comments.

The first person to notice it is a sound guy on a VH1 *I Love the '80s 3-D* shoot. He asks me what my affiliation is. I have no idea what he's talking about. "Do you have any idea what the actual meaning of that tattoo is?" Outside the obvious meaning of "never get a tattoo in Boise," I have no idea what he's talking about.

"Those three dots are the gang symbol for a major Mexican gang in East Los Angeles. Mi vida loca. Did you really not know that?"

Now that he mentions it, I do remember noticing the three dots when I volunteered in the LA county jail. Women had them on their hands or on their faces. I'd never seen the dots on the inside of a wrist but I'm sure rival gangs won't be sticklers about it when they gun me down in the 7-Eleven.

I do a search for "best place to get a tattoo cover-up in LA." The first one that comes up is Zans Tattoo on Venice Boulevard. The king of cover-ups is a rockabilly guy in a fedora named Rand. I like him. He laughs at my Boise tattoo story. "Oh no!" he says when I talk about the shit-talking baby part. "Are you kidding me?" he asks when I describe the girl's shaking hands. The first thing he assures me of is that he's going to fix that circle.

My friend Dan is worried that I'm going to spend the next five years trying to repair my bad tattoo and will end up with a dragon that goes all the way up to my forehead. I'm worried about this too. My only request to Rand is to keep it small. He sketches out an image of an old cracked mahjong tile. "This way you still keep the original tattoo but I'll use it as the design for the tile . . . get it?"

I hate it. It has no meaning to me whatsoever. I've never played mahjong in my life.

"You know what may be bothering me is . . ."

The entire tattoo shop is giving a "cool or not cool, Grandma?" stare down.

He asks me what I don't like about it. I'm not quite sure. As I'm trying to figure out what to say, the other tattoo artists come to his rescue and gather around the image he's sketched out. They all agree that it's the best tattoo that he's ever designed. "I'm not kidding. This is unbelievable." The receptionist gasps when she sees it. The last tattoo artist to see it drops the image back on Rand's station. "Fantastic, Rand. It's your best for sure."

Oh god, they're so clearly trying to boost him up. I've done it again; I've found the weak one. The one who's about to be fired or having personal trouble. I'm going to let him do the tattoo. I know it. Because he needs it. It will help him. Please god, let him not be single. Story of my life. "Well, *he* wants it. It would make *him* happy." A British guy tells me, "You and I will be wonderful together. You live close, I can bring dinner over, and we can watch *The Muppet Movie.* This is perfect for me." I'd liked aspects of that, but it wasn't anything I'd suggested. Nobody ever asked me what I wanted or wanted to do. It works for me because I do like a man to be in charge sometimes so I can giggle and complain about being fat and getting my period. In that order. I'm not sure what I would say if someone asked me what I wanted; I'd be so thrown. Or I'd worry that if I told them what I wanted they'd suppress who they were and only try to please me and I'd never see who they are. Love sucks.

I offer Rand the inside of my right wrist. "Go ahead."

As the needle digs into my skin, I stare at the sketch on the piece of paper that was passed around the room. It's not that bad. When people ask me what it is or why I got it, I'll say it was the last mah-jong tile my grandmother played before she died. Or that it's an homage to one of my favorite writers and fellow Hoosier Kurt Vonnegut, who died yesterday.

"You don't remember the mahjong game in *Cat in the Cradle?*"

The redo doesn't take very long. The way Rand has colored in the circle with red makes it look like I got a tattoo on top of a herpes sore. I can't look at it for very long.

"Thank you so much," I say and shuffle toward the door.

The receptionist stops me. "Hey! You have to pay!"

"Oh, right." She runs my credit card. Three hundred and fifty dollars.

I ask her if she wouldn't mind handing me one of the tattoo-removal pamphlets behind her.

She wants to know if I'm kidding.

"Oh yeah, I'm kidding."

A tall, willowy woman strides through the door, platform shoes and a million feet tall. Her backless sundress reveals angel-wings tattoos that cover her back. She glances down at me, gives me an "I'm beautiful, no?" smile, right as she notices my tattoo. She is incredibly beautiful. Please don't steal my husband, I think. Oh wait, I don't have one.

"Oh my god, what is that?" She takes her sunglasses off and bends down like Big Bird talking to one of the working-class kids of the neighborhood.

"Is that a Flintstones iPod?"

"No," I tell her. Give her a polite smile.

"Oh, okay. Sorry. Let me see it again. Oh! Oh! Is it money?"

"Yeah, it's money. Eye on the prize. Right? I'm kidding. No, it's not money."

"Okay. Okay. Hold on . . . I know! Is it toast?"

"No. As passionate as I am about toast, no."

Now she's got me wondering . . . what the hell is it? Really. I look down and study the tattoo along with her, trying to figure out what I'm looking at . . .

"Let's see, it's an old dirty cracked piece of concrete with a fucked-up circle and a gang symbol in the middle of it."

She wrinkles her nose like the tattoo smells bad too, and turns away from me toward the receptionist. The two of them share an eye roll.

"Yeah, I'm here for my eleven o'clock appointment. I'm just getting the last two feathers on my wings done."

I'm sitting in my car staring at my wrist. It's the most awful tattoo I've ever seen. I have a cracked piece of concrete on my arm. A symbol that says, "I can be talked into anything by anyone." I'm scared to drive my car. I don't even trust myself to do that, for some reason.

What will I tell my date, Kevin, the yoga guy from Venice, tonight? I'm going to tell him it's a tattoo I got for a short story that Kurt Vonnegut wrote called the "The Mahjong Tile," not well-known except to his die-hard fans.

The parking lot attendant, a Hispanic man in his sixties, with glasses and salt-and-pepper hair, is very handsome, Eric Estrada–like. He could very well be Eric Estrada; that's how bizarre and great this town can be. He sticks his head in my window, giving me a burst of cologne that smells like what my high school boyfriend wore. It's lovely. He's lovely. His hands are so smooth. His fingernails look buffed, the little moons so white and perfect. "Hello, sweet-heart, I'm sorry. I'm closing valet. If you want, you can street park." As he's talking to me, I'm admiring his hands and I see it. Three dots. Mi vida loca. Speechless, I stick my wrist out and put it next to his hand. His eyes narrow. "Mi vida loca," he says. "Did you grow up in East LA?" In my white Prius with the toddler seat in the back, I'm so flattered.

"No," I tell him. "North side of Indianapolis. Did you really think I could have grown up there? That makes me so—"

"No, I didn't, but those three dots are Mi vida loca tattoo. It's big-time, you know. I did a lot of bad things with gangs. I was a gang-banger, you know, all that stuff. Bad times. I'm out now. Never go back."

I ask him if the tattoo ever gets him into trouble, if people think he's in the gang. "Not when I'm working in Beverly Hills or Santa Monica, and you know, it could get you in trouble, but I think, hey, it's good. I look down and I remember, you know. It's who I was but it's not me. It's a good reminder, you know. Bad times behind me, good times right now, sweetheart."

He tells me to go ahead and park in the parking lot. "I'll keep an eye on your car."

Before I go in for my date with Kevin the yoga instructor, I give Erik Estrada my keys and ask if I can take a photo of our tat-toos next to each other. Nothing says gangbanger like posing for an Instagram photo.

Kevin is a tall suntanned man in a cardigan sweater. He smiles and nods at me while I'm talking. *Listening.* He's very attentive and kind and he's married. It's an open marriage. "Would you rather know someone in this life or be lied to?" he says with a smile, salsa dripping down his white cable-knit cardigan. This could work, actu-ally. Why not? I'm not looking for a relationship. It would be nice to know there was really no chance of it getting too serious. Maybe I'm one of these evolved hippies I've been reading about and fearing for so long. Kevin never notices my tattoo; he's far too absorbed texting his wife to tell her how much he likes me. No. This is not what I want to do. Not even for another five minutes. Without much explanation I stand up. "Thank you so much, Kevin. Tell your wife she's very lucky." I ask the hostess on the way out if valet is still open and she gives me a confused look. "Well, no, there's no valet." Hearing that they don't have a valet and have never had a valet doesn't worry me at all. Not even for a second.

Cold, Cold Water

I'm on an airplane flying to Portland, Oregon. It's my first trip away from home since David and I split.

Walking into the living room to say good-bye to Leo before I left this morning, before his dad came to pick him up, I considered pretending I heard someone calling my name outside—"Who's that? I'll be right back"—and running out.

After I finally did manage to say good-bye, I had that "I'm about to cry" bubble sound in my voice, which was more upsetting than if I'd just lain down on the floor and howled with tears. Leo asked me if I was crying. I told him of course not. Bugs had just flown in both of my eyes and I was eating a brownie that got caught in my throat "and it's so cakey." This made Leo mad. He's four, so brownies and bugs in his eyes are the stuff of fancy parties.

The plane is about to land and all I want to do is make it back to my hotel in time to Skype with Leo. I haven't spent that much time in Portland. I was here once before a few years ago doing my play *Bust* at a local theater, but that's been it. I have no idea how many bridges I'll have to cross or naked bike-rider parades I'll encounter that will slow me down.

I lean across the aisle and ask the no-nonsense composter-type lady sitting there if she's from Portland. The neon-green Crocs on her feet and bright red fleece pullover she's wearing have already answered my question, but I don't want her to feel racially profiled so I go ahead and ask her.

I've never seen anyone happier about being asked a question. It was like I'd asked an evangelical Christian if he knew anything about Jesus.

"Yes! I am. I am from Portland! I've lived there my entire life. I'd love to help you out. Please ask me. Ask me!"

In my best "you don't want to get stuck talking to me—I'm a manic depressive burden" flat tone, I ask her how long she thinks it will take to drive from the airport to downtown.

"Guess what!" Composting Lady, whose name I'm now changing to Public Transit Lady, says to me, still excited. "You don't have to drive! You don't have to! There is a train right there in the airport. You'll see it as soon as you get off the plane. It's called the MAX. M-A-X."

"I think the theater I'm working for is sending an airport pickup for me . . ."

"Oh well, maybe for your return flight."

I sigh. Traveling with Leo after he was first born had been so easy. We'd shove him in a pocket like a kitten, and off our little family would go to Vermont, New Mexico . . . Orange County.

After the first year, though, David started getting tired of being stuck in a hotel while I was onstage performing. It wasn't like I was coming home every night with my arms full of roses, smelling of champagne cocktails and gushing with tales of "not one but *three* standing ovations!" Most nights, I couldn't wait to get back to the hotel so I could complain to David about the row after row of sleeping old white men who were dragged to the theater by their wives against their will and viewed theater as nothing more than a planned nap time.

David, the greatest champion and supporter of my work, was also a man who wanted adventure, travel, and to be working *in* the theater. These are not things that happened a lot in a hotel room with a toddler. David started complaining that I was treating him like a glorified babysitter. Eventually, he couldn't take it anymore and decided to stay at home and glorify our actual twenty-something babysitter.

David doesn't like it when I call her "the babysitter."

"She's a human being, Lauren," he says to me. Her being a human being was never in doubt. You don't see doorknobs with cleavage like that.

She's twenty-one years old. I am not. If you take a handful of my neck skin, you will see from its elasticity that I am decidedly older than twenty-one. Or else I'm a chicken.

"What *time* is your return flight?"

Without thinking I tell her my actual return flight time. "Eight A.M." As soon as I say it I know it won't be early enough.

"Perfect! The first train leaves downtown at Pioneer Square at four forty-five A.M. You'll get to the airport in plenty of time."

The plane touches down, but she doesn't notice; she's too preoccupied with insisting I call the theater right now and cancel my pickup.

"You'll be able to catch them if you call now. The airport is twenty minutes away from everything. It was voted number one commuter airport in the nation. Portlanders love their airport. In fact, they put some googly eyeballs and a seat belt on a rolled-up piece of carpet that matches the carpet at the airport and named it the grand marshal of this year's Grand Floral Parade . . ."

Walking to the baggage claim, I know Public Transit Lady is

walking behind me. I can feel it. The first sign I see for the MAX, I crouch down and pretend to tie the laces of my loafers. She runs past me, yelling, "Hurry, the train's on time!" I watch her neon-green Crocs disappear down the escalator.

A roll of carpet as the grand marshal of a parade is a million kinds of wonderful. A train that takes you from the airport and saves the planet is as well. I know I should take the train, but I'm not going to.

Tonight will be the first night my sweet three-year-old blond boy is spending at his father's new apartment somewhere in the Valley. I don't even know exactly where he is. I don't care if I have to ride in a Hummer that runs on fuel made out of dolphin faces; I want to see Leo's little blond head tonight.

My airport pickup is not a spry retired teacher in a vintage Prius but a very tall gay man named Kelsey in a teeny-tiny car that he's just driven back from his parents' wind farm; he apologizes if it smells like dog. He tells me he's got exciting news for me that he wanted to wait to tell me in person—the hotel where I'll be staying while I'm in Portland is a LEED-certified building. I'm letting out a huge sigh of relief—"Oh good!"—even though I have no idea what that means, when I see the child's car seat in the back of the car. I forgot to tell the theater that Leo wouldn't be joining me until after his preschool let out for the summer in two weeks. Kelsey arranges travel for the theater. He knew I was traveling alone. The car seat is for his disabled pug.

"Things have changed since I was a kid," Kelsey says to me as he picks dog hair off the lid of his glass water bottle. "I'm from Pennsylvania. Missing two weeks of preschool when I was little would have meant missing two weeks of eating Play-Doh. If you live in Portland, pulling your kid for two weeks would mean they'd never learn to humanely slaughter a pig or say 'It makes me angry that I haven't had a turn holding the goat cheese' in French during the class trip to the local farmers' market." I love that. I've got to remember to ask Kelsey if I can use those lines in my show and act like I came up with them. He's so delightful, why stop at a few lines? I should steal his entire personality.

Leo's preschool teachers advised me that in times of chaos, routine is key. Whatever they tell me to do, I do it. I've also been leaning heavily on my friend Chuck's advice. Chuck's a gay midwestern motivational speaker whom I've known since high school. He told me to bring Leo with me. "No matter what, he should be with his mother." He's right. I should have brought him with me. Or not. I don't know. Chuck writes books about choosing to love and being nice to gay people, but last week he posted a photo on Facebook of his teenage son in a closet with his hands tied behind his back and duct tape over his mouth. "Look what the appraiser is going to find during his inspection today!" It's possible his parental instincts can be a little off.

"It's only two weeks," I tell Kelsey, hoping I seem stable enough to continue to employ. "I can handle it. Army parents are gone longer than that, right?" Kelsey gives me a quizzical look. Coming to do a play in America's top beer city and going to fight in a war. Same, same. I'm going to get my ass kicked in Portland.

Once I'm in my hotel room I set my computer up to Skype. We connect and I talk to David about how Leo is doing. Great, apparently. They're watching Leo's favorite Talking Heads videos, drawing pictures of monsters, and getting ready to read stories, but heads-up, the Human Being is there, so . . . Okay. I don't want to talk to him with her there. I don't want to abandon him, but I'm not ready for this. But he's okay. He's his normal fun hyper self. He's okay. This is so odd. I'm used to dragging myself into hell, but mostly my hells are familiar to me. This is a new one. Worrying about someone else being dragged down with me is not familiar. I ask David if Leo is ready to talk to me.

He's not. Okay. That's fine. As long as he's okay. Tell him good night.

Turns out, a LEED-accredited building means it's dark all the time. I call the front desk to ask how to turn the lights on. The front desk girl gives me her "Welcome to civilization, you caveman," speech and explains how in order to save energy the lights operate on a motion-detection system. If they don't sense a human in the room, they shut off.

I'm jumping up and down, waving my arms, yelling, "*I'm here! I'm here!*" Nothing. I knew it. I'm dead. Good, now I don't feel as bad about wiping with a towel.

Maybe I just need a cup of coffee. Seven P.M. may be a bit late for coffee, but I'm here to write a play about Portland and am supposed to be gathering material. Not sure how I should go about doing that. You know what? I'll grab whatever the local *Village Voice* is here and hope that there are some wacky things happening this week in the city.

I'm one step out of the hotel and a full-grown man wearing cutoff jeans and no shirt rides up the sidewalk on a miniature bike. He's wielding an enormous machete that he is swinging at anyone who passes by. It's dinnertime, the sidewalks are busy, and I'm sure I'm not the only one who would rather not see an arm get hacked off, so I run back into the hotel to get help. My screams for someone to "call 911!" are met with bored shrugs from the front desk staff. "Oh, that's just the machete guy. That's Ron."

Less than five minutes later, I'm about to walk into a coffee shop attached to a bike store when I hear what sounds like the wails of bagpipes, and here comes a man with purple hair riding a unicycle in a kilt and playing the bagpipes.

A chubby teenage boy walks by and looks up from the graphic novel he's reading and says, "I assure you it's way better when he's got the fire coming out of the pipes."

This play is going to write itself.

The barista is a twentysomething hipster dude. His beard is three times as long as his face.

"Hey, that's my favorite candy bar. Did you know that when you got it?" I point to the Butterfinger candy bar on his right forearm. He responds with a blank stare. He was flirty and nice to everyone in line in front of me. Why doesn't he like me? Do I look like some middle-aged blond lady from Los Angeles? Please god, don't let me look like what I am, because that's not what I am.

I order a pour-over and ask what it is I've just ordered. "Isn't all coffee some form of a pour-over at some point in the process?"

Words like "bloom" and "pour length" and "angle" and "Himalayan" are coming out of his mouth, but I'm not listening. He could be being cold to me to hide his attraction.

"Your total is eight fifty."

"Wow. Can I pay with two cards?"

My phone rings. It's David. I start to answer it and the barista points to a sign on the front of the register: IF YOU'RE TALKING ON YOUR CELL PHONE, DON'T BOTHER ORDERING.

"It's my kid . . . I'm going through a divorce and—" He stares at me with a mixture of hatred and boredom. I hit ignore and take my pour-over to go.

As I walk out the door, the barista calls after me, "Have a good day, LA." How does he know I'm from LA? Out, out, damn spot! I can't get the stench of that city off me.

Back in my hotel room, I'm not only depressed; I'm anxious, thanks to the coffee. Sure it's a green building, but it smells like black mold. I can't relax. I should go out. But what will I do? Wait a minute. What am I doing? I can do whatever I want. I'm . . . single now. In fact, this is the first night that I've been single, without my kid, in a hotel room, for years. Would you look at that? The depression has lifted.

Mama is going out tonight.

The concierge suggests I go to the Kennedy School. It's a converted old schoolhouse, and there are bars, restaurants, movie theaters, little nooks to smoke cigars, and a soaking pool. "Skip the soaking pool. It used to be amazing but now it's a bunch of depressed parents and their obnoxious kids. It's hell."

Thankful for the good advice, I hobble out on my high heels pretending to search for a bus stop and hail the first cab I see. Texting in a moving vehicle makes me yack; I wish I'd remember that before I started texting Jack. Is Jack my "ex" stepson now? No. That's awful. In fact, Jack's the only one who intimately understands the impact of what happened. In a way, he's the only witness to the family that was lost. Jack and Simone are the same age. Maybe that's gross, yet kind of "my dad's still got it!" David was an amazing father to Jack; I'm not going to ask him any questions where he feels pressured to trash talk his father. I have plenty of friends who *love* to do that. My text "Miss you, Jack. Don't get too high at work" sounds like I'm hinting for him to call me so I can talk about Simone and David. It is. That's why I'm worried it sounds that way. Jack's been living in Boston since he graduated high school. Jack and I talk on the phone now more than we ever used to. I haven't felt this close to him since he was in juvie. All the big bombs—divorce, death, and parole—really bring people together. It's been a year since I've actually seen Jack's face. I miss that face. "Your *face* misses my face," as Jack would say. My text was halfway done—"You're still my stepson even if"—and I have to throw the phone on the taxi seat and stare at the horizon to let the nausea pass.

I'm scurrying up and down the long, empty hallways of the Kennedy School. It's like a horror movie, and not just because I can't find a bar. It's the black-and-white photographs of the blank-eyed schoolchildren with bowl haircuts dancing around a may-pole circa 1919 staring out at me that are creeping me out. If a kid on a Big Wheel appears at the end of the hallway, I'm not waiting for his finger to say "Redrum." I'm out.

Finally, I pass by what I think must be a bar. It's so tiny I can't be sure. There are three empty barstools and a young male bar-tender behind the bar staring straight ahead and slowly cleaning a glass with a white-and-red-striped dish towel. If the lights in the hallway weren't on, I would've had to go back to my "I'm dead and I just don't know it" theory.

Nothing says "I'm a middle-aged white lady from LA" more than ordering a buttery Chardonnay, but I don't care. If this is death, sign me up. This Chardonnay is delicious. A young lesbian couple joins me at the bar. After downing shots of whiskey, they start making out. It's a graphic, slurping make-out. I lean my body to the left to give them some privacy, but it still feels like I've crawled into their mouths; the smacking noises are deafening.

The bartender and I make eye contact. I start sweating because I can't think of a good quip; their passion is so heavy and I'm so close to it. Should I reach over and tweak a nipple or something? They unattach with a *pop!* and I hear one of them whisper, "If I don't get you home right now, I'm going to lose my mind." Fol-lowed by fifteen minutes of clicking noises as they put on all their bike gear. Helmets, shin guards, shoes, reflectors. "Remember the days of 'I have to get you home, right now'?" I ask the bartender after we've watched them clomp out on their biker shoes. He doesn't answer. "Me neither," I say and sip my buttery Chardonnay. That was a lot of passion in a tiny haunted bar. I wonder if they were sneaking around. Recently, anytime I see people being openly passionate in public, my first thought is, look at the people having an affair.

An affair is inherently thrilling. Also, stressful. I imagine it would be the most incredibly exciting thing ever until it was the most awful, depressing thing ever.

"David is the kindest, deepest, most amazing man I've ever known." The Human Being said that to me one night after baby-sitting Leo. How sweet, I'd thought. There's somebody out there who worships him. That's got to make a middle-aged man feel good about himself. We all could use a little perk like that once in a while. I'll tell him she said that, I thought. I bet he has no idea she worships him like that. Her gushing about him reminded me of how I'd gushed about him after our trip to Baja.

David took me to Baja, Mexico, in the early days of our dating. Hiking around the Sea of Cortez, I'd suggested to David that we go swimming. The water was the most perfect clear blue I'd ever seen. It would be rude to not take off all our clothes and jump in. David warned me against it. "The cold water could give you a heart attack, Lauren. What if someone threw a lawn mower into the sea and we stepped on it with our bare feet? There are no hospitals around. We'll have a heart attack, bleed to death, and die." By the time he got to our clothes being stolen and us freezing to death after the sun went down in the middle of nowhere, I'd taken off my clothes and jumped in. The "spontaneous, fearless, adventure-seeker chick" was not a role I'd ever played. I wanted to show David that it was no big deal. That we could do crazy life things together, survive them, and enjoy the afterbuzz of near-death experiences together. The water felt fantastic. I turned back to shore expecting to see David waving his arms above his head and begging me to swim back. Instead there he was, walking over the jagged rocks in his bare feet—"Ow! Ow! Ow!"—in his tighty whities to join me. He didn't look any less nervous, but he was coming in the water. Blissed out of my mind, I'd started laughing and crying and laughing. The sight of him looking so nervous but doing it anyway busted my heart wide open. He didn't need to be a macho superhero about it. I didn't need him to not be scared to fall in love with him; I needed him to be scared and dive in anyway. By the time we were swimming to shore to check out what the group of teenage boys carrying brooms who were heading toward our clothing were up to, I'd fallen in love with the kindest, deepest, most amazing man.

Sadly, I never cheated on David. (I'm kidding. I'm glad I didn't. Being able to sob "I was never with anyone but you!" like a daytime soap star is so much more satisfying when it's true.) I hope I believe in love again. For Leo's sake. I hope that by the time he's a teenager I stop referring to marriage as "the festival of lies."

Well, this is fun. Look at me, out on the town. Woo-hoo.

The bartender dryly informs me that I look "very dolled up" this evening. I do? How does he know that this isn't my norm? My god, he thinks I'm a prostitute. What am I doing? I'm a mother on the road. I'm not even officially divorced. It's not appropriate to be sitting at a bar by myself boozing it up. No, no, no. Wipe that paint off your face, Jezebel, and go see a movie. That's exactly what I should do. Go sit in the dark.

Shockingly, I find the movie theater right away without the help of bloody handprints or a child's breathy voice singing "La la la . . . follow me." It's a living room–style theater where people watch the movies sitting on couches and La-Z-Boy recliners. The sign out front reads GEEK TRIVIA NIGHT. I thought it was the title of a movie. It's not. It's a trivia night—but on a level I didn't know trivia could reach. The place is packed. There must be about three hundred people shoved onto love seats and sitting on recliners. This was the wholesome place to be. It's Portland, so there's a bar. I'm ordering a beer that's described on the menu as "a bong hit in the bar" when the game starts.

"Where do Klingons go when they die?"

A high-pitched male voice calls out for clarification. "Uh, sir, would that be an honorable or a dishonorable death?"

There's no place to sit, and I notice that everyone is on teams. They all know one another. This may not have been the best thing to do when I'm alone. It was the worst thing. I'm old. I'm the oldest one here by far. I must have looked very dolled up to these trivia geeks.

"If you're looking to join a team, you are welcome to join ours."

A cute blond boy—he couldn't be more than twenty-three years old, maybe twenty-eight, I'm bad with ages—invites me join his team, which includes two other boys who are somewhere in their twenties. Their team name is the Nerdy Sanchezes. Their invitation touches my heart. How kind. I thank them and cram myself onto the love seat next to the cute blond one. You know what? I love people in their twenties. They're so much more open, so much more willing to take risks. In your twenties you want adventure. The Human Being would sit and talk to me for hours after she got done babysitting. I didn't want her to go home. Talking to a young girl was so interesting, I thought. I actually liked hearing about her hopes and dreams for the future, the frustration of living at home with her parents and trying to figure out what she wanted to do with her life. "Stop talking to her, Lauren, or she'll never go home," David would say to me.

"What two ingredients were used on the sandwich Ally Sheedy made in the movie *The Breakfast Club*?"

My teammates know every answer. No discussion needed. One

writes it down; the others glance at the answer, give a quick a nod, and wait for the next question. They don't look like they're having fun, but I sense that maybe they are.

A nerd fight over which font was used in the movie title *Jurassic Park* breaks out. The answer was multiple choice and a team has accused the hosts of the game of fraud: "Sir, none of them are correct. How dare you!"

The blond boy who called me over asks me if I'd like to come back to his house after the game is over to drink beer and watch him and his friends play *Magic: The Gathering*. Asking me this appears to be as painful to him as making eye contact. He glances up to see if I've heard him, but as soon as our eyes meet, he looks away. A shy, nerdy geisha. It struck me in the beginning of the evening as being a bit Aspergery but now I'm thinking that maybe it's because I'm simply too pretty for him to look at for any extended period of time. Or maybe that's the bong hits talking.

"I have no idea if that sounds like any fun at all," he says to me and hurries to put his headphones on, but I answer before he can block me out.

"I'm in! Where do you live?"

This was not the answer he expected. Me neither. "Why not? Sounds fun! I'll grab some snacks and some vodka. Wait a minute, who wants a Moscow mule? Yum. Let's do that, or, no, let's not. You have to get those tin mugs to really make them work. This is insane. What's your address? Don't worry about directions. I'll give the address to the taxi driver—I mean the bus driver! The bus driver!"

I'm writing down all the details, babbling away, giggling, taking orders, flipping my hair, and the Nerdy Sanchez boys are staring at one another with looks of . . . I can't tell what the look is. Shock? Excitement? Stress? Do I seem *amazing* to them?

What the hell am I doing? I'm supposed to be gathering material for a play. Am I going to write about making out with a twenty-three-year-old boy? No. I'm not. Remember how fun it was to declare, "I was *never* unfaithful to you, David"? Declaring "I never even kissed a twenty-three-year-old boy I met at Geek Trivia!" would be even better. If it was true. I gave him one tiny kiss, told him, "You're way too young. This feels disgusting, nothing personal, but this isn't happening. Sorry, I'd looked forward to telling myself that you worshipped me, but I can't."

The night ends with us standing in front of the Kennedy School, waiting for a taxi to take me back to my hotel, telling them about my divorce. The cute blond boy can't believe it. "Wow, it's such a Hollywood cliché—the babysitter?"

"She's a human being."

Back at my hotel, I'm brushing my teeth in the dark, wondering what this weird life zone I'm in is going to present to me next. I'd fooled myself early on into thinking that four years old was the "perfect" age for your parents to divorce. I mean, if we had to do it, *now* was the time. Leo polled his preschool class and discovered right away that he was the only divorced kid. "Just wait until you get to kindergarten," I told him. "You'll be the wise master advising the others on the perks of a two-house family." He didn't get it. How could he? He's four.

A few days later, Leo has arrived. David dropped him off on his way to Seattle. We did the handoff in the Portland airport. Leo is proof that I would have made a far better-looking boy. Seeing his face makes me swoon and my heart race like I'm in love. I *am* in love. Before I know what I'm doing, I'm promising Leo cookies dipped in frosting, helicopter rides, a *Skylanders* video game, and seven puppies unless he only wants six.

Leo and I ride the MAX back to the hotel. He complains that it takes too long.

Thank god he's here. Instead of going out in the evenings to gather material, I'd been sitting in the dark, drinking wine and watching *Intervention,* slurring at the TV, "Come on, lady! Get up off the front lawn and get it together! Jesus. Where's her family? Somebody help her!" Lucky for me, a lot of the addicts lived in Portland so I didn't feel it was a complete waste of time. The park bench where the heroin addict made her boyfriend sit and wait while she exchanged sex in the bushes for money was in Washington Park, a Portland area I hadn't yet explored but meant to.

Now we're in the elevator of the hotel heading out to explore the city. I'm fighting back the urge to ask Leo if he saw the Human kiss his dad. Instead, I keep it light and ask Leo if he had fun with the Human Being after I left. He gives me a funny look. I'm calling her by her name, so his confused look isn't because he doesn't know whom I'm talking about. He honestly looks like he's onto me. He knows that I shouldn't be asking him questions that will put him in the middle and that will only cause me pain. He knows.

"Well, did you have fun with her? She's fun. You did. I love her. You love her, so it's fun. To love someone. It's okay. So did you have fun?" Leo stares at me for a moment before he answers, "I don't know what you're talking about." He says, "You're not making any sense really," before he changes the subject to how many doughnuts he'll be having at breakfast. He tells me, "I think you're confused right now, Mama." How does he know not to answer me? It could have been the manic tone of my voice, sweaty armpits, and tears in my eyes that made him feel his mother was unhinged. Or maybe he's a warlock.

Two well-dressed men with their silky gray dogs get on the elevator. It's that expensive breed of dog that is really good about wearing vintage hats and high heels for photo shoots. They are talking about everyone's favorite topic, Portland.

"You know, Portland is known for being one of the cities with the least amount of people procreating. *Thank you, Jesus.* And it's also known to be one of the smartest cities in the world. So . . . you know. Two plus two."

Portland is actually a pretty kid-friendly place for the most part. They serve beer at indoor playgrounds, so it's easy to go out and feel like you're not just sitting around waiting to be an adult. But people in the Pearl District, a very high-end neighborhood with warehouses converted into fancy condos, where our hotel is, don't like kids. They don't realize that Leo isn't a kid. He's a little person wearing a four-year-old-boy skin suit. Gross, I made him sound like a serial killer. Or the son of one. The Pearl is more of a dog area. Once we're outside the hotel I'm about to encourage Leo to blend in and take a shit on the sidewalk when he says to me, "You don't like her because Dada loves her and not you, so now you hate her."

I don't know where it's coming from or how or why he says this—I have not mentioned anything to him about the affair, only, "You know how you fight with Riley at school and it's better if you don't play with him unless you want to get sand thrown in your face? Well, that's like Mama and Dada." Maybe he heard me on the phone or heard David say something?

My phone rings. I'm not in the best of moods, but I am glad to see that it's Lori Jo; hopefully she'll leave a message.

Lori Jo is a friend of mine I met in Seattle who recently moved to Portland. I love Lori Jo. She's an earth-mother kombucha drunk. She's always saying things like "Oh, Lauren, don't let me drive today. I've had too much kombucha. Oh my gosh, I really feel it today." Whenever she appears in my life it feels like a butterfly landed on my finger, and I don't want to scare it away, so when she calls me up and invites me to her house for a party Friday night, I accept, even though I'd have to leave Leo with a babysitter and he just got here, so that makes me feel guilty *again*, and even though she referred to it as a "salon." That's how much I like her.

A babysitter. The last time I was going to leave Leo with a babysitter, I called and canceled before she could get to the house. "You're not babysitting today. You're never babysitting Leo again," I'd said on her voice mail, hung up, and walked around looking for something to destroy. Five minutes earlier, I'd found the evidence of the affair. My whole life I'd imagined the moment of walking in on an affair and the dramatic scene that would follow. Slashing of tires. Screaming "I hate you! How could you do this to me!" and slapping everyone in the room including myself. Leo was in the apartment watching TV when I found out. Nausea made it impossible for me to even tip over a chair.

They are the two lovers who found each other and I'm the old wife, the employer they escaped from. I'm the putz. My therapist can tell me over and over again, "It has nothing to do with you. What those two did and do is not a reflection of you." What else is he going to say? "You are older and more demanding and they are scared of you"?

I'm glad to be out of the marriage, but boy do I feel like a sad, embarrassed, heartbroken asshole. He must have really hated me. Telling people what happened, I feel old and ugly. "We fell in love . . . ," they say. The ones who were cheating and who are now together are the sexy "we can't help it, we're soul mates" ones. I must have been horrible for someone to lie to me for so long. So unlovable. Someone who was easy to hurt. Maybe cheating on me felt like stealing a pen from Citibank. Men probably secretly admire David. And fear me. "What did she do to drive him to that?" I'll come up with an answer. I'll say I was too loving. Too sexual. Too funny. Too driven. And I made fun of him constantly and knew I didn't want to be with him early on but stayed with it anyway.

Months before, the Human had given me a coat of hers I'd admired over the years. A teal blue faux leather coat with a faux fur collar from Forever 21. Or Forever 51, as I like to call it. "I was going to give it away but you've always said how much you like it, so I want you to have it." I ripped that coat out of her hands, put it on, and ran to the mirror. It felt inappropriate to be wearing a twenty-year-old's coat, but hey, it did look good on me. It also felt inappropriate to take a hand-me-down from the babysitter. Wasn't it supposed to be the other way around?

Whenever David saw me in the coat, he'd give a sweet laugh. "Hey, I have to admit. You look pretty good in it; she was right!"

At the time it struck me as odd not that our babysitter could never make eye contact with me or that often she refused to take money for babysitting, but that at some point she'd said to David, when I wasn't around, that her coat looked good on me. It seemed like an adult thing to be saying to another adult, and she was a kid.

When I found out, instead of slashing tires or slapping anyone, I headed straight for that coat. I grabbed it off the coat rack to cut it up into shreds with a knife, burn it in the alley, tear it apart with my teeth, but instead I hung it up on a hanger and put it in the back of my closet. It was a cute coat. It shouldn't be a total loss.

When I see the babysitter the theater sets me up with, I'm relieved, even though David is nowhere in sight. She's a stocky twenty-nine-year-old with dyed gray hair and nose rings. After she meets Leo, she apologizes for being so low energy and promises to drink some coffee after I go. Right before she came over she'd had an argument with her boyfriend over whether hula-hooping was a career or not. "I don't even understand what we were fighting about. It *is* a career."

I love Lori Jo's house. It's a classic Craftsman-style Portland house. Smells like verbena and rosemary. The walls are covered with pho-tos of dogs and Buddhas, and Buddhas with dogs. A cool-looking chick walks by me with a tattoo of a jellyfish swimming across her chest. "I love your tattoo. Where did you get that?" I ask her. With an exhausted sigh she tells me she was born with it and walks away. She's right. I'm being exhausting. Trying too hard. Who's the out-of-towner old lady, chirping, "Hey what's that there picture on ya? Can I snap a photo?" Why am I so uncomfortable? I need to calm down.

This is the most active group of partygoers I've ever seen. There's no standing around talking with a drink in your hands. Everyone is busy doing something. It looks like a commune getting ready for the long winter ahead. People are grinding millet for bread, making homemade candles, sawing wood for extra chairs. I have no skills to offer. We'll be dead by sunrise because of me. I'd offer to put a tablecloth on the table but I don't know how to use a loom. Look out, dating world, I'm a real catch.

David would have been right at home here. He was the cook. Give him some apple cider vinegar and a few cloves of garlic and he's off. God, will I miss his salad dressing. I'll miss all of his cooking.

There's a group of women in the kitchen all huddled around a mixing bowl balling up some earthy mushroom-looking mixture. They all look like different versions of that French movie character Amélie. Quirky and unique. Vintage dresses, flapper-girl haircuts, boots with buttons, and hair with little bows. They look like the kind of women I would be friends with if I lived in Portland. Or rather whom I'd like to be friends with. I shove myself into the circle and offer to help make what Amélie #1 tells me are "energy balls." I roll the balls in hemp seeds and listen to Amélie #1 talk about how she just got back from getting her PhD on the flora and fauna of Botswana. Amélie #2 is in the middle of converting an old funeral home into a music venue that's going to have a sustainable food bar, and Amélie #3 just ended a vow of silence she took for one whole year. "I just didn't like what my words had been doing anymore."

These women are amazing. Yoga Amélie asks me what the play I'm writing is about. "I have a better story than that," I say and tell the Amélies about my failed marriage. Amélie #1 chides me. "Why did you put candy in front of a baby like that?" Yoga Amélie agrees. "If you are on a diet, do you bring chocolate into the house?" No, I wouldn't bring chocolate into the house, but the problem was that I wouldn't feel I had the right to tell someone else not to bring chocolate in. If that someone wanted a chocolate bar, that was their problem and I simply would have to be strong. The Amélies were right. They all stated it like it was a rule of life that we all knew. If your nose is running, you blow it. If the cops show up, the party's over. If your husband's handsome, hire babysitters who smell like bad butter if you want to save your marriage.

Lori Jo grabs me and leads me to the living room. "You have to meet John. You'll love him. Go talk to him, Lauren. Go!"

John is a handsome silver-haired gentleman standing in the living room with a two-year-old perched on his shoulders. The child is holding on to his head like a monkey. He asks me if I'd like to feed his son a cracker, says something in French to his son, and hands me a cracker to feed him.

"I love you brought your kid to a party," I tell him as I feed him the cracker. "I wish I'd brought my son, Leo, with me. But I get so worried about his bedtime and—"

"Bedtime?!" John says with surprise. "What, does the kid have a job or something?"

That's a good point. Leo should get a job. Why am I so uptight about stuff like that? Then again, I'm not sure Leo is the type to hang on to my head and eat crackers. He's so hyper.

"Well, children pick up on the energy of their parents," John says to me with a little smirk.

Don't think I haven't heard that one before, buddy. John is looking at me with a mixture of pity and amusement. Uncomfortable, I offer him a cracker; he refuses. "No gluten for me."

He asks if he can ask me a question. "Do you ever find living in LA that the concept of fame gets in the way of getting any real work done?"

Dang. I'd like to write that down but I don't have my journal with me. Yes, of course it does, and this is where I'm going to be raising my son as a single mother? If Leo grows up in LA, he'll be good-looking, but I want more for him; I want him to rich, too.

Lori Jo announces it's time for the salon to begin and all the guests are to go sit in the living room. Lori Jo asks me in front of all of her friends whether I'd be willing to go first. I'm not sure what I'm supposed to do. Lori Jo says that anything goes. Whatever I'm feeling. Sing a song. Read a poem. Whatever I'm feeling. I ask if it's okay if I get up, take off all my clothes, and stand in front of everybody sobbing? I get a pass. The cool chick with the jellyfish tattoo stands up; I clap a few times but stop when she shoots me a look. She walks to the front of the room and opens her notebook. "I'm going to be reading a poem I wrote called 'Naked and Sobbing.'"

The next night, I decide, that's it. We are going out on the town, Leo and Mama. I'm taking Leo out to dinner. Sure, it's past his bedtime, but who cares? Does he have to get up for his job at H&R Block in the morning? We get out of the Pearl District and I take him to an old vaudeville theater that's been converted into a pub, the Bagdad Theater & Pub. The minute we sit down at a table Leo starts making a big hubbub about wanting to watch a DVD. I look around at all the other kids with their families who are playing games with their fingers or staring off into space with big smiles on their faces, being surprised by their own thoughts.

"We don't do that anymore!" I loudly announce, but it's late and I'm getting stressed that it's the first night I've taken Leo out past his bedtime. What if he has some sort of awful meltdown and ruins the meal? I want to enjoy our first night out. So I get the DVD player, make a joke to the waitress about how "he just wants to see how *The Omen* ends" and throw my coat over him. He complains he can't breathe but I know he's fine. He's got a sleeve.

A drunken guy stumbles into the restaurant and makes a bee-line to sit at the table right next to us, like he came here specifically to meet me. He sits down and starts talking to Leo. "Look at you hanging out with your mama!" He's swaying from side to side and I can feel the eyes of the happy families on us. What's this drunk man about to do? You never know. He's talking with the shrill slur of a drunk doing his best to sound "friendly and harmless." "You're lucky, hanging out with your mama, aren't you? You are. You are one lucky, motherfucker. One lucky—"

Before he can say it again, I jump in with a friendly, "Oh, we're trying not to call him that anymore! He's just an asshole now. We're gonna wait until he's five to call him that. Make him earn it! Okay, you have a good night!" I shut the DVD player, grab Leo, and leave the pub. Leo's upset but I tell him that we'll get ice cream and I'll buy him a toy. I've got to stop promising to buy him toys every time he seems upset. It's a ridiculous thing to promise. Especially because it's pouring rain outside and it's eight at night.

There's a bookstore across the street. Perfect. Save us, Curious George.

A reading by a local writer is happening. He's in the middle of reading from his new book of poems, entitled *How I Plan to Take My Own Life*.

"Come on, Leo, let's go." I pull him back outside. Leo won't hold an umbrella. He's getting soaked. That guy was right. He is a motherfucker. Hold your umbrella! It's pouring rain. The city turns into an endless rainy tableau of suicidal people in hoodies smoking under bridges, whispering, "Help me . . . help me . . . ," as we run past them to find a bus stop, a tram stop, a llama farm, anything to get us back to the hotel.

The next morning, I make an announcement. "Leo, we got to quit smoking and drinking and cheer ourselves up. One last puff, buddy, and we're going to the zoo."

The zoo is lovely. There is a little drizzle but it's doable. After we see the elephants, we take a break on a grassy hill to have a snack. There's a stage in front of us that suddenly comes to life. College girls in khaki shorts and polo shirts come bounding out onstage. "Welcome, Portland Zoo visitors, to the Birds of Prey show!"

The show is incredible. The perky college girls in the khaki shorts introduce various birds of prey from around Oregon, but when the birds come out, they aren't carried out on someone's arm. They fly in from behind the audience, as if the bird was sitting in a tree and suddenly heard its name. "Oh, that's me—the spotted owl. That's my cue! Got to go!"

They all have very Portland names, like "Deschutes the Hawk," and they fly in to their own theme music.

Deschutes the Hawk tap-dances in the sky above the crowd to "Fly Me to the Moon."

Leo puts his arms around my neck and whispers into my mouth, instead of my ear, "I want to come here again. Today."

Halfway through the show, the girls stop the music. They come to the edge of the stage and quiet the crowd.

"Okay, Portland Zoo visitors, before we bring out our next special guest we're going to ask that everyone please make sure that there are no food items of any kind around you. If you have any food in your mouth right now, finish chewing, take a piece of gauze, and wipe your mouth. No sudden movements. Don't stand.

Don't wear red. No eye contact. Okay! Please welcome Larry the Vulture!"

A vulture with the face of an eighty-year-old ball sack flies in to the Barenaked Ladies singing, "It's been one week since you looked at me . . ." And instead of flying to the college girl who is madly giving signals and blowing a whistle to lead him to the stage, Larry looks at her and decides "Fuck it!" and lands right in the middle of the audience. He walks over purses looking for food and making babies cry, harassing and terrorizing anyone in his path. The college girls go crazy on their walkie-talkies: "LARRY IS DOWN! LARRY IS DOWN! FORM THE PERIMETER!"

They finally lure Larry to the stage with a bloody Cheeto, but not before he runs back out into the middle of the audience, opens up his wings, and shakes his ball-sack face as if to say, "I'll be back!"

People applaud while he's led off like the child molester he is. After everyone settles down, the college girls come over the loudspeaker again. "Please welcome our final special guest, Chinook."

"Somewhere Over the Rainbow" starts to play, the version by the Hawaiian guy on the ukulele that kills me. I look up and see a bald eagle that looks like it's been dropped from the clouds. Leo and I watch it glide slowly back and forth above us. I feel like crying.

Leo puts his little arm around my neck and whispers, "Eagles are Papa's favorite bird." Now I am crying. It *is* his favorite kind of bird. David would bring back photos from his fishing trips in Alaska of eagles perched on the end of the fishing boat.

Chinook lands on his perch. He turns around and strikes the dignified pose of the American bald eagle that he gets paid the big bucks to do.

That bird has a ferocious dignity. Everybody loves bald eagles. Leo asks me if I knew that the Human Being was scared of rivers when she was little. I tell him that I didn't know that. "She was scared that if she put her face in the river she'd see the Loch Ness monster."

David is not swimming in the Sea of Cortez with me anymore. He's back on the shore warning the Human Being not to go in and she's standing behind him feeling safe and protected. David's still scared to go in the water, but it doesn't matter. She doesn't see that. She sees the brave man who's saving her life. Warning her not to go in. Telling her all the things that could go wrong, and she's grateful.

David must be such a comfort to her. He was to me when I met him. This is happening. It's happened. They're in love. They're with each other. This is now my life. What seemed so surreal and awful now simply is. It is.

I pull Leo to me and kiss the top of his head. "She was scared to put her face in rivers? Wow. She sure is dumb."

Oops. That slipped out.

After the zoo, Leo and I ride the tram to the farmers' market.

We walk into the market, and it looks like everyone is moving in slow motion. Young organic farmers with earnest eyes and dirty fingernails slowly hand out blueberry samples; parents take care of one another's kids; college kids with Abe Lincoln beards play bluegrass music on washboards. Looking at all of this and all the people smiling and eating berries, I feel nothing. Not annoyed. Not superior. Not bemused. I'm not sure what's going on. I'm so used to always feeling something. What is this? For the first time in months—no, longer than that; years and years. For the first time in years, I feel calm.

I'm going to be okay. I am okay. This okay is deeper and has so much space around it. The end of my marriage to David will not be the end of me. I'm not going to get worse and worse. I have a family.

A huge family. I'm free. Free to nap and masturbate the days away and by masturbate I mean learn Italian. It's going to be okay. I feel completely . . . okay.

Or maybe I'm just hungry.

I get a slice of organic pizza for Leo and order myself an omelet with some kind of complicated sauce on it, and as I pull my money out of my pocket, a receipt falls out. I watch it fall for a moment, and then at that exact moment, I see a white butterfly fly up. I'm so blissed out that I honestly believe, for half a second, that my receipt has just turned into a butterfly.

I don't know how I'd do it, but I want Leo to have a life where he can believe, for more than half a second—for hours and hours— that a receipt can turn into a butterfly. He will have that kind of life. Things are not going to stay this bad. Things will settle. I love Leo. David loves Leo. Hell, the Human Being loves Leo too.

It starts to rain as we walk back to the hotel. I let it soak us. Leo is thrilled. We don't carry umbrellas anymore. Why should we? What if there was a rainbow? I look down on the sidewalk next to where we're standing and see a wig on the ground with throw up on it. Leo asks me what it is. I'm about to say, "The most disgusting thing I've ever seen in my life," when it hits me: it's not gross at all; it's sad. In the middle of all this bliss there's a human being who is clearly having a very rough day. I grab Leo's hand. "Come on, Leo. Somewhere out there, there's a transvestite with the flu and we have to help her."

ACKNOWLEDGMENTS

I'd like to thank . . .

Udesky—may we all have an Udesky in our lives. An incredible support and friend.

My editor, Becky Cole. She is the reason this book is here. Becky pushed me to go deeper with each story even though I insisted that I was shallow. I cannot thank her enough unless I get sued; then I'm going to blame it all on her.

The late Ann Richards, former governor of Texas; Lucinda Williams; Loretta Lynn; Margaret Cho; Miranda July; David and Amy Sedaris; Jane Campion; and Patty Griffin. None of these people are actual friends of mine, but it's not going to stop me from getting their faces tattooed all over my body.

Joe Donnelly, for his "this story is not good, but this one is" directness and wisdom.

Erica Beeney, for her incredible support and insights, her love of writing, and her fancy cheeses.

Gillian Vigman. At least two sentences in the book if not more were stolen from this hilarious and beautiful lady. (I have to overcompliment her since I've been stealing her personality for years.)

Jennifer Winters, for her mystical insights and ability to drink wine no matter what time of day it is.

Sandy Cioffi, for being my family, my Uncle Sandy.

SoulCycle in Santa Monica, for replacing writer's block with nausea.

Hilary Ketchum, for her constant support and ability to hold one-sided texting conversations with herself when I was too busy to talk.

Brady Harris, for his sweet music and incredibly healing company.

Kevin Wanzer and Matthew Vire and Scout . . . thanks for nothing. You guys don't give me enough presents or free food. But I'm willing to give you a second chance.

Sharon and Sid Weedman: Your voice mail messages of "Why isn't that book done? What the hell are you doing?" kept me hungry and driven.

Jeff Weatherford, for trying so hard to do the right thing to help me work and for reading my stories and giving me his blessings.

Greg MacDonald, who came up with the title of the book with the poetic help of autocorrect.

Mark Duplass, for the use of his retreat house to write.

Christie Smith, my Hollywood manager whom I'd love even if we didn't live in Hollywood—that's deep talk for our town.

Wine makers all over the world and Yerba Mate producers.

Christopher Evan Welch—who's dead now, but you never know who reads these things. He was my "crazy talented" friend who inspired me, and I miss him.

Trip Cullman, Arielle Tepper, Rachel Neuburger, and the Empty Space theater, for their commission of *Rash*, where some of the material for "To All the Gays I've Loved Before" was developed.